Gracious Laughter

"This Dove & Olive Branch." Courtesy of the Beinecke Rare Book and Manuscript Library, Yale University.

Gracious Laughter

The Meditative Wit of Edward Taylor

John Gatta

University of Missouri Press
Columbia, 1989

Library of Congress Cataloging-in-Publication Data

Gatta, John.
Gracious laughter : the meditative wit of Edward Taylor / John Gatta.
p.   cm.
Bibliography: p.
Includes index.
ISBN 0-8262-0704-9 (alk. paper)
1. Taylor, Edward, 1642-1729—Humor. 2. Comic, The, in literature.
3. Christian poetry, American—History and criticism. 4. Devotional literature, American—History and criticism. 5. Wit and humor—Religious
aspects—Christianity. 6. Puritans—New England—Humor. I. Title.
PS850.T2Z65   1989   88-27557
822'.1—dc19   CIP

∞™ This paper meets the minimum requirements of the American
National Standard for Permanence of Paper for Printed Library Materials, Z39.48, 1984.

For Arnold and Elsbeth Benz

Acknowledgments

For permission to incorporate adapted portions of an essay first appearing in *Early American Literature* (volume 10, 1975) into my fourth chapter, I am grateful to the current publishers of that journal. Thomas Gibbs of the Redwood Athenaeum in Newport, Rhode Island, allowed me to cite a brief passage from Edward Taylor's unpublished "Theological Notes" manuscript. And like other students of Taylor, I have benefited from the use of Gene Russell's *Concordance to the Poems of Edward Taylor* (Microcard Editions, 1973) and am pleased to acknowledge here this otherwise unspoken debt.

There are several whom I wish to thank more personally for diverse gifts of advice and assistance with the manuscript. Among them are James Cooper, Robert Daly, Paula Kot, Harrison Meserole, and Milton Stern. I am especially indebted to Michael Colacurcio for his learned guidance during the seminal stages of the project and to Raymond Anselment, Connecticut colleague and specialist in the English seventeenth century, for his trenchant criticisms and needed encouragement during the latter stages.

Charles Mignon generously allowed me to cite from his soon-to-be published transcription of the Nebraska manuscript containing Taylor's sermons "Upon the Types of the Old Testament." I am grateful as well for his thoughtful and detailed advice. Finally, I want to thank my wife, Julia, who though she is a cleric in Edward Taylor's sense did not disdain to help me in other clerical ways, and indeed in ways both including and surpassing those named in the usual spousal accolades. It is a rare grace to have found the theologian-critic I needed so near to home.

J. G.
November 1, 1988

Contents

When the good is in view, love entertains it, and joy delights, and sports, and playeth with it; love is like the Host that welcomes the guest, and joy is like the chamberlain that attends upon him, and is very ready and pleasing to entertain the promise, and the Lord Jesus Christ: this is the very guise of the heart, as I conceive.

Thomas Hooker, *The Soules Vocation*

Now the exhortation is thus, Rejoyce, & be exceeding glad . . . & therefore Luke renders it by a word that properly notes to leap as young things leape in their play, as lambs do, as the babe in Elizabeth's womb at the sound of Maries Salutation.

Edward Taylor, *The Harmony of the Gospels*

Introduction

The constellation of concerns lending pattern to this study of Edward Taylor begins with the matter of wit, in its diverse shapes, and expands to encompass humor, festivity, the comic imagination, play, and contemplative joy. As with the constellations overhead, one might wonder whether the finished tracing reflects anything more than the viewer's fancy. I would not deny that, from one angle of vision, play occupies a separate theoretical galaxy from the comic sense or that wit and humor can be worlds apart. But my working premise is that wit, comedy, and the ludic impulse do share a common universe—in the human mind, at any rate, and more particularly in the creative mind of our finest colonial poet. Taylor's peculiar blend of verbal wit, meditative earnestness, and comic exuberance is arguably the best index of his singularity as a sacred artist of Puritan New England.

The sensuous wittiness of the verse is no new discovery. From the first, modern readers of Taylor were struck by the brusque energy of this American anachronism of the metaphysical school, who could analogize the Eucharist as "Heavens Sugar Cake" and "Roastmeate," or could turn the primordial cosmos into a "Bowling Alley" wherein his Creator had "bowld the Sun." But Taylor's wit reflects more than frivolous ingenuity, more even than that "strength of thought" by which Dr. Johnson's classic definition saw dissimilar ideas and images combined in the *concetto.* As Karl Keller has already intimated, Taylor can be an arrestingly witty poet even in the humorous sense.

What remains to be explored is the precise relation between Taylor's play of wit—his ludic and comic propensities—and his all-enveloping religious commitment. Now that the poet's doctrinal orthodoxy has been settled beyond doubt, it is possible to sort out the subtler strands of that relation. In the argument that follows, Taylor's meditative exercise of wit is seen as the transformative link between his spirituality and his poetry. It identifies the rhetorical process by which the poet tried to reconcile doctrine and experience, type and antitype, Scripture and Sacrament, the public order of preaching and the personal order of his journey in faith, his meditative quest for God and his quest for inward assurance. More than for any other colonial writer, poetic wit served Taylor as a vehicle of spiritual search, a playful yet earnest turning of words, tropes, and types to release the latent power of the Word. Exploiting the self-allusive texture of Scripture beyond the established typological schemes, Taylor sought to demonstrate how types resonate with other types at the same time that they touch antitypal references that, in turn, play against each other.

In fact for Taylor, wit *was* his art. In its ideal application wit became a fleshly enactment of the covenant relation with absolute Spirit, a ritual performance leading toward the central Christian ritual of the Lord's Supper. Meditative wit offered one means for Taylor to aspire toward that integration of the soul's powers that Louis Martz takes to be the general ideal of seventeenth-century devotional poetry. Since God gave the Word, verbal and imagistic manipulation was something the poet could legitimately do, from the human side, in response to the Covenant of Grace. But like George Herbert before him, Taylor was well aware of the intellectual limits and prideful dangers of wit. His attitude toward it was correspondingly ambivalent. Only as transformed through a higher dedication could wit express the jubilant love of a regenerate will rather than the natural pride of ingenious ambition; and this renewal, like that of sanctification itself, could never be perfected in this mortal sphere.

Yet the poet's more gracious discovery and disclosure of a wit in some sense intrinsic to life transcended any claim to righteousness by works. As a heartfelt response to God and partial evidence of grace, this wit of love could express itself either in meiotically satiric and often self-disparaging forms or in more directly celebratory modes. Taylor thus developed his own poetic compound of "negative way" and "affirmative way" responses to the problem of expression.

In the one instance of diminishing wit, Taylor is apt to mock his own effort to represent holy things through earthly figures. By this deliberately inverting strategy of "reverent parody," he transmutes his necessarily defective artistry into an acceptable rhetoric of praise. In the more celebratory frame of holy jest, Taylor's jubilant wit acts to free the inherent dynamism of the scriptural Word by shaping fresh patterns of words. Jubilant wit also serves to penetrate the comic incongruity of the Incarnation, to dramatize the gratuitous energy and awesome extravagance of the divine will as underscored by Puritan belief, and to celebrate the prospect of eschatological delight.

In Taylor's poetic liturgies of the Word, two creedal suppositions in particular give endlessly repeatable cause for wonder and celebration. What the poet calls "blessed theanthropy," the union between humanity and divinity contained in Christ's person, commonly presents itself in the container imagery of the *Preparatory Meditations*. *Theanthropy* supports, in turn, the marvel of *theosis*, or deification, whereby human nature is seen to be exalted beyond remedy of the Fall to a glory surpassing that of the angels. In Taylor's verse this corollary doctrine commonly finds expression in alchemical or medical images of transformation. Though evidently connected to a Protestant theology of conversion, Taylor's preocupation with the double mystery of *theanthropy* and *theosis* developed in part out of his extensive reading in the Greek fathers of the Church. Within this highly optimistic anthropology, depravity figures as only a preliminary, albeit necessary, stage to be traversed ritually in the course of each *Meditation*.

Though Taylor's wit is not always funny, the jocular and festive aspects of the verse serve also the practical end of dispelling that familiar Renaissance-Galenic disease known as scrupulous melancholy. Far from being an incidental element of style, the poet's comic sensibility was thus rooted in pressing social and pastoral concerns, above all in the social sacrament of the Lord's Supper, as well as in personal spirituality and the religious tradition. Following the focal statement in chapter 1, this contextual problem is explored in chapters 2 and 3, together with a consideration of Taylor's rhetorical aesthetic and sense of audience. The last three chapters represent a more practical and particular application of criticism to Taylor's best verse, mainly *The Preparatory Meditations* and *Gods Determinations Touching his Elect.*

It may seem curious at first that a quality like verbal humor should be assigned to a Puritan divine, especially one fixed in Ezra Stiles's well-known account as "serious and grave." Granted, a fancy for jest was neither a dominant trait of the Puritan mind nor a prevailing feature of Puritan verse. There are ways in which Taylor fulfills the imaginative potential of the comic spirit despite, rather than because of, his immediate Puritan background. Yet as I try to show, distinctive sanctions for the idea of making "ernest out of game" were available to Taylor in his extended Reformed background as well as in his broader world of Renaissance and Christian thought. Simply stated, the aim is to understand how Taylor's exploitation of wit, play, and the comic spirit flowed from his peculiar grasp of Puritan and Christian poetics.

Uncovering this channel of mirth running through the marrow of Puritan divinity should further the ongoing scholarly project of reassessing early New England's religious culture. In a broader context than humor, we shall also find the poet's mystical temper allied to the contemplative, anti-utilitarian dimension of play. Studying Taylor's investment in ritualized play and contemplative wit therefore exposes further dimensions of the New England Soul.

Officially and consciously, Taylor expresses the standard Puritan invective against symbolism and holy festival in favor of historical typology and de-ritualized worship. Outwardly, his writing reinforces the usual anti-Catholic, polemical attack on all latter-day celebrations of sacred space and sacred time as the corrupted product of human invention. But beneath this exegetically firm surface of rationalistic iconoclasm, Taylor's poetry sustains an irrepressible current of symbolism and sacramentalism, a subliminal force even more encompassing than the Westfield minister's explicit devotional involvement in the sacrament of the Lord's Supper.

Finally, it is worth remembering that to focus on Taylor's artistic engagement with the "festival frame of spirit" and holy amazement is hardly to deny the dialectically opposed themes of sober remorse and Christian affliction likewise evident in his poems. For the current dispensation, Christian belief fastens inevitably on the truth of the *via crucis* and the Man of Sorrows. All the same, there is a perfectly orthodox sense in which Taylor felt bound to embrace the "comic" resolution of resurrectional joy as God's more comprehensive and ultimate truth. If life is one great preparation for the feast, Taylor held with the author of Ecclesiastes that "a feast is made for laughter." So even a Puritan like Taylor might come to value festive mirth, in due measure, both as foretaste of the heavenly banquet and as occasional restorative for the soul's earthly combat.

1 Divinity at Play

Another View of the Puritan Divine

In September 1696, Edward Taylor wrote his former Harvard roommate, Samuel Sewall, about the end of the world. A quarter century earlier, Taylor had withdrawn reluctantly from the eastern refuge of academe to launch a new pastorate in rustic Westfield, Massachusetts, a post he was never to abandon. But even after Taylor had fully accepted his vocation to live and die here, on the fringe of European civilization, he never lost his aptitude for scholastic debate. Now he zealously entered the latest stage of his amiable controversy with Judge Sewall, refuting the exegetical proposition that the sixth angelic vial poured on the Euphrates in Revelation 16.12 signified the impending dissolution of Spain's Catholic Empire in America toward the close of the ages.

In rising to Sewall's challenge, Taylor applied all the devices of Ramistic logic, rhetoric, and comparative scriptural reference that one expects of the Puritan preacher. Yet his exposition also shows a touch of the Puritan poet. Its sober logic is enlivened by persistent images of archery and competitive combat, together with forays into colloquial and neological diction. Stranger still, Taylor launches his discourse with a burst of facetious banter. Complaining with mock diffidence of his rusty forensic skills and disadvantaged setting "far off from the Muses Copses" where little but "Rusticity is Al-A-Mode," he bids his opponent expect no "Silken Rhetorick" or "Academick Eloquence." Likewise framing the conclusion of his case with apology, Taylor asks his old friend not to take offense at the liberality of "jesting expressions" interspersed through his exegesis. Their intent is "only to put to flight those Sediments of natures Constitution that otherwise would break down the Portraiture that is framed upon the minde with a Smiling Amicableness." In closing, Taylor admits to an unsettled

1

curiosity about the future "Res Antichristiana in America," exclaiming "Oh that the day was come that would reveale this Euphrates clearely."[1] Yet his contentious exercise lacks any sense of apocalyptic terror or urgency. The right ending of the world depends not at all, it would seem, on the predictive viability of Edward Taylor's hermeneutics but only on the inevitable unfolding of God's hidden designs. Within the circle of this confidence, the poet is free to regard his verbalized musing over text and event, for all its scholastic earnestness, as something of a sport.

A second revealing glimpse of Taylor's creative mind is afforded by the well-known courtship missive he sent to Elizabeth Fitch of Norwich, Connecticut, a little over two decades earlier. In its formal intricacy, the rhymed "Dove and Olive Branch" acrostic he wrote for the occasion projects an engaging charm. Yet the poem, in combination with the prose letter that accompanied it, reveals more than surface ingenuity. Taylor's intentions also go beyond the understandable urge to sweeten the bitter pill of Puritan marital doctrine, and of its carefully restricted approval of eroticism, with a little verbal fun.

In his letter, the ministerial lover expounds the paradoxical teaching that "Conjugall Love" should surpass "all other Love to any Creature" yet "must be kept within bounds" of subordination to God's glory. Taylor prefaces the numbered reasons of his argument, which has been aptly called a "mock sermon,"[2] with fanciful complaints about the vanity of capturing his love—"a Golden Ball of pure Fire"—with pen and ink. And in his poem he echoes the prose theme of restriction with the shaped motto, "The Ring of Love my Pleasant Heart must bee / Truely Confind within the Trinitie." Within this triangular emblem, around the visual figure and verbal invocation of the "cent'red heart," he sets a circular countermotto of infinity: "Loves Ring I send that hath no End."[3]

1. Edward Taylor, "The Pouring of the Sixth Vial: A Letter in a Taylor-Sewall Debate," ed. Mukhtar Ali Isani, 129.

2. William B. Goodman, "Edward Taylor Writes His Love," 514.

3. Edward Taylor, "The Dove Letter" and "This Dove and Olive Branch," as cited in *Edward Taylor's Minor Poetry,* vol. 3 of *The Unpublished Writings of Edward Taylor,*

The theological center of Taylor's playful ingenuity should therefore be apparent. To envision human love as bounded within the boundless love-circle of the Trinity is to realize the heart's expansion, not its amorous chastening and contraction. "My Love within my breast is so large," confesses Taylor in the prose communication, "that my heart is not su[ffi]cient to Contain it." Within the frame of this vision, a whole set of daring correlations between things human and divine takes shape. Taylor's homely "Post Pidgeon" and beloved Dove Elizabeth shadow the Holy Spirit of love; his fictive wedding ring suggests the sacred circle of Infinity; and his marital conjugation typifies that sublime union of the soul with Christ celebrated eventually in the final sequence of his *Preparatory Meditations* on texts from Canticles.

While the "Dove and Olive Branch" shows Taylor still searching for the proper form "to spell what Love can speake," his compound portrayal of "a True-Loves-Knot" here in poem and prose reveals traits conspicuous throughout his artistic career. Taylor sets up his characteristic interplay between poem and sermonic discourse, rationalistic logic and humanizing warmth, word and image, theology and homely actuality. Above all, the love poem exemplifies Taylor's enduring sense that he must exercise his play of creative wit within specially delimited boundaries of form and circumstance. In accepting these boundaries, however, he also freed his muse to fulfill a sacred service of praise.

Together the two samples of writing, addressed to a former classmate and a future wife, suggest a different face of Edward Taylor from that commonly associated with this ecclesiastically conservative, second-generation Puritan. They also throw light into a corner of the collective New England Soul not usually illumined by reports of the introspective anguish and uncertainty inspired by Puritanism. To be sure, there is warrant for portraying Taylor as an earnest defender of sectarian orthodoxy, a man zealous in his sabbath observance and sometimes crass in his

---

ed. Thomas M. and Virginia L. Davis, 37–41. Future references to this three-volume collection (including *Edward Taylor vs. Solomon Stoddard: The Nature of the Lord's Supper* [vol. 2] and *"Church Records" and Related Sermons* [vol. 1]) will be cited in the text as *UW*, with volume number.

polemics. Conversely, it is probably too easy to point up the sweeter, sanguine side of his personality and its qualified receptivity to mirth. The challenge in the ensuing argument is to reach beyond this simple observation, beyond what we have already glimpsed of Taylor's capacity for sportiveness and jest, to explore the broader dimensions and religious roots of his festive imagination. For Taylor's best poetry presents not only a distinctive brand of religious humor, which is readily overlooked, but also an exuberant play of mind, an enchantment with the sacred possibilities of verbal wit, and a preenactment of the festival celebration awaiting God's elect at the end of time. As such the poetry gives abundant exposure to those intuitive and emotive attributes of the New England Soul that some have declared wanting in earlier expositions of the New England Mind.[4]

Wit's Anatomy: From Mind to Humor

Most broadly conceived, Taylor's "wit" might name all of those human faculties of rational and creative intelligence exercised in response to God's approaches. This first, most comprehensive sphere of our investigation is centered etymologically in the Anglo-Saxon *witan*, meaning "to know." From its original sense of "knowledge," the term evolved into a synonym for intellect, the seat of consciousness, the general power of reasoning. During the later Middle Ages the five "inner" senses of wit matched the five "outer," or bodily, senses. From the medieval period through the seventeenth century, then, *wit* signified qualities of mind, attributes of wisdom and intellectual force, that were separable from rhetoric.[5]

This connotation survives, of course, in a few current expressions; and occasionally one finds Taylor drawing casually on it, as

4. The implied reference here, of course, is to Perry Miller's classic two-volume study *The New England Mind* (vol. 1, *The Seventeenth Century,* and vol. 2, *From Colony to Province*), whose presumably cerebral focus has been challenged by several later commentators, including most recently Patricia Caldwell, *The Puritan Conversion Narrative: The Beginnings of American Expression,* 36, and Harry S. Stout, *The New England Soul: Preaching and Religious Culture in Colonial New England,* 38, 325 n. 19.

5. Beyond the *Oxford English Dictionary,* a convenient reference point for such information is William F. Thrall, Addison Hibbard, and C. Hugh Holman, *A Handbook to Literature,* 509–11.

in *Meditation* 2.75, where the speaker's reason has run temporarily "out of 'ts Wits."[6] Yet by the time of the Renaissance, through a second line of usage, the word had also begun to acquire its close connection with rhetoric. To excel in the three primary divisions of Renaissance rhetoric—invention, disposition, and eloquence— was invariably to possess a strength of thought that went under the name of *wit*.[7] Within this progressively narrower but still expansive field of definition, Taylor's "wit" might be identified with his verbal artistry as such. Now and then, as when celebrating Samuel Hooker's skill in framing "Brave Apophthegms" or when tallying the reach of angelic eloquence, Taylor invoked the very word *wit*—approvingly—in this sense. In any case, the problem of conceiving a forceful rhetoric was never far from his mind.

At the same time, sacred poets had to be constantly reminding themselves how unmistakably their flashes of verbal wit were struck from God's flint. Those familiar Puritan complaints against "witty" styles of preaching in the established church were motivated above all by the fear of succumbing to pride in creaturely accomplishment. But the Puritan, whether in Old England or New, was never alone in counseling vigilance against the temptations of artistic pride or in reflecting a deep-seated ambivalence toward the very notion of rhetorical wit. George Herbert, whose attitude toward wit was fraught with ambiguities, exemplifies much the same concern. Purified and consecrated to devout use, Herbert's wit might be a potent weapon of evangelical persuasion; but the poet likewise saw it as "an unruly engine," liable to swerve at any moment toward the self-exalting perils of mere cleverness. To write with creative ingenuity seemed almost inevitably to imply an assertion of personal ego. Wit could also seem to demand the obscuring of plainest truth in a maze of subtle trickeries.[8]

6. *The Poems of Edward Taylor,* ed. Donald E. Stanford, 218. All subsequent verse citations, identified in the text by poem and series numbers (or by *Poems* and page number), are to this edition unless otherwise indicated.

7. This relation is evidenced and elaborated by William G. Crane, *Wit and Rhetoric in the Renaissance: The Formal Basis of Elizabethan Prose Style.*

8. Sam Westgate addresses these matters intelligently in "George Herbert: 'Wit's an Unruly Engine' "; also helpful is Ernest B. Gilman, *The Curious Perspective: Lit-*

For all its liabilities, the wit of human artists assuredly could carry sacred import for the seventeenth-century reader. Continental theoreticians such as Baltasar Gracián and the Italian Jesuit Emmanuele Tesauro held that God set forth his wit more or less directly, in the books of Scripture and Creation, as well as indirectly. Divine wit found indirect expression in the wit of the human artist, a manipulation of mind that assembled the remote terms of conceits scattered throughout nature. What Joseph Mazzeo has termed the "poetic of correspondences" rested on a conviction that the universe was a web of universal but hidden analogies sporadically made manifest through the poet's inventive turning of words and juggling of thoughts. As Ernest Gilman sums up Tesauro's outlook, "God himself is the efficient cause of wittiness, the creator of a witty universe." Through the language and events of Scripture as well as through the phenomena of nature, "Wit is the method by which the creator confers significance on the creation—and by which the conceited poet explores and imitates the working of the divine mind."[9]

Such statements, especially Tesauro's characterization of rhetorical wit as a "vestige of the Deity in the human mind,"[10] advance no small claim for the sacred dignity of the creative faculties. Samuel Coleridge's nineteenth-century definition of the Secondary Imagination would scarcely claim more. And nothing attributed so far to these continental students of wit contradicts the central views of Protestant rhetoricians like Sir Philip Sidney and George Puttenham in Elizabethan England. Like meditation, wit is a unitive act of the human creature founded on the original unity of Creation.

By the time one enters a Jacobean-Caroline setting, wit has become a specialized synonym for the metaphysical mode. Wit still signified originality and force of mind but also came now to be associated with an energetically terse and learned style that

---

erary and Pictorial Wit in the Seventeenth Century.

9. Gilman, *Curious Perspective*, 71; Joseph Mazzeo, "A Critique of Some Modern Theories of Metaphysical Poetry."

10. Cited in S. L. Bethell, "The Nature of Metaphysical Wit," in *Discussions of John Donne*, ed. Frank Kermode, 140.

relied heavily on paradox and striking metaphors to uncover similitude in the midst of apparent unlikeness. In its own age the "new wit" was an identifiable if variable phenomenon. Here was a novel realm of thought and expression, as Thomas Carew would have it, set under the universal monarchy of John Donne. Subjects of the English realm could otherwise differ in defining this newness, associating it with a startling celerity of thought in poetic expression, with a lapse of decorum in forms of catachresis distinct from true imagination, with a fondness for recondite learning and scholastic terms, with Izaak Walton's "strong lines," or with Alexander Pope's "School of Donne."[11]

Before the era of neoclassical criticism, writers were inclined to agree at least that wit was an essential constituent of poetry, not a decorative embroidery to art or a largely extrinsic quality inferior to judgment. Yet the precise relation between wit, on the one hand, and the Hobbesian faculties of mind, Fancy and Judgment, on the other, remained obscure. Was wit to be equated mainly with Hobbes's innovating Fancy, and thereby opposed to Judgment? This common tendency seems to be reflected in the opening lines of Taylor's *Meditation* 1.29, where the poet's "shattred Phancy" accompanies his venturesome "Wits" as they "run a Wooling over Edens Parke." But at other times writers might presume a multiple definition of wit encompassing both Fancy and Judgment.[12]

More vexing questions arise as modern scholarship tries to order its overview of this period's richly diverse landscape of English verse. Was there in fact a seventeenth-century poetry of wit, a grouping or style or school of writing that might be named "metaphysical," pace John Dryden and Samuel Johnson? If not, and if categories like "metaphysical" or "School of Donne" are expunged from the critical vocabulary, can another organizing term more legitimately account for the currents of sympathy that do seem to run among devotional poets as memorably distinct as Donne, Herbert, Crashaw, Quarles, and Cleveland?

11. George Williamson outlines the range of possibilities in *Six Metaphysical Poets: A Reader's Guide*, especially 3–10, 100–104, 233–59.
   12. Ibid., 19–25

The unsettled status of such questions on the British side of things is bound to influence judgments of Edward Taylor's position on the American strand. That Taylor was a late-blooming, American variety of the "metaphysical" species was a familiar judgment of his earliest critics. Lately it has become common to deny him that honor or opprobrium. Taylor looks either too Protestant or too untutored in taste to belong in the tradition of Donne. He is said to be an emblematist, a lonely primitivist experimenting in the wilderness, an exemplary Puritan writer of the Ramistic school, a meditative lyricist, or a typological poet—but not a metaphysical poet.

There is no point in insisting on a comprehensive application of the "metaphysical" rubric to Taylor at a time when the term has passed from critical favor. The general category remains, in any case, a poor substitute for close analysis. Yet given the limited scope of any such term, one must also hesitate to call Taylor a "typological poet" if the term is taken to be all-encompassing and antithetical to the practice of those English devotional poets with whom he evidently shared much. Neither does typology define the sole subject matter or structure of his art. Likewise, the emblem approach helps to explain one source of a poet's material without necessarily defining the principles of literary execution applied to it, the poet's method.

We return, then, to an affirmation that *wit*, in some connection with the metaphysical mode, remains a valuable frame of reference for addressing at once a style of writing and a habit of mind. Ernest Gilman shows the broad and dynamic scope of the term in its critical application either to a literary or a pictorial medium. It is therefore a unitive category in several senses. For a reading of Taylor, the major relevance of wit in the special seventeenth-century sense lies in its verbalization of wondrous surprise. Yet Taylor's poetry does not dramatize the apprehension of new discovery and holy admiration as an end in itself but as the affective end of his meditative vision.

To anatomize this sector of wit's operation in Taylor it may help to reinvoke briefly the standard terms of older discussion. Attempts to define the wit of metaphysical or baroque poetry traditionally begin, of course, with the notion of the *concetto* as captured by Johnson's familiar if less than approving description in his *Life of Cowley*. The new wit is "a kind of *discordia concors*; a combination of dissimilar images, or discovery of occult resemblances in things apparently unlike." In the conceit, "the most heterogeneous ideas are yoked by violence together." Because of the exaggerated, difficult nature of the conceit, the reader's first reaction to it is supposed to be, in Johnson's words, "sudden astonishment" followed by "rational admiration."[13] As widely removed spheres of thought, image, and experience are brought into unexpected alignment, a moment of new insight may occur. In this mode of potential discovery, the poet's searching intelligence tries to draw the scattered fragments of experience—and his own divided powers—into some freshly realized if tentative order.

Despite the vivid amazement that wit engenders, the rough meter and blending of learned and colloquial diction in the conceited style, its shock value should not be overdrawn. Later scholars like Earl Miner and Rosemond Tuve wanted to explain at length the logical and rhetorical processes at work in the English metaphysical lyric, showing how the conceited style moves above a structure of carefully reasoned argument. So also the latter-day inclination in studies of Taylor is to minimize the strain and surprise provoked by his metaphors, either by denying outright the paradoxicality of his poetry or by insisting more plausibly that his conceits would not have seemed as shocking to his contemporaries as they do to us. It is true that Taylor's images lose something of their initial jolt once we have read the exegetical commentary provided by Thomas Wilson or have consulted a typological treatise by Samuel Mather. A look into the emblem books is bound to make the terms of certain Taylor metaphors less independently remote than they first appeared.

Still, the arresting aspect of the conceit is undeniable. Although the surprises of conceited wit should not be confused with sensationalism, they remain surprises all the same. The design of the metaphysical religious lyric is usually to arouse sentiments of

13. Samuel Johnson, *Lives of the English Poets*, ed. George Birbeck Hill, 1:20–21.

wonder and devout admiration in the reader. If readers do not learn wholly new truths—and after all, applied gospel teaching fills a limited field of discourse—they must at least be led to apprehend some of the old ones in a new way. So the more crucial astonishments of baroque wit may unfold in a fairly subtle, interior way. M. M. Mahood has written persuasively of Herbert's "delicate balance of his reader's expectations and surprise"; a similar sense of contrast bonded to continuity informs Earl Miner's useful discussion of wit as "definition and dialectic."[14] Perhaps the current risk, then, is that too narrow a concern with a poet's rational structures of intellection and use of source materials behind the scenes will obscure the genuine surprises set before us.

In fact, genetic source study cannot undo the sense of arresting incongruity that pervades Taylor's metaphors. We are still left with the charming singularity of a redeemer woven by "Eternall Wisdoms Huswifry" in *Meditation* 1.41, the curious use of laboratory apparatus to dramatize the gracious alchemy of Christ in *Meditation* 1.7, and the memorable depiction of Christ's spiritual body as "Heavens Sugar Cake" in *Meditation* 1.8. In Taylor's best-known image, that of God as cosmological bowler of the sun in *Gods Determinations*, the distance between tenor and vehicle is glaringly remote; and there is no explaining away the effect of whimsical surprise. Some of Taylor's conceits—those, for instance, where the eating of the Son's body becomes lurid cannibalism—may seem as indecorous as they are astonishing; others unite discordant elements under tension if not with violence. Yet the poet's best metaphors always act to stimulate a wonder of recognition.

That figures like the sugar cake from heaven have originating antecedents in Scripture and other traditional sources need not lessen their revelatory impact. Again there is need to distinguish material from method, origin from essence. Thus, we can profit-

14. M. M. Mahood, "Something Understood: The Nature of Herbert's Wit," in *Metaphysical Poetry*, ed. Malcolm Bradbury and David Palmer, 132; Earl Miner, *The Metaphysical Mode from Donne to Cowley*, 118–58.

ably learn from Alan B. Howard that various details in Taylor's portrayal of a "Royall Coach" in *Gods Determinations* were apparently drawn from the Song of Solomon. But given the poet's quaintly peculiar handling of the vehicle, we should question whether a resonance like this indicates Taylor's "rather traditional decorum" in opposition to the amazements of "Metaphysical" wit.[15] Taylor's imagery here is "traditional" only by derivation; judgments concerning its "decorum" and rhetorical effect must be based instead on how the writer chooses to develop it in his own imaginative context. It can be all the more wonder-provoking when the poem's reader is brought to realize anew how the wit of divine Love has already deigned to use a startling trope or figurative pattern in Scripture. The poet is no less a wit because his model, the Holy Spirit, turns out to have been one also.

As Taylor's modern readers have long recognized, this poet compacts divine and human frames of reference through a distinctive form of homely metaphor. The poet himself wrote of his "Hyperboles" and "homely Style." In Austin Warren's account, the shock of discovery in Taylor's use of homely conceits "comes from the modernizing, the provincializing, of the Infinite." No arena of worldly activity is deemed too humble to supply the writer with tropes for his drama of faith and salvation. Taylor's figures of encounter with the Infinite come from kitchen and loom, garden and barnyard, sickroom and dung heap, marketplace and playground. This emphatic approval of domesticity finds parallel sanction in Herbert's counsel to country parsons that "Holy Scripture . . . condescends to the naming of a plough, a hatchet, a bushell, leaven, boyes piping and dancing; shewing that things of ordinary use are not only to serve in the way of drudgery, but to be washed, and cleansed, and serve for lights even of Heavenly Truths." In Warren's fuller characterization of the "Baroque" tradition of poetry and prose, to which he sees Taylor belonging, a stylistic fondness for "polar mixtures" and

15. Alan B. Howard, "The World as Emblem: Language and Vision in the Poetry of Edward Taylor," 361–62.

"bold figures" is supported by an "incarnational" Christian philosophy "admissive of miracle and hence of surprise."[16]

With good reason, then, Warren understands Taylor to be above all a "wit" in his poeticizing. To be sure, there are ways in which his brand of wit differs from that of his baroque or metaphysical precursors in England, just as many distinctions can be observed within the English grouping. In Taylor one finds no direct counterpart to Donne's much discussed skepticism, no felt division between the "old theology" and the joint influence of "new philosophy and new science." What skepticism can be discerned in Taylor is mostly self-skepticism. Nor is Taylor's writing a "Scholastick" verse in the sense Johnson had outlined. It is even less an aristocratic verse, by which measure Warren restricts the company of "metaphysicals" to Donne, Carew, and Lord Herbert of Cherbury. But Taylor exploits the full range of verbal devices ordinarily attributed to metaphysical (or, as Warren would have it, "baroque") wit. He is immensely fond of ploce and polyptoton, paradox and pun.[17] If toughness of line and span of metaphorical diction are the relevant criteria, Taylor emerges as more of a metaphysical poet—to a hostile neoclassical judgment, as more of a perpetrator of false wit—than most of his English models.

But as Earl Miner reminds us, the wittiness of metaphysical verse is not merely a question of imagery.[18] It is as much or more an attribute of mind, Johnson's "strength of thought" in the disposition of ideas. Especially for Taylor and Donne, this vigorous play of mind displays itself in a kind of darting flamboyance, a riddling and adventurous disposition. Moods of bright exuberance appear within an air of restless persistence.

16. George Herbert, *A Priest to The Temple; or, The Country Parson*, in *The Works of George Herbert*, ed. F. E. Hutchinson, 257; Austin Warren, *Rage for Order: Essays in Criticism*, 2, 8.

17. William Manierre, "Verbal Patterns in the Poetry of Edward Taylor"; Norman S. Grabo, *Edward Taylor*, 148. Manierre defines *ploce* as the "repetition of words within a relatively brief context" and *polyptoton* as the "repetition of a single root in different inflectional forms." The most straightforward case for Taylor's status as a metaphysical poet is Wallace Brown's "Edward Taylor: An American Metaphysical."

18. Miner, *Metaphysical Mode*, 123–24.

Clearly the seeds of still another sense of wit, humorous wit, were already inherent in the playful boldness and unexpected juxtapositions of the conceited style. The instant of amazement triggered by the *concetto* bears an evident resemblance to the punch line of a jest. Most attempts to explain risibility, however unsatisfying in the end, recognize the same elements of sudden perception, manifest incongruity, and veiled likeness that animate the metaphysical style. And though a connotation of *wit* as humor was not so inevitable in Taylor's era as it is today, it was nonetheless much in evidence. As early as the sixteenth century, jokes were being termed *witty*. Herbert more than once associates "wit" with the laughable in "The Church-Porch," his introductory passage to *The Temple,* just as the Elizabethan John Lyly revels through any number of comic innuendoes in his *Euphues: The Anatomy of Wit.* In fact *wit,* which in current usage generally points toward a sharper, more intellectual mood of jocularity than do the good-natured frolics of *humor,* had begun to take on comic import well before the latter word.

Within the foregoing context we come at last to the thesis that a comic vision of reality, linked to a broader conception of wit as its practical mode of realization in the sacramental act of composition, substantially influenced Edward Taylor's creativity. For Taylor this vision excluded the sort of wit associated with factitious triviality, with clever sophistries directed toward nothing higher or deeper than worldly distraction. Conversely, that which Taylor called the "festival frame of spirit"[19] should open far enough to encompass matters only tenuously related to amusement—including play in its several ramifications, dance, delight, music, and contemplative rapture. The poet could find religious sources of this festivity in selected tributaries of Reformed teaching, if not in its mainstream, and what was lacking there his library and antiquarian temper enabled him to draw from the fuller reservoir of Christian tradition.

---

19. *Edward Taylor's Treatise Concerning the Lord's Supper,* ed. Norman S. Grabo, 199. Subsequent references to this work will be cited in the text as *TCLS*.

Taylor's Play: Reverent Parody and the Comic Imagination

Though the sense of play and entertainment of the comic spirit are rarely sought in New England Puritanism, they are a telling feature of Taylor's best poetic voice. In certain prose works such as the newly printed *Harmony of the Gospels,* as well as in failed poems such as the *Metrical History of Christianity,* Taylor can be oppressively literalistic and pedantic. But when his affections were most deeply stirred in his dutiful course of meditating on the great facts of salvation, he was able to bring his verses alive with flourishes of sacred play and rituals of verbal celebration. Taylor at his best emerges as a richly comic poet, a wit even in the humorous sense, though much of his playfulness surpasses risibility.

Neither was this vitalization of wit, or the brusque exuberance so often noticed in his style, merely a chance product of temperament. Within the central achievement of *Gods Determinations* and the 214 *Meditations,* Taylor exploits diverse forms of the ludic and comic imagination he found latent in Christian theology. As a verbal response to grace, Taylor's wit was apt to express itself within two main channels: in the negative, indirect rhetoric of meiotic satire and self-disparagement; and in the more directly affirmative way of celebratory joy.

In the first channel, one remarkable form of holy wit Taylor embodies is a specialized outgrowth of the conceit that might be called "reverent parody." By reverent parody I mean something quite different from the "art of sacred parody" under which Louis Martz has discussed the appropriation of profane love-literature toward devout ends.[20] Taylor's parody shows itself rather in his distorted imitation of Holy Writ. The bulk of Taylor's poetry fastens obsessively upon the images, phrases, and typological patterns of Scripture; yet the poet so manipulates his borrowed figures, so suffuses them with a homely and whimsical aura of the anthropomorphic, that they only reinforce by contrast the dignity of their inspired source.

In this case, surely, the hyperbolic distentions of metaphor that

20. Louis L. Martz, *The Poetry of Meditation: A Study in English Religious Literature of the Seventeenth Century,* 184–93.

warp mimesis cannot be intended to ridicule the original model, as does most parody. On the contrary, Taylor's extraordinary uses of the homely metaphor bespeak an extraordinary reverence that would never wound the Source. By its own inverting logic, yet drawing on a sense of polar continuity between *ridiculum* and *admiratio* as old as Aristotle and Cicero, reverent parody aims instead to magnify the Lord. Its very obliqueness offers a fresh way of stirring gratitude for the tropes given in Scripture, corresponding to that rarer sort of parody whose distorted replication may even—as the handbook puts it—"imply a flattering tribute to the original writer."[21]

Taylor recognized from the outset the futility of locating signifiers wholly adequate to the thing signified, particularly in the case of a sacred thing. No poet could directly represent the sweetness of divine intercourse in verse, however vividly he might know it in devotional experience. John Calvin taught that any attempt to figure God in visible images must sully God's invisible majesty, for even Moses was allowed to see only God's "backparts."[22] Yet for Taylor a rhetoric of praise was futile only from the absolute perspective. From the angle of human contingency it was not only possible, but blessed and obligatory.

Acutely aware of how far the splendor of the invisible God surpasses all human efforts to image in word or figure, Taylor also felt called by God to write. From his acknowledgment that "Grace excells all Metaphors,"[23] he obviously did not move to abandon metaphor altogether. Neither did he ordinarily try to escape the natural failure of sacred art by following the Herbertian rhetoric of poised simplicity or by aspiring to employ the "Silver Metaphors and tropes" (2.153) of a high-mimetic style. Instead of competing

21. Thrall, Hibbard, and Holman, *A Handbook to Literature*, 341; Gilbert Highet, *The Anatomy of Satire*, especially 68; Marvin T. Herrick, *Comic Theory in the Sixteenth Century*, 36–64.

22. John Calvin, *Institutes of the Christian Religion*, ed. John T. McNeill, 1:99–103. Lynn Haims gives a provocative analysis of the larger problem of iconophobia in "The Face of God: Puritan Iconography in Early American Poetry, Sermons, and Tombstone Carving."

23. *Edward Taylor's Christographia*, ed. Norman S. Grabo, 253. Subsequent references to this work will be cited in the text as C.

with the high-flying "Orator from Rhetorick Gardens" (2.44) by seeking metaphorical vehicles congruent with their imageless tenor, Taylor chose to exploit his inevitable failure to achieve the congruence. The character of this negating choice has much to do with defining the poet's unique style.

Essentially, Taylor's wit of reverent parody is founded on a reflexive, *via negativa* principle of inversion. By deliberately disparaging his own efforts to contain the treasures of holy reality in vessels of earthen metaphor, the poet hoped to turn his ineluctably defective artistry into an acceptable language of praise and introspective piety. Taylor might transcend his defect by exposing it to determined mockery, ridiculing it beyond the usual human judgments of worth. His tropes often press beyond their own limits by openly surrendering to them, so that what the poet releases in postures of futility he may recover as a higher gift. What is more, that deliberate embrace of failure other critics have sensed in Taylor seems to contain for him a peculiarly comic dimension.

To construe this abasement as self-satiric comedy is not to deny traditional precedent for the poet's laments. By derivation they fit under the familiar rubrics of deflating rhetoric and the inability *topos*, just as Taylor's radical metaphors develop out of traditional catachresis, hyperbole, and the *genus humile*, or "base style," of classical rhetoric. Yet it is revealing to discover how many of the self-effacing disclaimers in the *Meditations* achieve their deflation in a decidedly humorous way. Taylor's words are not just inadequate but "Drivle" (2.142) and "incky, Goose quill-slabbred draughts" (2.43), his verse "slippery" and mere "Tattling" (1.21), his metaphors "but dull Tacklings tag'd / With ragged Non-sense" (2.36), "ragged Stuff, / Making the Sun seem like a Mullipuff" (1.22). When he aspires to lofty invention, his thoughts "in Snick-Snarls run." Even the ordeal of composing under an uncooperative muse comes out sounding more idly fanciful and mischievous than it does anguishing:

Thus my leane Muses garden thwarts the spring
    Instead of Anthems, breatheth her ahone.

But duty raps upon her doore for Verse.
That makes her bleed a poem through her searce.

(2.30)

I also crave thy pardon still because
    My Muses Hermetage is grown so old
Her Spirits shiver doe, her Phancy's Laws
    Are much transgresst. She sits so Crampt with cold.
    Old age indeed hath finde her, that she's grown
    Num'd, and her Musicks Daughters sing Ahone.

(2.122)

The poems ridicule their author's personal and spiritual ambitions no less than his writing. A creature of "Folly," he has only "an Acorn Cup" of a soul to set beneath the oceanic effusions of divine grace. Before the palace of his redeemer he stands "More blockish than a block, as [a] blockhead" (1.28, 1.24). Drawing from a store of self-derisive epithets so extensive one could smile, Taylor accounts his love "a shrimpy thing," his head "a Bog of Filth," his members "Dung-Carts that bedung at pleasure" (2.161[A], 1.45).

Even when Taylor elects to describe objects outside himself, he is inclined to betray his stylistic design of meiosis through his handling of imagery and diction. Without warning the silver skies of heaven can become an inverted beer bowl; and God the healer becomes a pharmacist who mixes up physical cordials. The water Moses releases with his rod becomes a river of beer for Israel "to bath and bibble in" (2.60[B]).

Without dispelling the oddity of these juxtapositions, comments by Samuel Mather and Calvin help disclose the inner logic of satiric contrast. For Mather, the failure of unreformed Christians to perceive the chasm between godly dispensation and human invention was quite literally a laughing matter, albeit one to be restrained within "holy" bounds:

See here the difference between God's Ceremonies, and Mens; between religious Ceremonies of Divine Institution, and of Humane Invention. Divine Ceremonies are full of Light, full of Spirit, full of Gospel-Marrow and Mystery. But Humane Ceremonies in the Worship of God, are full of

Darkness and Vanity, thick Darkness, their is no Light, no Signification
in them; As Men cannot *bless* their own Ceremonies, and make them
effectual for spiritual Ends: So they cannot so much as make them *suitable*
and *significant*; they are commonly so Foolish, so impertinent and
ridiculous, that it is hardly fit to name them in a Pulpit, lest they provoke
Laughter.

As for Instance; for I will give you an Instance or two, because there is
an *Holy* Scorn and an *Holy* Laughter.[24]

Calvin admitted that we must think and speak of God, though all
our efforts to do so were "an insipid fiction." "Whatever by
ourselves we think concerning him is foolish," he warned, "and
whatever we speak, absurd." If images such as the golden cher-
ubim, veil, and mercy seat of the divine presence were permitted
under the Old Law, it was only because they signified that our
minds are to be "lifted above themselves with admiration." Such
images served only the self-canceling function of showing how
"images are not suited to represent God's mysteries."[25]

In highlighting the comic disparity between earthly vehicle and
divine tenor, between scriptural figure and domestic replica,
Taylor likewise dramatizes his conviction of God's unspeakable
transcendence. By making his tropes manifest the very absurdity
of trying to trace the ineffable, he is able to draw a new, comically
devout aesthetic from the sober truth that "My Rhymes do better
suite / Mine own Dispraise than tune forth praise to thee" (1.22).

The point is not that Taylor scorns his writing in a worldly and
immediate sense, as viewed in competition with others, but that
for him any product of human ingenuity falls ludicrously short of
comparison with God's eternal majesty. Human construct amounts
to nothing more, relatively speaking, than "Wits Wantonings,
and Fancies frollicks plump" (2.56). Even "Angells Wits are Child-
ish tricks" (1.13) when set against the supreme glory. For that
matter, Taylor knew that the tropes figured so brilliantly in Scrip-

24. Samuel Mather, *The Figures or Types of the Old Testament*, 207. It had long been
suspected, but is now established beyond doubt, that Taylor knew this work: see
Charles W. Mignon, "Christ the Glory of All Types: The Initial Sermon from
Edward Taylor's 'Upon the Types of the Old Testament,'" *William and Mary Quarterly* 37 (1980): 287.

25. Calvin, *Institutes*, 1:103, 124, 102.

ture itself paled beside the antitypal reality of Christ. If Christ is indeed "the image of the invisible God" (Col. 1.15), the Bible paints only an image of an image. Calvin went so far as to grant that for providential reasons God's book set forth its sublime announcement of the Kingdom "largely in mean and lowly words."[26] The gospel portrait, too, amounts to something less than the living God.

Cognizant of all this, Taylor believes he can write well enough to justify persistence, well enough to satisfy part of his temporal calling. Given God's friendship he knows he will be able, even in this life, to make his "rough Feet . . . thy smooth praises sing" (1.39); and the buoyant witticism in this phrasing helps belie his otherwise abject note of apology. So too, in the final stanza of *Meditation* 1.27, he contradicts his own apology by praying in verse exactly what he says he cannot:

Were't not more than my heart can hold, or hord,
    Or than my Tongue can tell; I thus would pray,
Let him in Whom all Fulness Dwells, dwell, Lord
    Within my Heart: this Treasure therein lay.
    I then shall sweetly tune thy Praise, When hee
    In Whom all Fulness dwells, doth dwell in mee.

One of the more telling enactments of self-dispraising wit in Taylor is his image of the babbling child. Taylor's finest artistry could please the infinite Father only as a benign sort of amusement, much as the capricious antics of a child engage the human parent. The reach of man's intelligence toward the unlimited heights of divine wisdom is as comparatively frivolous as "Childrens catching speckled Butterflies" (2.37). In images like these, Taylor's self-satiric edge is softened, and several poems indicate that the erring, inarticulate child may also be the adopted heir of salvation. Often Taylor describes his poetic speech as a "Lisp of Non-sense" (1.17).[27] Yet for Taylor there was considerable consola-

---

26. Ibid., 1:82.

27. It is telling that around 1628 Francis Quarles could without hesitation equate "non-sense" with "wit": Quarles, *The Complete Works in Prose and Verse*, ed. Alexander Grosart, 3:240; cf. 2:225–26.

tion in the knowledge that "Non-Sense very Pleasant is / To Parents, flowing from the Lisping Child" (1.34). If destined to spend his mortal life as God's juggler and lisping child, he would learn to play the role for all it was worth.

In fact, Taylor leveled his most biting sallies of deflationary wit not against his own person but against the crowd of sins and devils he caught rioting within his heart and parading senselessly through the world. The world itself, to the extent of its infection with depravity, acts out a cruel parody of its creation in pristine beauty. Its deepest learning is only a "mock Wisdom" (C, 128). And in Taylor's technique of caricature, the unholy foolishness of depravity often shows itself in gaming and scatological imagery.[28] "A Knot of Imps" play "at barly breaks" (1.43) in the poet's soul. Satan, that "fool" and "Cursed Elf," uses the same spot as a "Bowling Ally" wherein to amuse himself with "Nine Pins, Nine Holes, Morrice, Fox and Geese" (1.40, 2.32).

The poet finds so many reveling passions competing here that he speaks as one stranded in the thick of a rural carnival:

Was ever Heart like mine? Pride, Passion, fell.
    Ath'ism, Blasphemy, pot, pipe it, dance
Play Barlybreaks, and at last Couple in Hell.
    At Cudgells, Kit-Cat, Cards and Dice here prance.
    At Noddy, Ruff-and-trumpt, Jing, Post-and-Pare,
    Put, One-and-thirty, and such other ware.
                           (1.40)

Mine Heart's a Park or Chase of sins; Mine Head
    'S a Bowling Alley. Sins play Ninehole here.
Phansy's a Green: sin Barly breaks in't led.
Judgment's a pingle. Blindeman's Buff's plaid there.
Sin playes at Coursey Parke within my Minde:
My Wills a Walke in which it aires what's blinde.
                           (2.18)

In the end, naturally, all of this fooling turns out to be folly indeed, as Grace "befooles" Satan's design to "outwit" holy wisdom (C, 90, 120, 254; Meditation 2.32).

28. See Robert D. Arner, "Edward Taylor's Gaming Imagery: 'Meditation 1.40' "; Calvin Israel, "Edward Taylor's Barleybreaks"; and Elizabeth Wiley, "Sources of Imagery in the Poetry of Edward Taylor," 49–52.

That victory points toward the joyous ramifications of Taylor's wit, toward an exuberant energy that complements the more frowning uses of satiric parody considered thus far. Indeed the meiotic rituals of debasement are in a sense only "preparatory" play before this more buoyant, festive, and affirmative sanctification of verbal wit.[29] Only rarely might Taylor provoke immediate laughter; he is otherwise apt to sound by turns whimsical or facetious, coy or celebratory, irrepressibly eager to play with his material in one way or another. And like the meiotic dimension of reverent parody and the satiric representation of depravity, Taylor's jubilant wit springs from a complex of theological motives. One of these, involving the self-allusive interplay of word and image enacted within the scriptural Word, is treated in the next chapter. Other motives for the poet's celebration can be found in: (1) the archetypal *discordia concors* of God's Incarnation in Christ; (2) the apprehension of grace as playful extravagance; and (3) the delightful prospect of eschatological joy.

For Taylor the most conspicuous model of comic incongruity lay in the Christian mystery of the Incarnation. He was not the first writer to express astonishment that the Creator and Lord of eternity had assumed a creaturely nature in time, that a boundless Wisdom had bound itself in human flesh. Cotton Mather, for one, called the hypostatic union an "astonishing thing."[30] That an infinite God should have voluntarily abased himself to the wretched state of humanity to restore his own blighted creation gave plentiful cause for wonder. Yet Taylor showed not only ceaseless astonishment but even something of genuinely comic amazement before a picture of Incarnation in which, as he puns, "Thy Person infinite, without compare / Cloaths made of a Carnation leafe doth ware" (2.24). It was fortunate to the point of ludicrousness that the divine Sun should

---

29. It is this buoyant side of Taylor's wit that Karl Keller underscores as all-pervasive, most directly in *The Example of Edward Taylor*, 163–88. An appreciation of Taylor's energetic wit likewise informs the readings of Everett Emerson, *Puritanism in America: 1620–1750*, 112–21, and Albert Gelpi, *The Tenth Muse: the Psyche of the American Poet*, 15–54.

30. Cotton Mather, *A Companion for Communicants*, 23.

. . . array
Itselfe with Clouds, and to a Glow worm go
For Light to make all o're the World light day.
                              (2.41)

All the more startling was the miracle of human salvation and
deification accomplished through this mediation. That sinful humanity should be singled out for such lavish favor was a turn of
events so unfathomable that "Should Gold Wed Dung, should
Stars Wooe Lobster Claws, / It would no wonder, like this Wonder,
cause" (2.33). Taylor represents standard Reformed doctrine in
preaching the necessity of Jesus' death on the cross. Yet his imaginative soteriology, or doctrine of salvation, follows the Eastern
church fathers in its stress on saving results of the larger process of
Christ's Incarnation, dwelling especially on Christ's personal union
of natures and the fulfillment of this eternal union in resurrection
and ascension. Taylor shows regret that the "Brave Flower" of
Christ had to be plucked and pressed with violence to make a
physic for his soul, but he is more entranced by the marvel that
"this mangled Rose rose up again" (1.4). That poignant empathy
with Christ's experience of the Passion so prominent in Lutheran
piety is barely felt in Taylor. And like most Puritans, Taylor reveals
little curiosity about the human personality of Jesus. What mattered for him was simply the fact, the amazing phenomenon, of
heaven's love wedded to humanity, and this fact he committed
himself to driving upon the heart through every conceivable turn
of rhetoric, with all the wit and meditative passion he could muster.

As the Word becomes flesh, so the poet incarnates something of
divine truth through the fleshly medium of words. His words
imitate the Logos by their echoing response to God, by their
enlivening address to himself and others. His wit, a carnalizing
faculty, undertakes the active process of mediating between
changeless truth and present revelation, between God and the
self.[31] Thus, the Incarnation gave particular warrant to the pun-
gent vulgarity and polar extravagance Taylor favored in his meta-

31. William J. Scheick, *The Will and the Word: The Poetry of Edward Taylor,* 93–114,
elaborates on the role of Logos theory in Taylor's poetic.

phoric style. Commenting on the homely materials presented in the Eucharist, a New England contemporary of Taylor's exclaimed at how Christ had condescended to our infirmity by making "choice of Things that are most vulgar to us, to be the sacramental Signs of the choicest and most precious Benefits that are to be had from him."[32]

For that matter, the Christian faith as a whole appeared an absurdity to the world by virtue of the radical paradoxes and scandal of particularity centered in the Incarnation. Its story, replete with drastic incongruities, sounded fantastic enough that the Apostle himself admitted—in famous words Taylor cited— that the Christ he preached was "unto the Jews a stumbling block: and unto the Greeks foolishness" (1 Cor. 1.23; *TCLS*, 78). By a further paradox, the wisdom of this faith could be imparted only "by the foolishness of preaching" (1 Cor. 1.21), since "faith cometh by hearing, and hearing by the word of God" (Rom. 10.17). The sober charge of evangelism, then, called Taylor as poet-preacher to become one sort of comedian and holy fool for the sake of Christ.

Another religious spring of Taylor's comic imagination is not so apparent: his conviction of the gratuitous freedom and energy of the divine will, his sense of grace as playful extravagance. Though otherwise grounded in Jewish and Christian belief, this is one of the few ludic impulses to which the Puritan-Calvinist tradition could give special impetus. If in static attributes the Puritan deity was described as awesome, merciful, and omniscient, he was also a dynamo of energy and activity. In the beginning, the primeval God acted to shape chaos into visible forms under no compulsion and for no practical necessity whatever, but purely to satisfy his good pleasure.

Conservatively, one can see how the Puritans felt compelled to enshrine motives of godly whim for fear of suggesting that their Lord was bound somehow by human processes of reasoning or that he had to create and sustain the world because he lacked something without it. God's will, on the contrary, was wholly self-

---

32. Samuel Willard, *Some Brief Sacramental Meditations*, 5–6.

sufficient. The divine life reflected the very essence of freedom, of voluntaristic energy. God existed at the first for his own sake, with the generation of the Spirit from Father and Son enacting a dynamism complete unto itself. Like St. Thomas, Samuel Whiting wrote of God's continuing subsistence as "pure act"; for William Ames the *sufficientia* and *efficientia* of God were the two pillars of faith.[33] Though immutable and impassible, this Lord was never passive. If God chose to bind himself to reasonable activity and steadfast love within the conditions of human covenanting, he did not do so for reasons penetrable by human logic. And he certainly did not do so for reasons of human merit. What God created must be good *ipso facto*, but that he created at all was a mystery beyond utilitarian explanation. As Calvin and the rest intoned repeatedly, God acts out of his own good pleasure, out of sheer delight, rather than need.

If this pleasure principle cannot be construed in a crassly anthropomorphic light, it does envision God's exercise of a freely active disposition recognizable in human terms as play. In the same vein, Taylor in his *Christographia* sermons affirms the Deity's nature as a "Sovereign being" who "hath all right to Dispose, and impose at his pleasure" (*C, 67*). Though fulfilling his own eternal decrees, "He was in no necessity to Create the World; nor to suffer man to Sin" (*C, 15*). Not even the redemption of fallen humanity or the election of saints could be forced on God by any logic of duty. It was, in the words of *The Shorter Catechism*, "out of his mere good pleasure" that God elected some to eternal life in the covenant of grace.[34] Increase Mather reiterated that God's covenants were "voluntary Transactions," the terms of reconciliation propounded by the Father as "an Act of His holy Will and Pleasure" rather than from "any necessity of nature."[35]

33. Whiting is cited in David D. Hall, *The Faithful Shepherd: A History of the New England Ministry in the Seventeenth Century,* 59; William Ames, *The Marrow of Theology,* trans. John Eusden, 84, 92. Taylor's father-in-law, James Fitch, expounds on the theme of divine self-sufficiency in *The First Principles of the Doctrine of Christ,* 5–9.

34. *The Shorter Catechism with Scripture Proofs,* 6; Taylor adds his endorsement in *Christographia,* 54.

35. Increase Mather, *The Mystery of Christ,* 7.

As repugnant as this capricious accent may seem from one point of view, it also points toward the joyously sublime principle of play. And according to the Hebraic Wisdom tradition, that enigmatic female personification called Wisdom once sported in playful "delight, rejoicing always" (Proverbs 8:30) with and before the Lord, in the elemental acts of Creation.[36] The play of God is a notion whose import extends well beyond the terms of Reformed orthodoxy, with variant expressions in Catholic Christianity as well as in Hindu forms such as the myth of *lila* or the cosmic dance of Shiva.

God's unforced activity, then, is the very essence and prototype of play. As Johan Huizinga defines it, play is above all a "free," "superfluous," and "voluntary" activity containing that which "transcends the immediate needs of life and imparts meaning to the action." It fills no bodily need, offers no earthly profit. Play is thus allied to contemplation, that pure enjoyment of God in holy leisure that crowns all other activity. Josef Pieper cites St. Thomas to this effect, but the connection could apply as well to Taylor: " 'because of the leisure that goes with contemplation' the divine wisdom itself, Holy Scripture says, is 'always at play, playing through the whole world.' "[37]

Grace enters this equation when the circle of God's play touches man, when the free, gratuitous motions of the divine life penetrate human life. Taylor often follows convention in representing grace as a thing, an enlivening substance. Even so, his liquid imagery usually manages to convey a more dynamic sense of grace as the play of superabundant energy. *Meditation* 1.1, for instance, variously represents the force of gracious love as a sexual urge, as the Spirit's fire, and as a tumbling succession of fluids. God's "Matchless love" is at first a living water that overflows the vessels of earth and heaven. But in its rushing course it becomes in turn the salt tide of the sea, the blood of the Savior, and a fluid of unquenchable flame welling up in the heart.

---

36. See Samuel Terrien's chapter on "The Play of Wisdom" in *The Elusive Presence: The Heart of Biblical Theology*, 350–89.

37. Johan Huizinga, *Homo Ludens: A Study of the Play Element in Culture*, 26, 19; Josef Pieper, *Leisure the Basis of Culture*, 41.

A more dizzying kaleidoscope of liquid comparisons pours out of the typic rock of Aqua-Vitae in *Meditation* 2.60[B]. Taylor mentions everything from sea water, river water, wine, and oil to beer, blood, nectar, and dishwater. The sheer surplus of figures conveys the unrestrained extravagance of "All Glorious Grace" in what he elsewhere calls its "overflowing fulness."[38] This curious superfluity recalls the nearly redundant language of the prologue to St. John's Gospel with its paean to the fullness of "grace upon grace." At the same time the fluid, tumbling rush from one liquid to another sweeps away the static seriousness of any individual metaphor, suggesting the unfettered richness of grace as divine energy.

Knowing the dynamism of God's delight and its communication to humankind as grace, the Christian may be expected to respond in kind. A third component of Taylor's comic imagination involved celebrating the prospect of eschatological joy, that sheer delight of subsisting in God experienced after the example of God's own freeplay. St. Augustine restricted the principle of "enjoyment" to the will's rest in things satisfying for their own sake, especially God, relegating all else to the lower category of "use."[39] Looking beyond his anti-utilitarian defense of the New England Sabbath day, Taylor presents a vision of bliss in the eternal sabbath as the predictable outcome of *Gods Determinations.* And progress toward this end defines the usual shape of the *Meditations.* The typical *Meditation* begins, after posing some question or problem, by painting a comically dire picture of the soul's state. Like the typical psalm, however, it progresses toward a close that reaffirms the promise of salvation and projects a future of endless delight. The more depraved and desperate Taylor's opening view of the soul, the more exultant and amazed our sense of the saint's ending in felicity.

Beyond these structural tactics of suggesting ultimate joy, Tay-

38. Edward Taylor, *The Harmony of the Gospels,* ed. Thomas M. and Virginia L. Davis with Betty L. Parks, 1:303. Subsequent references to this work will be cited in the text as *Harmony.*

39. See Augustine's *De Trinitate,* in *Augustine: Later Works,* ed. and trans. John Burnaby, especially 66 (and n. 13), 80, 85.

lor often gave more immediate expression to his jubilant hopes. Many a *Meditation* finds him rhapsodizing on the "glee" and "delight" of sainthood, jumping for joy at the hypothetical prospect of glory, or urging himself to share in the "holy cheere" of heaven:

But thou my Lord, (Heart leape for joy and sing)
Hast done the Deed: and 't makes the Heavens ring.
                                        (1.31)

One may doubt whether Taylor sang, danced, and leapt for joy in real life, but there is no end to this carrying on in the playing field of his writing. As Huizinga observes, "*Poiesis,* in fact, is a play-function,"[40] in which light Taylor's resolve to "play" the divine praises takes on new layers of meaning (2.153). In the sermons too, Taylor is constantly declaring the soul's espousal with God to be a source of "rapture," "Delightsomeness," "Sweetest Consolation," "comfort," and "unspeakable delight."

By extension, an atmosphere of ecstatic joy is often visible in the natural life of the entire cosmos. That insight offered still more support for the poet's playful manipulation of metaphors. Only some of Taylor's gaming imagery operates as satiric wit to mock the world's depravity; the rest conjures fanciful impressions of that frolic merriment suffusing creation within the vision of a divine comedy. One of the *Meditations* explicitly compares the sport of human salvation to the game God began to play when he set in motion all natural processes:

Thou madst this World: dost it thy play-house keep
Wherein the Stars themselves play Hide-and-Seek.
It is thy Green, where all thy Creatures play
    At Barly-Breake and often lose their fleece.
But we poore wee our Soules a wager lay
    At Nine-Mens Morrice, and at Fox and Geese.
    Let me not play myselfe away, nor Grace.
    Nor lose my Soule, My Lord, at prison base.
                                        (2.35)

40. Huizinga, *Homo Ludens,* 14.

Animating the temple of the world, therefore, is the same gracious Life concentrated more intensely in the glorified body of Jesus and the tabernacle of heaven. "Art thou my Temple, Lord," asks the poet in *Meditation* 2.20, "Then thou Most Choice / Art Angells Play-House, and Saints Paradise." Several poems celebrate the carefree play of angels, the poet's enravished soul playing in their midst (2.68[A]), the dancing "Scip, and play" of Love within the regenerate saint (1.36, 76–78). In others the "bright Wonder" of some real or fancied marvel in nature is used to analogize the greater wonder "that fore us playes" in God's saving acts (2.24). But even when Taylor draws on natural facts for the sake of analogy only, exploiting the usual pious puns along the way, he ends up painting a vividly pulsating cosmos in which the stars dance in rhythm with the communion of saints:

The world play in a Sneale horn Hide, and Seek
May, ere my thimble can thy fulness meete.
                                             (2.46)

Doe Fables say, the Rising Sun doth Dance
   On Easter Day for joy, thou didst ascende.
. . . .
   And shall not I, furled in thy glorious beams,
Ev'n jump for joy, Enjoying such sweet gleams?
                                             (2.67[B])

The Earth a dancing fell when thy bright day
   Of its uprising shining all about
   Angells put on their glorious robes to tend
   Thy tryumph over death and as thy freinds.
                                             (2.158)

Meethinks thy smile doth make thy Footstoole so
   Spread its green Carpet 'fore thy feet for joy.
And Bryers climb in t'bright Rose that flows
   Out in sweet reechs to meet thee in the sky:
   And makes the sportive Starrs play Hide-and-Seek
   And on thy bodies Glory peeping keep.
                                             (2.76)

For Taylor part of the game inherent in life derived from God's coy, flirtatious methods of pursuing his saints. Such courtship sometimes threatened to turn faith itself into a dark jest of hide-and-seek. But Taylor could accept the game, with all its stalking and amorous spying, as offering its satisfactions to both sides. At least God seemed entertained by the sport of letting his "Love play bow-peep" (2.96) with the poet on earth.

For the Puritan especially, joyous delight in God was not merely a legitimate satisfaction. It was a serious duty and a critical sign of sanctity. An obligation of this sort could plainly become self-defeating. Still, what the catechisms and worthy divines announced to be man's chief end beyond glorifying God was the enjoyment of God, both in this life and the next. And though Reformed spirituality held no monopoly on it, this Augustinian statement resonates with a peculiar literalness in the Puritan tradition. In his *Explicatory Catechism*, Thomas Vincent explained that "to enjoy God is to acquiesce or rest in God as the chief good, with complacency and delight." Alluding to Psalm 34, Vincent goes on to specify that the "rest" of which he speaks is no passive negation, appearing instead in the active experience of one who "tastes and sees" the Lord. Richard Baxter fixes the paradox even more pointedly: "this Rest contains a sweet and constant action of all the powers of the soul and body in this enjoyment of God. It is not the rest of a stone, which ceaseth from all motion when it attains the centre."[41]

This Reformed preoccupation with the soul's emotive disposition as it grew toward the ideal of dynamic joy seemed to have developed naturally out of a need to confront the insufficiency of holy works. Though one could and should act to prepare the heart for conversion, and though doing good did the saint good in any number of subtler ways, the naked deed produced no saving merit. As much as the soul's godly motions in the world counted as evidence of saving grace, they counted less than the interior flux of the Spirit as shadowed in one's outward demeanor. After

41. Thomas Vincent, *An Explicatory Catechism*, 3; Richard Baxter, *The Saints' Everlasting Rest*, vol. 1 of *The Doubleday Devotional Classics*, ed. E. Glenn Hinson, 24. Taylor was well acquainted with Vincent's catechism.

passing through the valley of contrition and humiliation, could the convert's reply to God's lively delight be anything less than delight? "Oh when Divine Shines, Love, and Sweetness are returnd in upon the Soul from God as the Fruite of Holiness in its highest ascent," wrote Taylor, "inexpressible must needs be the Joy, and Comfort of the Soule" (C, 179). You ought to "Cheare up," he tells the poor, drooping soul, for possessed of true faith "Its a Shame for thee to ly Sulling thy Glass with Sighs, and plastering thy Cheeks . . . for feare thou shouldst be Condemned for thy sins." They may not yet have closed with Christ in whose countenance "appears too much the image of Spirituall Death. . . . How Languid is their Holiness? How palefaced is their profession?" (C, 362, 194).

Moreover, while Reformed doctrine considered the soul to stand passive in the actual reception of grace, the soul was subsequently obliged to exercise the grace it experienced. This interior activity, another version of festive dynamism, involved stirring the affections and drawing grace toward the end of enjoying God. Registered emotionally as delight, the exercise of grace might be played out through prayer, meditation, or even through the exercise of poetic wit. Taylor echoes other Puritan divines when he urges "the right improovment of those gracious Influences comming . . . upon our Souls so as to draw out the Soule Satisfying delight of God" toward our "felicitating . . . with the Divine Sweetness therein." "Oh this is Sweet indeed," he adds, "This is called the injoying of God" (UW, 1:11).

Taylor's odes to joy and demonstrations of playful zeal do not nullify the sorrowful aspect of journeying in faith. The Westfield pastor would think the theological virtue of hope trivialized if construed as the equivalent of unregenerate optimism or simple good feeling. Nor was Taylor's sense of the sacred uninformed by that sublime fear with which Moses and St. Paul encountered the Almighty. The holy amazement fostered by the comic imagination, as broadly and seriously conceived, stands in a dialectical rather than negative relation to the *mysterium tremendum et fascinans*.[42] Still, there is a sense in which comic resolution is ulti-

42. See M. Conrad Hyers, "The Dialectic of the Sacred and the Comic," in *Holy*

mate in the divine plan. Consequently, not even Jesus' reputation as suffering servant kept Taylor from urging parishioners to live after holy delight. Responding directly to the relevant objection, Taylor argued that Christ's "delight" and "Soule joy" outweighed his familiarity with grief. If the "outward man" of Jesus was weighed down by sorrow, the more essential self preserved "the Sweetest Soule Comfort imaginable" (C, 179).

Delight and amusement of more profane origin could also be exploited for devout ends. Whatever else the Puritan "plain stile" may have meant, it surely did not mean that preachers were to forego raising the affections of their listeners with the bait of rhetorical pleasure. Even those like William Perkins, John Cotton, and Thomas Hooker who expressly favored "plainness" over the showier floridities of pulpit eloquence had to be concerned about evangelical persuasion. They knew that to teach and persuade effectively one not only had to use dramatic figures but also had to exploit their motivating power of delight. Richard Sibbes admitted that "it was the study of the wise man, Solomon, becoming a preacher, to find out pleasant Words, or words of delight" as a means of affecting the heart. John Bulkley of Colchester commended Roger Wolcott's *Poetical Meditations* with the reminder that the art of writing "does greatly delight and entertain us, and at the same time Instruct or Teach."[43]

Bulkley's conjunction of instruction and entertainment was shared by Renaissance rhetoricians of every religious persuasion. Not everyone went so far as Thomas Wilson in advising preachers "now and then [to] play the fools in the pulpit," tickling ears with the judicious interspersion of "pleasant saws and moving laughter." But no one could dispute Wilson's conclusion: "delight theim and win them; weary theim, and you lose them forever."[44] To lose

---

Laughter: Essays on Religion in Comic Perspective, ed. M. Conrad Hyers, 208–40

43. Sibbes and Bulkley are cited in Perry Miller and Thomas Johnson, eds., *The Puritans: A Sourcebook of Their Writings,* 1:66, 2:681. Notable assessments of the Puritan plain style include Larzer Ziff, "The Literary Consequences of Puritanism," in *The American Puritan Imagination: Essays in Revaluation,* ed. Sacvan Bercovitch, 34–44, and Lawrence A. Sasek, *The Literary Temper of the English Puritans,* 39–56.

44. Thomas Wilson, "The Art of Rhetorique," in *The Renaissance in England: Nondramatic Prose and Verse of the Sixteenth Century,* ed. Hyder E. Rollins and Herschel Baker, 591.

an audience meant nothing, a Puritan would say, if the preacher's vanity was the principal casualty, but to risk losing souls otherwise won by a means ordained to salvation was a more fearful thing altogether.

The Aristotelian conjunction "to teach and delight" was also, as Sidney made clear in his *Defense of Poesy*, the only effective means of teaching in poetry. If the reader or listener was not somehow moved to respond, the writer had exercised his art in vain. And for the Puritan, a rhetorical art exercised in vain, satisfying only the ingenious instincts of the artisan, was the very height of vanity. It was therefore a duty of poet or preacher to entertain. This principle remains a constant beneath the successive waves of controversy about style that agitated the English-speaking world during the era of Protestant dissent. Even a narrower conception of art as didactic fastening of the Word could never be fulfilled in practice unless the word given in instruction was entertaining enough to take root. Some Puritans were eager to question that which seemed to them demonstrative of merely human eloquence, but none would quarrel with the trinity of values St. Augustine upheld in his praise of the eloquent man: "he who is eloquent should speak in such a way that he teaches, delights, and moves."[45]

45. Augustine, *On Christian Doctrine*, trans. D. W. Robertson, Jr., 136.

2 Pills to Purge
New England Melancholy

The Diagnosis of Puritan Sorrow

If Taylor's rhetorical invocation of delight to draw the heart toward salvation is well rooted in theology, clearly it is no less grounded in spiritual psychology. And as we examine more closely this psychological matrix of the poet's comic aesthetic, we confront the presumed antithesis of joy: the traditional problem of religious melancholy. Taylor's practical concern with spiritual infirmities related to melancholy, as experienced personally and as observed in members of his congregation, is demonstrably related to his practice of verbal wit. To appreciate just how the problem of despondency figures in his writing, we need to recall something of the moral and medical background of humoral psychology.

At the time Taylor began to write his poetry, the physiology originally supporting the Renaissance theory of bodily humors was already becoming outmoded. In fact, the final blow to the medical principles behind humoral psychology had been struck by William Harvey's discovery of blood circulation in 1628. Yet the psychological concept of melancholy continued to draw interest through the English Renaissance and beyond Taylor's lifetime. Everyone recognized the symptoms of pathological melancholy, and the representation of character types based on the various humors was a commonplace in dramatic literature. In writers such as Shakespeare, Ben Jonson, and John Donne, the literary uses of this traditional concept of melancholy could be highly complex.[1] But even for the less gifted authors of theoretical trea-

1. The topic is discussed in Lawrence Babb, *The Elizabethan Malady: A Study of Melancholia in English Literature from 1580–1642*, and Bridget G. Lyons, *Voices of Melancholy: Studies in Literary Treatments of Melancholy in Renaissance England*. Most of my general background information is drawn from these two works.

33

tises, *melancholy* was a word rich in physical, psychological, and spiritual meaning.

That Taylor could have been unaware of this tradition or could have remained conceptually unaffected by it is thus inconceivable. Going no further than the books in his library, he would have found the topic discussed by authors like Thomas Shepard, Benjamin Colman, William Ames, and Cotton Mather. He also owned a collection of Anne Bradstreet's poetry with its long poem "Of the four Humours in Mans Constitution." As practicing physician for the Westfield community, he was familiar with Lazerius Riverius's *Practice of Physick* (translated by Nicholas Culpeper), which featured an elaborate diagnosis of melancholy from the medical standpoint together with assorted herbal prescriptions for its cure. It should come as no surprise, then, that Taylor's poetry often alludes to melancholy or mentions terms that a contemporary audience would have immediately recognized as symptomatic of the splenetic illness.

The Practice of Physick describes in simplest terms how to recognize the disease caused by an excess of melancholic humor, associated with black bile: "Melancholy is a Doting or Delerium without a Fever with fear and sadness."[2] Among its more obvious symptoms were a sullen, morose temperament, a sustained inclination toward grief, and morbid fear. Authorities as diverse as Riverius and Richard Baxter agreed that "overmuch sorrow" might be either a symptomatic result or a chief cause of the sickness. This ambiguity explains some of the complication in attitudes Taylor and other Puritans would adopt toward melancholia.

Two other ways of interpreting the melancholic state arose to challenge Galen's medical scheme, which came into much favor during the late sixteenth and early seventeenth centuries. The first, drawing heavily on Aristotle, tried to set the melancholic condition in a favorable light. What had been pathological in the Galenic formulation became, in this scheme, a heroic virtue: melancholics were persons inspired by a kind of superior madness similar to Plato's idea of divine frenzy. A second way of interpreting the passions connected with melancholy derived

2. Lazerius Riverius, *The Practice of Physick*, 48.

from the medieval habit of placing them under the rubric of moral philosophy. Consequently, "overmuch sorrow" came to be regarded as a sin—particularly, the sin of *acedia*. This approach, highlighting ethical and philosophical rather than clinical considerations, found expression in a variety of expository books produced around the turn of the seventeenth century.

The ideological focus of still another brand of treatise fell somewhere between the two extremes of Galenic materialism and moralized instruction. Affirming melancholy to be at least as much a disease as a vice, these books projected a mainly clinical and sympathetic attitude toward it. At the same time they rejected the notion of heroic melancholy and often insisted that the entire matter be considered within a theological framework.[3] It is this mixed, medical-cum-theological strand of the tradition that contributes most to an understanding of Taylor's imaginative response.

A prominent early example of the "middle way" of understanding melancholy is Timothy Bright's *Treatise of Melancholy* (1586), which takes pains to distinguish melancholy proper from remorse of conscience. Bright found the scrupulous—those whose "heartes are . . . overtender and rare"—to be especially liable to affliction by melancholy's dark fumes. Although he lent such victims his consolation and encouragement, Bright also felt compelled to point out the moral "disadvantage of the melancholicke complexion." If not sinful in itself, the humoral malady offered Satan an occasion to effect the downfall of godly souls. For a melancholic was naturally predisposed toward despair, which Bright considered not merely the converse of spiritual presumption but its logical consequence. Morbid self-doubt bred presumptive curiosity, which could lead in turn to despair. Contemplatives and scholars were asking for trouble, then, unless they took care to keep their speculations firmly grounded in the scriptural Word.[4]

That "overmuch meditation" and "too importunate enquiry" might precipitate despairing melancholy was likewise a lesson of Robert Burton's famous *Anatomy of Melancholy.* To be sure, Burton's flamboyant and expansive *Anatomy* takes a less consistently dis-

3. Lyons, *Voices of Melancholy,* 3–5, 7–10.
4. Timothy Bright, *A Treatise of Melancholy,* 188–89, 190, 192, 199, 207.

paraging view of the melancholic state than does Bright's *Treatise*.
For the most part, though, Burton endorsed the prevailing view of
melancholy as a disease with spiritual ramifications. The first to
identify a distinct species of "Religious Melancholy," he attributed
the perturbation of religious scrupulosity not only to physiological
imbalance but also to unhealthful conduct and, ultimately, to supernatural forces. "The principal agent and procurer of this mischief is the Devil," he wrote, whose "ordinary engine . . . is the
melancholy humour itself, which is the Devil's bath." Accordingly,
Burton prescribed a mixture of cures. Neither "sole physicke" nor
"good advice alone" was accounted a sufficient remedy.[5]

Although Burton was of course no Puritan, his sense that melancholy "is a disease of the soul on which I am to treat, and as much
appertaining to a divine as to a Physician" sums up a typically
Puritan attitude toward melancholy and toward spirituality in
general. That a divine was first and foremost a "physician of the
soul" had been a central assumption of English Puritanism from
its earliest days.[6] Indeed, the metaphor of the theologian as spiritual physician arose so naturally from evidences of interconnec-
tion between soul and body that for some Puritans it was scarcely
a metaphor. And in his *Bonifacius*, a book Taylor owned, Cotton
Mather's well-known psychosomatic musings led to the counsel
that physicians cultivate "the art of curing by expectation" and
"consolation," pursuing the useful question of "what the mind
will do toward the cure of the body."[7]

Conversely and more crucially, the Puritan stress on subjective
religious experience encouraged many learned theologians to
play physician, to minister to the symptoms of physical and
especially of mental disease as a way of promoting the cure of
spiritual afflictions. Thus, a whole literature of the genre known
as "cases of conscience" enjoyed a tremendous vogue during the

5. Robert Burton, *The Anatomy of Melancholy,* ed. Floyd Dell and Paul J. Smith, 29,
938, 940–41, 959.

6. Ibid.; see chapter 1, "Physicians of the Soul," in William Haller's *The Rise of
Puritanism*, 3–48.

7. Cotton Mather, *Bonifacius: An Essay upon the Good*, ed. David Levin, 103–4.

seventeenth century.[8] If these writings were devoted only in part to prescribing solace for souls troubled by melancholy, scrupulosity was nonetheless a favorite "case of conscience" in the treatises of such eminent writers as Ames, Baxter, William Perkins, and the Anglican Jeremy Taylor. In his *Whole Treatise of the Cases of Conscience,* Perkins devoted special attention to the problem of "ministering and conveying . . . comfort to the mind of him, that hath confessed his sinnes" and yet remained "in Distresse of Mind." Ames, whose *Conscience with the Power and Cases Thereof* was in Taylor's library, added further distinctions in response to the question, "What is to be done when the conscience is scrupulous?"[9]

Unlike these works by Perkins and Ames, Baxter's *Preservatives against Melancholy and Over-much Sorrow* addressed itself almost exclusively to the problem of an oversensitive conscience. Granting that this form of humoral disease had physical causes, Baxter felt certain also that the Devil had a hand in cases of "overmuch Sorrow." It was in Satan's interest to cast the righteous into melancholic illness to seduce them first "to Overmuch sorrow and fear," then "to distracting Doubts and thoughts," and finally "to murmur against God, and to despair." Like his predecessors, Baxter earnestly charged those susceptible to melancholy to avoid exercising their "Thoughts now too deeply nor too much" since "long Meditation is a Duty to some, but not to you." Rumination, as Baxter perceived, sets the stage for melancholic self-absorption: "As Milstones wear themselves if they go when they have no Corn; so do the thoughts of such as think not of better things than their own Hearts." The victim of overserious self-regard could hope to escape his dungeon only by forcing the mind toward higher things—if, that is, he still had "any Power of . . . [his] own Thoughts."[10]

8. See Samuel Eliot Morison, *Harvard College in the Seventeenth Century,* 1:263. John T. McNeill discusses Puritan spiritual healing in its wider historical context in *A History of the Cure of Souls,* 263–67, 275–77, and Perry Miller remarks on the attention American Puritans gave *melancholia* in *The New England Mind,* 2:233.

9. William Perkins, *The Whole Treatise of the Cases of Conscience,* 55, 113; William Ames, *Conscience with the Power and Cases Thereof,* 19.

10. Richard Baxter, *Preservatives against Melancholy and Over-much Sorrow,* 84, 28.

Here precisely was the rub. Those vexed by internal demons had little chance of curing themselves through a simple act of self-will. Understanding as much, Baxter made several recommendations to those caring for distressed melancholics. If the melancholic could not divert his or her thoughts from the old round, another person might. This second party might read grieving melancholics "informing comforting Books, and live in a loving cheerful manner with them." It was absolutely imperative that the patient be "pleased, delighted," distracted from "sad and troubling words and things." In short, the melancholic's sadness somehow had to be replaced by delight and "Godly Cheerfulness."[11]

Implicit in Baxter, then, is a suggestion that delight might be an appropriate anodyne to melancholy. The same thought informs Bright's recommendation that melancholics embrace "all cheerful sights" and delightful impressions while keeping "good cheere . . . in Christ," or Cotton Mather's command that counselors raise for them "as bright thoughts as may be, and scatter the clouds."[12] If mirth was only one of the medicines capable of raising therapeutic delight, it would seem an altogether predictable one. Moreover, the view that mirth is an acceptable means of countering symptomatic melancholy finds direct support in contemporary sources inside and outside the Puritan tradition.

Burton, for example, held that comic wit was a singularly effective means of producing that healthful state of delight and spiritual "good cheere" recommended by writers like Timothy Bright. For Burton the therapeutic force of gaiety could scarcely be exaggerated. Because of its capacity to "expell grief," mirth was prescribed by physicians "as a principal engine to battle the walls of melancholy, a chief antidote, and a sufficient cure of itself." Among the approved varieties of therapeutic mirth in Burton's formulary were "jests, conceits," and "merry tales."[13]

Though Taylor may not have seen Burton's *Anatomy*, which was read in colonial New England, he would have encountered similar sentiments in his copy of a treatise by Benjamin Colman, *The*

---

11. Ibid., 70–71, 78, 86.
12. Bright, *A Treatise*, 242, 222; Mather, *Bonifacius*, 104.
13. Burton, *Anatomy of Melancholy*, 481.

Government and Improvement of Mirth. Colman stressed the pre-
ventive more than the restorative powers of mirth. He saw "regular
Mirth" and "the Habit of Chearfulness" as contributing greatly to
the spiritual health of Christians, whereas "Melancholly People
commonly make drooping Christians, to the disadvantage of
Religion." So long as it was "sober" and "decent," mirth helped
engender the spiritual joy God intended for his children. Working from this premise, Colman combed the Scriptures to find
evidence of heaven's blessing on jocularity when applied toward
virtuous ends. He pointed to Solomon, who said "I commended
Mirth"; to the Apostle's injunction to "Rejoice evermore"; to
Sarah's confession that "God has made me to laugh . . . so that all
who hear will laugh with me"; to the repeated call of the New Testament to "Be of good cheer"; and to the many calls to joyousness
echoed throughout the psalms. It was "Davids Sanguine Temper," after all, that "lead him to his Psalmody."[14]

In offering scriptural proofs for his moral argument against
gloom, Colman was following well-established precedent. Baxter
had prefaced *Preservatives against Melancholy* with the words of
Psalm 42, "Why art thou cast down, O my Soul? and why art thou
disquieted in me?" Others had similarly confirmed that spiritual
joy defined the normative disposition of Christian believers. And
several Puritan writers in England had been willing to endorse
properly restrained mirth as a refreshment for mind and spirit.
With due qualification, Perkins's *Direction for the Government of the
Tongue according to Gods Word* (1593) even stressed the duty of the
human race to exercise its divine gift of laughter.[15]

After Perkins's example, Colman went beyond many of his
predecessors by insisting on "not only the Lawfulness, but the
Loveliness and Obligation of Civil Mirth." Christians who failed
to show mirthful delight in their religion gave poor witness to the
unregenerate while opening the way to melancholic depression in
themselves. Though this good cheer was never to replace Christian earnestness, "'Tis a gross Opinion to think the Gravity,

14. Benjamin Colman, *The Government and Improvement of Mirth*, 20–26, 33–35.
15. Raymond A. Anselment, *'Betwixt Jest and Earnest': Marprelate, Milton, Marvell, Swift, and The Decorum of Religious Ridicule*, 13–14.

Sobriety, Moderation and Mortification to the Word, which agrees to the Christian character, cannot consist with Occasional Mirth, or with Habitual Chearfulness." Yet the serious demeanor of the biblical Christ and his repute as the lamb of affliction threatened to belie Colman's thesis on the duty of mirth. Undaunted, Colman came up with an apology recalling one we have already encountered in Taylor's *Christographia*:

> Indeed there was nothing Morose and Sour in the Conversation of our Lord: and I wish we could learn from thence, and always remember it, that Evangelical Holiness and Mortification do require no such thing of us. He was Courteous, Obliging, Affable to all that sought unto him; only severe & inexorable to mens Sins. 'Tis true, we read of his Tears, but never of his Laughing; and his Style was—A Man of Sorrows: Yet we know also he did not shun Mirth on proper Occasions, nor censure it in others. I have already observ'd, how he honour'd the Joyful Solemnity in Cana with his Presence; wherein he sufficiently countenanced Regular Mirth, and indeed Sanctify'd it; for it would be silly to question whether the Guests were Merry there; there was the Joy of the Bridegroom, and his Friends rejoyced to hear his Voice.[16]

One could cite other complaints against melancholy even from the vast, mostly sober expanse of Puritan prose. It may be enough to remember John Bunyan's "Apology" to *The Pilgrim's Progress*. Introducing a book that features a graphic image of the Slough of Despond, Bunyan calls out to his prospective reader, "Wouldst thou divert thyself from melancholy?" And in the secular sphere, a belief that mirthful stories helped "purge melancholy from the minde, and grosse humours from the body" was commonly invoked to justify the circulation of entertaining popular literature and jestbooks. "Doctor Merryman" is a potent foe of melancholy in more than one piece of seventeenth-century writing. And the worth of cheerful play in expelling depressive humors is a familiar theme in English playwrights like Shakespeare, Jonson, Thomas Heywood, and John Marston. Even within the domain of Puritan New England, as Samuel Eliot Morison discloses, the extracur-

---

16. Colman, *Mirth*, 20, 36–37, 91. Taylor nonetheless stood at odds with Colman over the question of standards for admission to the Lord's Supper.

ricular reading of students at seventeenth-century Harvard featured plentiful drafts of witty, erotic, and scatalogical verse, including one collection bearing the revealing title, "Witts Recreations augmented, with Ingenious Conceites for the Wittie, and
Merrie Medecines for the Melancholie."[17]

From the picture given so far one might almost suppose the
Puritans to have been thoroughgoing apostles of mirth. If therapeutic wit could laugh Puritan Everyman out of his ill humor, how
could one fail to endorse its exercise as a godly and needful thing?
Yet each of the previously cited proponents of mirth also made
sure to outline the evils of carnal gaiety. There was an impious
splenetic form as well as a sanguine form of laughter: Bright
called them, respectively, "false" and "true" laughter. Perkins
quoted Solomon's "laughter is madness," warned against setting
one's heart even on lawful recreations, and indicated deep suspicion of mirth "so farre forth, as it hath not the feare and reverence
of the Name of God to restraine it." Among the sins forbidden by
the third commandment, as interpreted by the *Larger Catechism*,
were actions that involved "in any way perverting the word, or
any part of it, to profane jests."[18]

Even as Ames defended words "uttered in jest or sport, or by
way of merriment" because "they may have a lawfull and honest
use," he admitted the jesting could be evil if its application were
otherwise. Baxter showed more suspicion of ill-directed mirth
and recreation. After all, the Devil's cure for melancholy is to
drink and play it away, and "the end of that Mirth is incurable
Sorrow." Similar cautions against "the foul abuses" of mirth toward "vice and carnality" appear in Colman, who is careful to
distinguish "Carnal and Vicious Mirth" from its worthier counterpart. Even the decidedly un-Puritan Burton, who listed the
sight and touch of a beautiful woman among his cures for melan-

17. Louis B. Wright, *Middle-Class Culture in Elizabethan England*, 405–17; Lyons,
Voices of Melancholy, 15, 53–63; Baab, *Elizabethan Malady*, 14–15; Morison, *Harvard
College*, 1:127. Helen C. White cites a passage from Arthur Dent's *The Plaine Mans
Pathway to Heaven* recommending use of "merrie bookes" as a "speedy remedy"
for the "dumpishnesse" of melancholy, in *English Devotional Prose: 1600–1640*, 232.

18. Perkins, *Cases of Conscience*, 349; *The Confession of Faith; the Larger and the
Shorter Catechisms*, 170.

choly, reproved some versions of hilarity. He found little to praise in those content simply to play their lives away: like grasshoppers who enjoyed the summer but gave no thought to the winter, they would "for a little vain merriment . . . find a sorrowful reckoning in the end."[19]

But the idea of embracing mirth met with still deeper oppositions in the Puritan soul than these selective cautions would indicate. In short, the challenge of curing scrupulous melancholy would not have received the attention it did from Reformed theologians if the disease had not become in some manner endemic to Puritan belief. There were reasons why the New Englander's Old English cousin so often filled the role of malcontent on the Elizabethan stage, and there was perhaps some basis in fact for that aura of Puritan "gloom" with which Hawthorne surrounded his acutely earnest ancestors in fiction. As Samuel Morison remarked, "There was much opportunity for love and laughter in colonial New England, though not as much as there should have been." The greater part of Puritan writing may indeed betray what Perry Miller called the "interminable high seriousness" of a people "who lived far too uninterruptedly upon the heights of intensity."[20]

In large measure the Puritans inherited their fretting humors along with their Protestantism. Though scrupulosity presented itself throughout the literature of the Catholic Middle Ages, it grew to new, epidemic proportions with the Protestant Reformation. Familiar mechanisms of piety were swept away, and with them the objectifying psychology that lent stability to the strivings of many an intense Christian. Human exertions still mattered after Wittenberg, but in less apparently predictable ways. At the cost of obscuring the evangelical doctrine of Christian liberty, the legal system of popular Roman Catholicism had enforced a commonsense doctrine of mental security with a wisdom of its own. But as the rule of *sola fides*—or, in the Calvinist scheme, *sola gratia*—came to be more rigorously applied, and as the uncer-

19. Ames, *Conscience*, 97; Baxter, *Preservatives*, 96; Colman, *Government*, A4; Burton, *Anatomy of Melancholy*, 486.

20. Samuel Eliot Morison, *The Intellectual Life of Colonial New England*, 24; Perry Miller and Thomas Johnson, eds., *The Puritans: A Sourcebook of Their Writings*, 1:59.

tainties of personal election loomed up more forbiddingly in the path of sanctification, crises of self-centered anxiety were inevitable. Interior frustration would seem the all-too-natural consequence of believing that one must ferret out the signs of election without effecting the desired New Birth. The problem of assurance, with its concomitant anguish of self-analysis, was not unique to the Puritan conscience, as the career of Martin Luther clearly illustrates. In practice, few heirs of the Reformation found predestination the "comfortable" doctrine Calvin supposed it to be. Among those knowledgeably committed to living after Reformed precepts, it would have been the rare acrobat who could walk the narrow line between despair and presumption without falling or feeling the strain.

In the Puritans, however, the introspective habit could become so fully and methodically developed as to constitute an obsession. Sacvan Bercovitch has fixed on "the dilemma of Puritan identity" wherein the endless strivings toward radically passive and humble self-denial become coextensive with the self-assertion of a heavily subjective spirituality.[21] These contradictory pressures, added to the duty of pursuing regular and vigorous self-examination without the release of sacramental confession, were bound to produce melancholic symptoms. Divines like Thomas Hooker and Thomas Shepard fully expected the regenerative process to be long and painful. Indeed, the usual morphology of conversion required candidates for visible sanctity to relate their firsthand experience of deep remorse, of the piercing grief that seized them when they came to know the reality of sin. The first of "two basic stages of repentance" represented in New England conversion narratives involves display of the heart wound suffered under legal fear. In his "Spiritual Relation" Taylor describes similar youthful impressions provoked by his sister's rendition of the creation and nativity narratives.[22]

21. Sacvan Bercovitch, *The Puritan Origins of the American Self,* 18–21.

22. Patricia Caldwell, *The Puritan Conversion Narrative: The Beginnings of American Expression,* 67. Taylor's "Spiritual Relation" appears in *UW,* 1:97–104. In addition to Caldwell's book and Perry Miller's writings, standard accounts of New England theologies of conversion are to be found in Edmund S. Morgan, *Visible Saints: The History of a Puritan Idea*; Norman Pettit, *The Heart Prepared: Grace and Conversion in Puritan Spiritual Life*; and Darrett B. Rutman, *American Puritanism: Faith and Practice.*

Intense grief over the "true sight of sin" was supposed to engulf the soul only during the various preparatory phases of the conversion process—in Taylor's scheme, that period of "Conviction" and "Aversion" encompassing "Contrition" and "Humiliation." By the time the journeying soul passed into "Conversion" proper, which Taylor classifies as the second part of "Repentance," it ought to be registering vivid sensations of joy and delight. Nonetheless, it was often hard to tell where godly remorse shaded into pathological depression; it was easy to "get stuck" in the preliminary stages. Dutiful introspection bore a troubling likeness to that ruinous rumination leading to neurotic self-absorption. Then too, the mortal self was never quite done with experiencing "Conviction"; in his relation Taylor confesses he does "dayly finde something" in his heart by way of "Soule abasement" (*UW*, 1:97).

Whereas the conditional assurances of the preparationist doctrine widely taught in New England helped to mitigate certain doubts, they seem to have spawned or prolonged others. Even when the Puritan preacher assured his congregation that "assurance" may indeed be theirs, he will be found to refer only to a reasonably grounded hope—not, as we might suppose, to a full-blown certainty. To offer this last would smack of presumption. The practice of sifting through one's personal motives may have been more pronounced among the second and third generation of American Puritans than it was at the founding, but a rumination conducive to melancholy was the continuous plague of the New England conscience from the time of Thomas Hooker's earliest writings in the Old World through the era of Jonathan Edwards, a self-confessed melancholic.[23]

On balance, then, the mood of American Puritanism might be described as more pervasively melancholic than comic. Or at least the comic spirit did not hold visibly dominant sway. Yet we have already observed how the traditions of Reformed theology sustained in New England offered distinctive encouragements for an

---

23. See Austin Warren, *The New England Conscience*, 7–27; Gail T. Parker, "Jonathan Edwards and Melancholy," 193, 201, 203.

imagination of wit, humor, and play. Harrison T. Meserole reminds us also that early New Englanders were often university trained and "the inheritors of a well-established Renaissance tradition of wit."[24] Neither was Taylor the only writer in Puritan New England willing to expose a playful wit. Comic ingenuity found expression in scores of seventeenth-century anagrams and acrostics, becoming a curious staple of Puritan elegiac verse. Beyond these verbal displays by poets such as John Fiske, John Wilson, and John Saffin, a few other notable cases come to mind: rollicking satire from the pen of Nathaniel Ward, mock-epic levity from Benjamin Tompson, occasional whimsy and comic hyperbole from Anne Bradstreet.[25] Yet the major poems of a popular writer like Michael Wigglesworth, together with the *Meditations* of Philip Pain and even the "Charracteristicall Satyre" of John Saffin, are pretty serious business. Compared with other New England writing of its time, Taylor's poetry emerges as unusual if not unique in the manner and extent to which it exploits comic principles.

Since Taylor's *Meditations* speak repeatedly of a melancholic's yearning for sanguine piety, one should not expect the differences between Taylor and less comic Puritan writers to derive from any immunity to melancholy on Taylor's part. Rather, as someone acquainted with the depressive state, this poet would have grown sensitive to its symptoms and attentive to methods of relieving it, including jocular wit. It makes paradoxical sense to find him especially attuned to the comic spirit while especially susceptible

24. Harrison T. Meserole, "'A Kind of Burr': Colonial New England's Heritage of Wit," in *American Literature: The New England Heritage,* ed. James Nagel and Richard Astro, 11–28.

25. Beyond the article cited above, the general topic of wit and humor in colonial New England receives mention in Austin Warren, *Rage for Order: Essays in Criticism,* 5–6; Harrison T. Meserole, *Seventeenth-Century American Poetry,* xxx–xxxi; Larzer Ziff, *Puritanism in America: New Culture in a New World;* Miller and Johnson, *The Puritans,* 2:392–93; Robert D. Arner, "Wit, Humor, and Satire in Seventeenth-Century American Poetry," in *Puritan Poets and Poetics: Seventeenth-Century American Poetry in Theory and Practice,* ed. Peter White, 274–85; Jeffrey Walker, "Anagrams and Acrostics: Puritan Poetic Wit," in *Puritan Poets and Poetics,* 247–57; and Stephen Fender, "Edward Taylor and the Sources of American Puritan Wit," 228–34. Fender takes the case for cultural receptivity further than I should care to by arguing that "witty writing was the rule rather than the exception in American colonial literature" (228–29).

to melancholy. As Kierkegaard, another self-confessed melancholic, opined in his *Journals*, "It belongs to the imperfection of everything human that man can only attain his desire by passing through its opposite," so that "the melancholy man has most sense of the comic." No wonder the *Concluding Unscientific Postscript* tries to puzzle out links between the religious truths of existential suffering and the comic sense.[26]

And no wonder the *Meditations* abound with complaints that the poet's soul is "dull," "sad," "lumpish," or "lowring." "Let some thing spoute on me," Taylor prays in *Meditation* 1.37, "Then I shall in a better temper bee." Often this chronic depression shows itself in recognizable symptoms of pathological melancholy. Thus, the poet's spiritual maladies make him "leaden," cause him to groan and sigh. He is afflicted by "Clouds of Dumps" and "bitter gall," a "befogg'd Dark Phancy" and "Clouded minde." When clutched by the sickness he finds himself "All black" and "Not sweet." Time and again he asks to be drained of all "ill Humors" and thereby cured of his "griefe." At other times he dares to mention the illness by name:

Dull! Dull! my Lord, as if I eaten had
    A Peck of Melancholy: or my Soule
Was lockt up by a Poppy key, black, sad:
      Or had been fuddled with an Hen bane bowle.
      Oh, Leaden temper! . . .

                    (2.69)

But Taylor knows there is more to do than simply to bewail his state. He tries to argue himself out of the ill humors, exhorting himself to "cheer up, Soule" (2.93) while supplicating heaven for release:

Then why shouldst thou, my Soule, be dumpish sad,
    Frown hence away thy melancholy Face.
Oh! Chide thyselfe out of this Frame so bad

26. *The Journals of Soren Kierkegaard*, ed. and trans. Alexander Dru, 90, 387; Soren Kierkegaard, *Concluding Unscientific Postscript*, trans. David Swenson and ed. Walter Lowrie, 390–468.

Seing Christs precious bowells thee Embrace.
One flash of this bright Gem these bowells bring
Unto thyselfe, may make thy heart to singe.

(2.123[A])

Let some, my Lord, of thy bright Glories beams,
    Flash quickening Flames of Glory in mine eye
T'enquicken my dull Spirits, drunke with dreams
    Of Melancholy juyce that stupify.

(2.73)

Fortunately too, the poet's resolution to compose sacred verse is
already a first step toward dispelling the clouds of melancholy:

I do constrain my Dumpishness away
    And to give place unto a Spirituall Verse
Tund on thy glorious joys and to Conveigh
    My notes upon the Same, and my heart seirce
        From all such dross till sweet tund prais pierce through
        Those Clouds of Dumps to come thy throne unto.

(2.145)

But for the choicest therapy Taylor looked to the sanguine
vitality of wit exercised in the poems themselves. Regularly urging his congregation to get and maintain the "festival frame of
spirit" requisite to feasting on the Lord's Supper, ordering them to
"be not morose," he used the *Meditations* to play out the rhetorical
challenge of exciting the right mood of affections in his representative soul. Harnessing wit for its power as a medicine no less
than as a bait of pleasure, he aimed to stir up a mood of delighted
anticipation of the feast. The prospect of the sacred meal is set
before the soul's gaze in such an attractive, winsome light that one
would press to realize it in experience and to attain the regenerative condition it demanded. Any melancholic distempers hinder-
ing acceptance of the banquet might be relieved. The comic spirit
was well suited to inspiring hopeful expectation and the "true
sight" of eschatological joy. It was therefore one of Taylor's more
potent "motives to move" souls toward the life-nourishing bene-

fits offered in the symbolic elements of the Supper. It was one way of raising the soul's hunger for a taste of the divine:

Stir up thy Appetite, my Soule, afresh,
   Here's Bread, and Wine as Signs, to signify
The richest Dainties Cookery can Dress
   Thy Table with, filld with felicity.
   Purge out and Vomit by Repentance all
   Ill Humours which thy Spirituall Tast forestall.

                        (2.104)

Taylor's sponsorship of "a festival frame of spirit" was no invitation to that worldly frivolity reproved by Colman under the label of "Carnal and Vicious Mirth." Like the Samuel Hooker limned in elegy, Taylor's ideal Christian was "Grave" but not "Morose," ready to "attend the Sacred Writ with joy" (*Poems*, 478–79). Still, Taylor's persistent call to "be not discouraged," to be "of good cheer" (*TCLS*, 221), stands out against the contemporary background.[27] At the contrary extreme, Michael Wigglesworth filled his diary with confessions of scrupulous melancholy yet frowned on nearly all forms of mirth and recreation, much less the idea that merriment could be spiritually beneficial. And in another autobiographical piece written while a tutor at Harvard, he rejects the counsel of someone who had spoken "in Commendation of seasonable laughter and Merriment, as that which may be a means to Recreate ones tired Spirits, and prolong ones Life." "Let me rather live a Melancholy Life all my days," he exclaims, "than by Merriment run into a course of provoking my God."[28]

Though not so mirthless as Wigglesworth, Taylor's opponent Solomon Stoddard also believed there were better ways to banish impious humors than to laugh them away. "Many young persons . . . give themselves up to Mirth and Jollity," he complained, "and neglect the opportunities of Salvation." They ignore the sober warnings of their elders because "they hate to live a Moping

---

27. Though most prominent in *TCLS*, Taylor's commands to "Cheer up" under the "Cheering & Comfortable" influence of grace appear as well in *Harmony*, 1:65–66, 99; 2:475; 4:48–50.

28. *The Diary of Michael Wigglesworth, 1653–1657*, ed. Edmund S. Morgan, 27, 46, 69, 77, 80, 91; citation in Morison, *Harvard College*, 1:123.

Melancholy Life, to be confessing their Sins, and crying to God for Pardon; but if they were afraid of Hell, that would make a mighty change in their Carriage, a sense of Hell-Fire would soun feare them out of those Humeurs."[29] Conversely, Stoddard did not hesitate to complain that his ministerial colleague to the south was provoking needless fear and grief over Sacrament days.

It is at least true enough that Taylor considered every Christian duty-bound to the painful rigors of introspection. Despite the risk of triggering despondency, God demanded an earnest scrutiny of the soul's estate: "Thou bidst me try if I be in the Faith" (2.155). But there was a drop of consolation even in the bitter gall of melancholy, so long as it came in limited season and quantity. For mental anguish was most likely to seize the deeper, "twice-born" soul. In this minor sense, where melancholy could almost be seen as a mark of peculiar favor, remnants of the heroic melancholy tradition survived to influence Taylor's outlook.

More essentially, Taylor's symbolic scheme in the *Meditations* presumes an ameliorative progress from splenetic torpor to sanguine delight. Thus *Meditation* 2.32 passes from the poet's initial "dulness" of melancholy, his "Leaden Whistle," to a "song of Love . . . full of glee." The disease of melancholy—not the scrupulous form, always, but melancholy in general—signifies all that blocks the fervor of raised affections otherwise set on the enjoyment of glory. If Taylor's diagnosis and cure of the humoral malady are not the controlling principle of the *Meditations,* the poems do suggest a pattern of equivalence between depravity and the leaden disposition, between grace and sanguinity. The relevant background can often help to explain the imagery of individual poems. One connotation of the blood imagery introduced in many *Meditations,* such as *Meditation* 1.1, is the sanguine contrary to black bile. And in *Gods Determinations,* Taylor offers a full-scale treatment of scrupulous symptoms linked to the pathology of meditative melancholy.

29. Solomon Stoddard, *The Efficacy of the Fear of Hell,* 21.

Wit, Meditation, and the Word

Though one form of self-indicting introspection might contribute to Puritan *melancholia,* Taylor also conceived of meditation as a conjunctive act leading toward holy joy. Through meditation one looked to achieve a practical unification between heart and mind, between the self and God. For Taylor, the essential purpose of meditation was to conjoin a soul situated in the phenomenal world with the divine will revealed in Scripture. As such, the poet's meditative process of pondering the scriptural Word found a natural expression in the conjunctive activity of verbal wit.

Earlier scholarship tended to link Taylor's mode of meditation with formal patterns of Catholic spirituality established before the appearance of Richard Baxter's *Saints' Everlasting Rest* (1650). More recently, Barbara Lewalski has stressed its pervasively Protestant character.[30] Taylor's digressive spontaneity and peripatetic mood nonetheless transcend the usual sectarian categories of Catholic and Protestant, reflecting a style most aptly labeled "Augustinian." These same qualities are reflected in the verbal techniques of the poet's wit. Yet the biblical propensities in Taylor's meditative method do signal a Protestant allegiance and are combined with a recognizably Puritan investment in covenant theology. Both Taylor's practice of meditation and his language of wit converge in the intertextuality of Scripture. Two other traditional subjects of meditation—the self and the creatures—appear in variant combinations throughout his writing. But the organizing focus of the written meditations, as well as the main source of their figures, is the canonical Word. Meditation on the Word was for Taylor, as for other leaders of Protestant devotionalism, the cornerstone of personal spirituality and sacred art.

The Reformed emphasis on fidelity to the Word sometimes took the form of Levitical literalism. Unlike Luther or Richard Hooker, Puritan "precisians" were apt to regard the Bible as all-sufficient and authoritative in every matter of worship, doctrine, and church

---

30. Barbara Lewalski, *Protestant Poetics and the Seventeenth-Century Religious Lyric,* 388–426.

government, not merely in the truths necessary for salvation. Those of such a literalist persuasion insisted the church could approve no practice lacking explicit warrant in Scripture.[31] But as a group the Puritans were something other than uniformly literalistic in their approach to the Bible. This point surely applies to the case of American Puritans, particularly in matters of evangelical piety as distinct from those of institutional or civil legality.

Puritans believed the Bible contained the Word of God and in a thoroughly real sense *was* that Word. Yet they were not willing to equate the Word unequivocally with the words printed across the page. They taught neither "fundamentalism" nor "verbal inerrancy" in today's sense of the terms. For all their attachment to the canonical writings, they knew that these too could shape themselves into the new idols of Reformation religion. Of course sacred writ was to be read, devoutly and often, in public and private. Yet the dynamic power of the Word would never be released through a bare repetition of the words. The text had to be opened, turned, and applied before it would speak forth the Word. It was only by the inward testimony of the Spirit, not by any amount of gazing on or intoning from the tangible book, that the Word unleashed its generative power. And it was a major responsibility of the Puritan preacher to turn and break open the Word, pouring out its liberating essence onto receptive hearts.[32]

The same principles obtained in private meditation, Baxter's "preaching to oneself." To release the living Word contained in Holy Writ, one had to turn the written letters, bend and play with them, break them inwardly upon the recalcitrant soul. "Words are no such trifles as trifling Persons make them," Taylor urged, yet

31. See Horton Davies, *The Worship of the English Puritans*; Miller and Johnson, *The Puritans*, 1:41–55.

32. See Ziff, *Puritanism in America*, 29; John T. McNeill, *The History and Character of Calvinism*, 310; and John Calvin, *Institutes of the Christian Religion*, ed. John T. McNeill, 1:liv, 79–81, though on several questions of exegesis Calvin's approach differed from what came to be the dominant "Puritan" one. Luther restricted the authoritative essence of the Bible to a smaller *trostbuch* within it. Samuel T. Coleridge, especially in *Confessions of an Inquiring Spirit* [printed 1840 and ed. H. Hart, 1853], later argued that it was best to think of the Bible as containing the true Word of God "in reference to its declared ends and purposes" rather than as constituting the Word of God "in all parts unquestionable" (68).

special effort was needed "to minde, Weigh, meditate, & ponder this greate Word; the Lord Christ" (*Harmony,* 1:282, 7). Here was no place for blockish passivity. Thomas Hooker's well-known discourse in *The Application of Redemption* certifies it to be a matter of vigorous spiritual exercise, relentless search, a tenacious "coasting of the mind and imagination into every crevis and corner." Meditation was, in short, hard work.[33] As a resolve to dig out the roots of personal sin, the object circumscribed in this discourse, Hooker's meditation could be painful, even melancholic, work.

It could also be play. In Hooker a lively and adventurous movement of the meditative mind gave ample purchase to the imagination, mitigating the laborious rigor of self-examination typically (in both senses) emblematized as a spiritual "chewing of the cud." Often too narrowly defined on the basis of its treatment in the one section of *The Application of Redemption,* Hookerian meditation could elsewhere offer a more joyous prospect, a more direct focus on the Word of promise contained in Scripture, a more conspicuous concession to verbal and mental play. In *The Soul's Vocation* Hooker advises the uncertain soul to search out and lay hold of the biblical promises just as a child finds the mother's breast after "muzzling about a dry chip," or as one discovers the sweet marrow inside a bone. The promises are full of consoling comfort so far as "you . . . chew them, break them, and bestow thy heart on them" through meditation. Particularly for the convicted believer, meditation thus becomes a lively roaming after truth, an experimental turning of the Word, an interior motion led by an adventurous intellect. Herein it resembles what John Dryden called the "nimble Spaniel" of wit, which ranges restlessly through the field of memory till it finds its quarry in "delightful imaging." The promises strike fire as love and joy only after a meditating soul allows its holy desire to wander freely, like the Spouse in Canticles, "from this thing to that thing, from this place to that place," never ceasing "to see if it can gain notice of Christ."[34]

---

33. The Hooker selection appears in Miller and Johnson, *The Puritans,* 1:304.

34. Thomas Hooker, *The Soul's Vocation,* Doctrine 3 and Doctrine 7, in *Salvation in New England: Selections from the Sermons of the First Preachers,* ed. Phyllis Jones and Nicholas Jones, 85, 95–96; *The Works of John Dryden: Poems 1649–1680,* ed. Edward

This principle of digressive spontaneity lay at the heart of Puritan resistance to set prayers and homilies. It also helps to explain the restlessly probing quality of Taylor's poetry. To release the Spirit from the otherwise dead letter of Scripture, one had to follow its untutored leadings, albeit within certain specified bounds. Those bounds, reflected in the formal divisions of a Puritan homily, likewise curbed the imaginative options in meditation—such as the re-creation of scenes from Jesus' earthly ministry—that had appeared more widely in Catholic methods. Sober attention to categories of exegetical understanding was apt to replace the sensuous visualizations of place featured in Ignatian meditation.

At the same time, Protestant meditative theory gave fresh encouragement to other sources of literary imagination and, as Baxter illustrates, found room to endorse at least some applications of sensuous imagery. Compared with the Ignatian regimen, the Reformed approach could better claim to capture the shifting winds of the Spirit by virtue of its broader field of biblical subjects opened to meditative perusal, its rejection of a rigid time frame for the exercises, its freer response to spontaneous discovery in the form of what Joseph Hall called "occasional meditations." Even within the more regulated format of "deliberate meditation," Hall objected to schemes that left the mind "too much fettered" in its search. Above all it is the mood of darting curiosity, of free-wheeling search through the great magazine of Scripture, that links Taylor's distinctive style of poetic wit to the meditative traditions in which he was steeped.[35]

Niles Hooker and H. T. Swedenberg, Jr., 1:53.

35. *The Works of Joseph Hall*, 1:114. Theories of Protestant meditation have been examined in several studies, whose main findings are drawn together in Lewalski, *Protestant Poetics*, 146–67. See also Louis L. Martz, *The Poetry of Meditation: A Study in English Religious Literature of the Seventeenth Century*, 153–65; U. Milo Kaufmann, *The Pilgrim's Progress and Traditions in Puritan Meditation;* and Ronald J. Corthell, "Joseph Hall and Protestant Meditation." Informative studies of meditative theory and practice as developed in colonial America include two pieces by Norman S. Grabo: "Puritan Devotion and American Literary History," in *Themes and Directions in American Literature,* ed. Ray B. Browne and Donald Pizer, and "Catholic Tradition, Puritan Literature, and Edward Taylor." See also Ronald A. Sudol, "Meditation in Colonial New England: The Directives of Thomas Hooker and

As Louis Martz has demonstrated, those traditions derived in the main from meditative teachings set forth by St. Augustine centuries before the Reformation. In contrast to the Ignatian method, the Augustinian manner favored "tumbling" meditations, exploratory sallies or digressions of mind designed to recapture and focus glimpses of the divine illumination mirrored in the human soul.[36] This iterative approach and sense of interior illumination influenced Catholic writers as well as Protestants; on the Catholic side it bore some affinities to Salesian meditation. And since St. Augustine is common property of Catholic and Protestant traditions, it seems more accurate to characterize Taylor's meditation of exploratory wit as "Augustinian" than as "Protestant." In any case, the several schemes of Christian meditation shared a sense of quest for loving union with God, realized as the soul unified its powers of memory, understanding, and will. A purely cerebral and trivial wit, one that failed to draw forth the affections and to engage the larger self, could not contribute to the spiritual discipline of meditation. In this pejorative sense Thomas Hooker denied meditation to be "a flourishing of a mans wit." But in this same discourse on meditation Hooker's darting movements of mind, his boldly conceitist imagery bordering on the humorous, all disclose a good deal of wit. Like meditation and in consort with meditation, sacred wit enacted an integrative process that promised to repair part of the damage sustained in the Fall.[37]

Taylor's reliance on the conjunctive power of meditation does show a distinctly Puritan cast in its involvement with the federal theology. A central purpose behind Puritan meditation was to establish whether the covenant promises of grace did indeed

Ebeneezer Pemberton"; Louis Martz's older but excellent treatment in his foreword to the 1960 *Poems of Edward Taylor,* ed. Donald E. Stanford; and the illuminating account, with special attention given to Taylor, by Ursula Brumm, "Meditative Poetry in New England," in *Puritan Poets and Poetics,* 318–36.

36. Louis L. Martz, *The Paradise Within: Studies in Vaughan, Traherne, and Milton,* 16–31. The Augustinian traits in question are generally deduced from Book 10 of *The Confessions* together with several sections of *De Trinitate*

37. Ernest B. Gilman, *The Curious Perspective: Literary and Pictorial Wit in the Seventeenth Century,* 234, alludes to seventeenth-century belief in the ability of wit to help repair the alienating effects of the Fall.

apply to oneself, whether the general decree of Election had a claim in the first-person singular. The project could be excruciating, but to judge from the *Meditations* Taylor's doubts were generally outnumbered and supplanted by verifying signs. Without reaching to affirm universal salvation in the technical sense, the writings of divines like Taylor and Thomas Hooker—notably, Taylor's 1694 sermons on the Lord's Supper—carried an assumption that the promises would finally obtain for any soul earnestly drawn to embrace them. For the Lord's promises were "Rich, Quick'ning things" (2.12), and to believe less was to risk calling God a liar:

Dost thou adorn some thus, and why not mee?
    Ile not believe it. Lord, thou art my Chiefe.
Thou me Commandest to believe in thee.
    I'l not affront thee thus with Unbeliefe.

                    (1.25)

The ingenious turn of logic evidenced here begins to suggest the larger role of wit in Taylor's meditative quest for assurance. The work of redemption had already been achieved through God in Christ and became accessible through the promises held out in the Covenant of Grace. The Elect soul could do no more by way of saving work; yet it still had to lay hold of the covenant by aligning its personal destiny and will with the truths spelled out in divine Revelation. A prospective saint like Taylor's speaker in the *Meditations* had to look into the Word, finding his name written there; at the same time he had to consult his own soul to find the corresponding stamps and badges marking him as Christ's own. As a meditative poet, Taylor committed himself to seeking out tokens of the New Covenant congruence in semiotic configurations of word and image, a technique that one critic calls an enactment of the Covenant of Grace through "Metaphors of Promise" and that another describes as "a language of correspondence" developed out of metaphor, typology, and allegory.[38]

38. Michael North, "Edward Taylor's Metaphors of Promise"; Parker H. Johnson, "Poetry and Praise in Edward Taylor's Preparatory Meditations."

Lacking intrinsic merit, the fortuitous analogies produced from the "game" of wit were nonetheless "ernest" vehicles by which the soul could discover its comparable consonance with the Word. In vulgar terms, the wit of composition accomplished a sort of matching exercise; on the sacred plane, it tried to release the Word stored in Scripture, creation, and church ordinance in such a way that Revelation could find the self and vice versa. When the poems manage to make good on this experience of "Mutuall propriety," they convey an unmistakable impression of exuberance and joy that chases away melancholy.[39] It is as though Taylor has suddenly struck the answer to a comic riddle on finding that he truly is the glass, the purse, the lily, the "Golden Angell" of God, that he has been as good as tucked inside the leaves of Sharon's Rose, bedded all the while in the "Circumcisions Quilt" of Christ. And beyond its relevance to Puritan categories, the shock of joyous recognition bears a religious kinship to the familiarly witty conclusion of a gospel parable or a Zen *koan*.

To invite the crucial episodes of consonance that imparadise the soul, Taylor allowed wit to circle freely around the objects it encountered in the world. The phenomenal world served less as the poet's central dwelling place than as a colossal playhouse to be ransacked for whatever signs of earnest congruence it might present. In several respects, to be sure, the *Meditations* are set in carefully ordered patterns; and a rigidly predictable scheme determines the choice of subject matter in sequences like the typological poems in *Meditations* 2.1–2.30, 2.58–60[B], 2.70, and 2.71. Taylor's wit nonetheless claimed a space for unpredictable movement, for play. It is precisely on account of this digressive spontaneity in Taylor, a quality related to his erotic zeal and his "roughness," that Donald Stanford once observed the meditative structure of his poetry to be looser and more irrational than that of earlier English verse written in the great meditative tradition.[40] Likewise in Karl Keller's analysis it is neither Taylor's selection of

39. Such is likewise the conclusion of Johnson, "Poetry and Praise," 92, and of North, "Taylor's Metaphors," 15.
40. Donald E. Stanford, *Edward Taylor*, 18.

sources nor his theological interpretations that render him unusual as a New England typologist. It is rather his wit of meditation, his irrepressible urge to play with the conventional types to underscore their delightful import and to draw out their personal applications.[41]

Although much useful attention has been given to Taylor's poetic handling of typology, the wit of his meditation on the Word extends beyond his manipulation of persons, rituals, and events from the Old Testament to demonstrate their prefigurement of the Gospel. For when Taylor explored the typological interplay between the two testaments in figures of shadow and fulfillment, he was presuming the essential unity of the Scriptures; and the special character of his presumption had important literary consequences. As William Jemmat explained, "The same Testator made both Testaments, and these differ not really, but *accidentally*; the Old *infolding* the New with some darknesse, and the New *unfolding* the Old with joyous perspicuitie." Meditative wit helped to reconstitute the perceived unity of the Scriptures by dissolving all "accidental" boundaries into the undivided radiance of Christ, by running after the saving Word and drawing it to the surface wherever it might lie in the biblical text and however it might have been obscured in the shadows of human corruption. But Taylor's poetry shows as well a distinctive awareness that each testament possessed an endlessly self-reflexive texture of its own. Enfolded into every book of Scripture were the imagistic keys to any number of other books, in both testaments. As George Herbert marveled, "This verse marks that, and both do make a motion / Unto a third, that ten leaves off doth lie." The *Meditations* exploit a fertile image like that of food or light not only by setting out the expected typological parallels but also by gathering up the rich

41. Karl Keller, " 'The World Slickt Up in Types': Edward Taylor as a Version of Emerson," in *Typology and Early American Literature*, ed. Sacvan Bercovitch, 175–90. Less theoretically, Karen E. Rowe, *Saint and Singer: Edward Taylor's Typology and the Poetics of Meditation*, 48, 118, 125, 248, offers many sensitive readings that expose Taylor's "clever wordplay," "piquant humor," playful manipulations, and effort "to insert himself humbly, nimbly, even wittily into the figural equation."

variety of relevant allusions scattered throughout the several parts
of each testament.[42]

As subsequent perusal of individual poems can demonstrate,
Taylor was intrigued to find a chosen Old Testament type pointing not only directly forward to its new covenanted antitype but
also laterally to other types, which in turn reached to invoke still
other New Testament figures. Moreover, the scriptural figures
suggested further analogies with types visible in the world: Taylor exclaims over "The glory of the world slickt up in types" (2.1).
Thus, though "The glory of all Types doth meet" in Christ, the
narrative of Christ as "Pend by the Holy Ghost" in Scripture is
anything but one-dimensional. It is the story compounded of all
others, a flame of wonder "fan'd / From evry Chaff, Dust, Weedy
Seed, or Sand" (2.79).

The larger effect of Taylor's rippling style of allusion is to dramatize the unity-in-complexity of biblical revelation without violating
Reformed teachings on the "one sense of Scripture."[43] Described
in tropes Taylor might have appreciated, the Bible comes out
looking less like the classic medieval terrace with its several
distinct levels of meaning and more like an elaborately inter-
stitched tapestry, woven of many colors and brighter in one
hemisphere than another but drawn into a continuous circle.
Beyond the usual temporal dialectic generated by its typological
structures, Taylor's poetry often conveys a rarer sense of "spatial
form" through its wit of multiplying allusion. This quality of
associative spontaneity, exemplified most notoriously by a poem

42. William Jemmat's dedicatory epistle to Thomas Taylor's *Christ Revealed; Or,
The Old Testament Explained*, A2, A3; cf. Gordon E. Slethaug, "Edward Taylor's
Copy of Thomas Taylor's *Types*: A New Taylor Document"; *The Works of George
Herbert*, 58. As Herbert's expression suggests, Edward Taylor was not alone in per-
ceiving the self-allusive texture of Scripture, an insight with precedent in
Augustine's hermeneutics, among other places. Taylor was nonetheless unusual in
the manner and creative intensity with which he exploited the insight in his
poems.

43. The practical significance of "one sense" hermeneutics is discussed by
Kaufmann, *Puritan Meditation*, 27–41. On the Protestant assimilation of spiritual
elements and figural extensions of the literal sense into the notion of a "compound
sense," see Lewalski, *Protestant Poetics*, especially 85, 121, and Raymond Anselment, introduction to *Christ Revealed*, by Thomas Taylor, viii, xx n. 6.

like *Meditation* 2.78, or by the bizarre, overwhelming confluence of mundane and speculative exegesis in *The Harmony of the Gospels*, also distinguishes his better work. It has much to do with his penchant for leaping abruptly from one conceit to another.

In its experimental eclecticism, Taylor's meditative wit becomes at least as absorbed in reflection upon secondarily derived doctrine as upon the immediate biblical text.[44] His sermons advise meditation on the doctrine of the church, the doctrine of God in Christ as defined by the hypostatic union, the doctrinal significance of the Lord's Supper, and the "mystery of redemption" (*C*, 316, 102–3; *TCLS*, 203, 138). In fact, the art of theologizing is itself a form of "play": the theologian is one who spins out provisional human abstractions beyond the revealed text of Scripture. Taylor capitalized on this insight through his custom of developing a fantasia of tropes around favorite points of doctrine.

Taylor's writing also shows eclecticism in the formal methods and genres of meditation it embraces. Beyond their immediate generic identity as meditations from Scripture, the poetic *Meditations* often satisfy as well the traditional category of meditation from the self. In addition they often qualify, together with *Gods Determinations*, as a form of Baxter's "heavenly meditation." And in the poems on selected "occurrants," Taylor records his practice of meditation from the creatures.

Synthetic in its meditative method, the poetry reflects the Ignatian temper (also associated with Donne and, more selectively, with Thomas Hooker) in its imagistic violence, its sporadic discourse, its engagement with interior struggle and holy fear, and reflects the Salesian in its homeliness, its loving intimacy with God, its externalized rituals of holy "entertainment" and peace.[45] It pursues Baxterian foretastes of heaven as well as Augustinian fits of heavenly recollection, seizing moments in the past—like

44. The point is conveyed by the full title of the *Preparatory Meditations*, in which Taylor identifies his poems as written "Chiefly upon the Doctrin preached upon the Day of administration" of the Lord's Supper.

45. Martz contrasts the Ignatian and Salesian temperaments in *Poetry of Meditation*, 144–49; Sudol, "Meditation in Colonial New England," extends the distinction to an American context.

that celebrated in "The Experience"—when the soul temporarily recovers visible possession of the divine image.

It is not even safe to fix Taylor's method uncritically within the current broad-gauged definitions of "Protestant Meditation." For if Protestant meditation on Scripture is supposed to apply the Word to the self rather than the converse, such is not always Taylor's practice. As several commentators point out, Taylor often inserts himself into a previously established typological setting.[46] He may begin a poem focusing on some biblical event or personage he develops to apply to his own state; he is also apt to follow something like the reverse procedure. One cannot always tell whether the Scripture is being applied to the self or vice versa because Taylor wished above all to demonstrate their joint communion in the Spirit, their interpenetration. Taylor's meditative method identifies itself as "Protestant" by virtue of its conspicuously close kinship to the poet's preaching, its fascination with exploring verbal nuance over sustained visual impression. But as the prevalence of container and tabernacle imagery suggests, the larger Catholic principle of mystical indwelling takes precedence over the more didactic "uses" of Protestant homily. All in all, the relatively freewheeling and eclectic method of Taylor's meditation in verse seems closest in spirit to the Augustinian example of digressive wit. This same wit extends a roaming imagination of compound allusion throughout Scripture.

Neither does the poet's specific attachment to Puritan doctrine inject as much anguished uncertainty into his meditative awareness as may first appear. Behind the stylized exorcising of presumption in the hypothetical ending of most *Meditations* is a barely disguised confidence in the speaker's redeemed status.[47]

46. Keller is the main expositor of this point in " 'Slickt Up in Types,' " though Lewalski's *Protestant Poetics* and Anselment's introduction to Thomas Taylor's *Christ Revealed* illustrate that Edward Taylor was not unique in seeking a personal appropriation of the types.

47. For an exposition of how Taylor's confidence may be associated with "full assurance" according to Calvin's theory of spiritual growth, see Michael Schuldiner, "The Christian Hero and the Classical Journey in Edward Taylor's 'Preparatory Meditations. First Series.' " Schuldiner believes that stages in Taylor's developing assurance can be identified quite precisely with poems in the First Series of *Preparatory Meditations* and that *Meditations* 1.40–41 mark attainment of the final stage.

Imitating well-known scriptural paradigms, the if/then structure of such a conclusion enacts the everlasting claim of the covenantal promises as grasped provisionally from the human side and as inclined toward their necessary completion in the age to come. For the *Meditations* to end where they do is to acknowledge, with entire aptness, that we are still living in a "preparatory" stage of becoming, within the earthly sphere of wit and movement and change. From God's side, the covenant relation nonetheless persists changeless and unquestionable. Sometimes, in fact, Taylor allows his last word in a *Meditation* to sound more openly declarative than conditional, as in *Meditation* 1.2: "I have enough. Enough in having thee." And in *Meditation* 2.138 Taylor shows how the grinding labor of meditative discipline, paired to true faith in Christ, is bound to yield delight. Drawing on figures from Canticles, he first sets down analogical links between meditative wit and the pleasant sight of lambs in "leaping play and joy" and then illustrates more overtly how the digestive process of meditation distributes "Choice Spirituall Cheer / Through all the new man by its instrument."

The poet assigned the ultimate source of this saving "Cheer" to God, for neither meditation nor its vehicle of verbal wit produced any new nourishment for the soul. From one theological angle, moreover, the Puritans insisted on the passive condition of the will in conversion. Still, the passivity in question never precluded exertions, whether internal or external, by which the soul responded to God's gracious influences. Indeed, activities like wit and meditation expressed a human initiative of desire necessary in all true lovers of God. A worldly confirmation of this principle appears in the way Puritans favored "games of wit" over "games of hazard" because "games of wit" gave fuller play to humanity's divinely endowed powers of intelligence and purposeful invention.[48] Though as a Puritan Taylor considered himself incapable of inventing new metaphysical truths, such a limitation was not so remarkable, so unreasonable, or so inhibiting to creative imaginings as has been supposed.[49] He would have thought it more than

48. William Perkins, "Concerning Recreation," in *English Puritanism from John Hooper to John Milton*, ed. Everett H. Emerson, 159–66.
49. The hypothesis that a Puritan belief in cosmic predeterminations left no room

sufficient merely to discover what he might learn of God's truth, to declare and celebrate God's joyous marriage to humankind. No less than Richard Crashaw's, Taylor's was thus a "witt of love"[50]— that is, a meditative dedication with no pretense to independent worth or originality of essence.

---

for tension, drama, or paradox in Taylor's poetry is ably refuted by Sargent Bush, Jr., "Paradox, Puritanism, and Taylor's *Gods Determinations*."

50. Martz, *Poetry of Meditation*, 62–64.

3 From Depravity to Festival

The Aesthetics of Depravity

If Taylor's physical isolation from an urbane Renaissance culture makes it hard to conceive of him as a genuine poet of wit, his Puritan religious commitment continues to raise doubts about whether he was even a genuine poet. Half a century after his work was discovered for our age, the impression lingers among readers or potential readers that such a writer must have been artistically either "too Puritan to be good or too good to be Puritan."[1] Such doubts stem in part from the suspicion, warranted or not, that Taylor's sectarian environment imposed a blighting restriction of subject matter and imaginative scope. But a further problem presents itself in theological strictures enunciated by the Puritans themselves. Not only might their oft-stated abhorrence of iconic idolatry call into question the legitimacy of any figural art, but their rhetoric of total depravity would seem to deny the capacity of human beings to create such art. From a Reformed perspective, the world itself, which supplies the significative body of literary art, is likewise fallen, as is language, the medium through which the sacred poet must strive to express the inexpressible. At the same time, no Puritan in either England left us a developed *ars poetica* to justify versifying beyond the terms of Cotton Mather's well-known counsel to relieve arduous study with "a little recreation of poetry."[2]

The record of Taylor's steady devotion to his craft for more than

---

1. Kathleen Blake, "Edward Taylor's Protestant Poetic: Non-Transubstantiating Metaphor," 2.

2. Mather is cited in Perry Miller and Thomas Johnson, eds., *The Puritans: A Sourcebook of Their Writings*, 2:686. The problem of piecing together scattered expressions of a Puritan poetic theory is discussed by Robert Daly in chapter 2 of *God's Altar: The World and the Flesh in Puritan Poetry*, 40–89.

forty years attests to the seriousness and deliberateness with which he conceived his poetic vocation. But how does one square this accomplishment with his own self-demeaning assessments? Repeatedly throughout the *Meditations*, Taylor declares his writing a failure. His "Rough Voice" and "blunt Tongue" yield nothing better than "A sorry Verse" to set before the Almighty. "Spoild" by sin, his words and tropes fall hopelessly short of bridging the referential chasm between sign and substance (1.23, 1.45, 1.7).

Deeper scrutiny of the problem, not to mention the undoubted existence of the poems, suggests that Taylor's confessions of literary futility cannot be read at face value.[3] One must recognize, at the start, that his supposition of depravity does not in itself distinguish him from other Christian writers of his era. But Taylor does reveal a distinctive aesthetic in his practical response to this challenge, a response informed by his subtly paradoxical sense of poetic decorum. By this twofold standard of decorum he finds his expression from one angle futile, from another sanctified. Moreover, Taylor's apprehension of the Fall is supplanted by his awareness of humanity's regenerative restoration and "deification" under grace.

This deification principle, held as it is in tension with depravity doctrine, points toward a sustaining poetic theory scattered throughout Taylor's prose and poetic writings. In previous decades of scholarship, Taylor's self-conscious preoccupation with the communicative contingencies and referential incapacities of language may have seemed oppressively Puritan. Yet from the standpoint of postmodern critical theory, such a concern sounds less parochial and carries strangely contemporary resonance. For Taylor, neither written texts nor human selves could be read as coextensive with the Absolute. But whereas Taylor denied the sufficiency of language as referential sign within the scheme of static semiotics, he affirmed its value within a dynamic grammar of ritualized play.[4]

---

3. On the "inability *topos*" as a traditional rhetorical device applied by Taylor, see Stephen Fender's "Edward Taylor and the Sources of American Puritan Wit," 16; on the rhetorical use of "deflating" images, see Rosemond Tuve, *Elizabethan and Metaphysical Imagery: Renaissance Poetic and Twentieth-Century Critics*, 196–214.

4. My formulation here draws on that of Michael Clark, who has interpreted the

To approach Taylor's aesthetic, one could do worse than to examine the "Prologue," the first poem printed in Donald Stanford's edition of *The Poems of Edward Taylor*. Whether this poem of unknown date was written to introduce the *Meditations* only, as is ordinarily supposed from its position in the manuscript, or to define the corpus as a whole, cannot be known for certain. But as more than one reader has observed, the "Prologue" is in any case a logical starting point for search into Taylor's poetic philosophy.[5] The immediate issue raised here in the frame of God's eternal "designs" is the relation between the poet, as a type of fallen yet redeemed humanity, and the challenge of producing sacred verse. From the standpoint of the eternal Logos, weighed against the standard of absolute truth, the Christian writer's ambition to magnify God must be counted stark presumption:

> Lord, Can a Crumb of Dust the Earth outweigh,
>   Outmatch all mountains, nay the Chrystall Sky?
> Imbosom in't designs that shall Display
>   And trace into the Boundless Deity?
>   Yea hand a Pen whose moysture doth guild ore
>   Eternall Glory with a glorious glore.
>
> If it its Pen had of an Angels Quill,
>   And Sharpend on a Pretious Stone ground tite,
> And dipt in Liquid Gold, and mov'de by Skill
>   In Christall leaves should golden Letters write
>   It would but blot and blur yea jag, and jar
>   Unless thou mak'st the Pen, and Scribener.
>   (*Poems*, 1)

Thus far a negative answer to the opening rhetorical query would seem all too inevitable. One is tempted to seize the self-

---

aesthetic of Taylor and other Puritans against the matrix of present-day theory in three stimulating essays: " 'The Crucified Phrase': Sign and Desire in Puritan Semiology"; "The Subject of the Text in Early American Literature"; and "The Honeyed Knot of Puritan Aesthetics," in *Puritan Poets and Poetics: Seventeenth-Century American Poetry in Theory and Practice*, ed. Peter White, 67–83.

5. See, for example, Charles W. Mignon, "Edward Taylor's *Preparatory Meditations*: A Decorum of Imperfection."

demeaning connotations of Taylor's figurative "Crumb of Dust" as confirming the Puritan's abnormal pessimism about human nature, in contrast perhaps to the Anglican's high confidence in human glory and artistic calling as manifested in poets like George Herbert and John Donne. And compared with Herbert, a writer echoed throughout his poetry, Taylor *was* no doubt more emphatic about the chasm separating natural man from God, more fixed by the polar opposition between Old Adam and New. Taylor the preacher could insist that "all" man's nobler qualities "were Spoiled, and broke to pieces by the Fall" (*C,* 314). This difference probably does have a real, albeit problematic connection with the distinction commonly drawn between Thomistic, Catholic views of original sin, as shared by some versions of Anglicanism, and the Calvinist sense of total depravity.[6]

Yet Herbert shared with Taylor a conviction of personal depravity and expressed grave concern over his fitness to present acceptable praise, as evidenced in poems like "The Temper I and II," "The Sinner," and "Sighs and Groans." The two poets were one in their belief that no human writer could be worthy, on the absolute scale, to set forth divine truth on earth or to converse with heaven. Taylor's frequent expositions on this theme should be read against Herbert's apostrophe in the poem "Miserie." "My God, Man cannot praise thy name," wrote Herbert, for "Thou art all brightnesse, perfect puritie," and "How shall infection / Presume on thy perfection?" Richard Hooker, the quintessential Anglican, likewise offers the dampening admonition that the "safest eloquence" of feeble-brained humankind concerning God "is our silence."[7]

Attention to the peculiar context of New England Puritanism should not, therefore, obscure the essential continuity of belief between Taylor and Herbert as devout, English-speaking Chris-

---

6. For other samples of language for total depravity as corrupting "the whole man" and leaving him "wholly defiled in all the faculties and parts of soul and body," see *The Shorter Catechism with Scripture Proofs,* Question 18, 5; the Westminster Confession in John H. Leith, ed., *Creeds of the Churches,* 201; John Calvin, *Institutes of the Christian Religion,* 1:252–53; and William Ames, *The Marrow of Theology,* trans. John Eusden, 120.

7. *The Works of George Herbert,* ed. F. E. Hutchinson, 101; Hooker is cited in Kenneth B. Murdock, *Literature and Theology in Colonial New England,* 39.

tians of the later Renaissance.[8] For that matter, Christian writers of other eras—including our own—have likewise shared their vexation with the problem of sacred ineffability and the chronic failure of words. Nor do religious writers stand alone in betraying anxiety over the communicative limits of language.

So Taylor's obsession with his putative inability to write, though individual in its mood and expressive idiom, is hardly unique. Neither is it an inevitable result of his Puritanism. One looks in vain among his fellow poets of colonial New England for comparable signs of theological scruple over the artist's role. Though Urian Oakes takes a self-deprecating posture at the start of his address "to the Reader" when he confesses "I am no poet," he never touches the general problem of religious presumption raised by any attempt to write sacred verse. His confession remains a personal gesture of apology for suspected defects in talent. And Michael Wigglesworth, who was otherwise ready enough to worry, shows no diffidence about daring to poeticize— or about claiming heavenly sponsorship for such efforts in his prefatory poem to *The Day of Doom*. Only Anne Bradstreet, in a few lines of her "Contemplations," conveys anything like Taylor's religious and theoretical concern over the necessary failure of art. But she does so only momentarily, in a passing mood within the larger course of her contemplations. Elsewhere, in her "Prologue" to the *Four Quaternions*, she indicates a good deal of self-consciousness about her position as a female writer, but none about the specter of theological arrogance raised by a creative act in potential rivalry with the definitive Word.

In comparison with other colonial poets, then, Taylor brings a distinctive burden of theological self-consciousness to his craft. And in comparison with other Christian poets of the seventeenth century, he defines his poetic identity through the particular manner and logic of his response to the common challenge of ineffability and fallen artistry. Plainly, Taylor did not choose to

8. In *Protestant Poetics and the Seventeenth-Century Religious Lyric*, Barbara Lewalski establishes Taylor's continuity with the major English lyricists of his day and rejects the notion of a "Metaphysical-Puritan dichotomy" (389). In several respects I believe the point should be extended to affirm a general Christian continuity and to question a Protestant-Catholic dichotomy.

retreat into Richard Hooker's "safest eloquence" of silence. The "Prologue" suggests the grounds on which he moved beyond the potential debilitation of depravity.

Before the end of its second stanza, the "Prologue" has already begun to qualify its apparent dismissal of human creativity: all earthly art, no matter how gifted its maker or materials, is an exercise in vanity "Unless thou mak'st the Pen, and Scribener." Despite its lack of intrinsic merit on the scale of infinity, poetry can thus reveal an acquired worth in its mediation of divine power. For this creative possibility to obtain, however, the poet must first know something of the enabling experience of regeneration. To write graceful verse is, presumably, a sign of having been animated by grace. And to become "*Thy* Crumb of Dust" (emphasis supplied) instead of an anonymous clod is to pass beyond the limits of personal egoism toward an identity in which the human "I" and divine "thy" can interfuse. Such a poet is not merely permitted but positively "design'd" to trace those "designs" earlier associated with display of "the Boundless Deity":

I am this Crumb of Dust which is design'd
    To make my Pen unto thy Praise alone,
And my dull Phancy I would gladly grinde
    Unto an Edge on Zions Pretious Stone.
And Write in Liquid Gold upon thy Name
My Letters till thy glory forth doth flame.

But Taylor's climactic transformation of his original Adamic trope takes place in two subsequent lines of prayerful imperative centered on the verb *Inspire*: "Inspire this Crumb of Dust till it display / Thy Glory through't: and then thy dust shall live." With this pointed re-creation of the original Genesis scene of human creation, the poet's sordid humanity appears in the new light of an *imago Dei* bearing the "designs" of God's own nature. Having inhaled the breath of natural life, this clay may hope to receive the headier breath of the indwelling Spirit. Thus inspired—and Taylor's usage plays deliberately over the word's literal sense—the poet becomes a prophetic agent capable of displaying the divine "Glory through't." In the transforming light of redemption, both the regenerate self and its productions shine forth as "jems" rather than as obscure and inert clay.

Anticipating Emerson's assurance that "one man is a counterpoise to a city," Taylor finds that the worth of a single soul laden with divine life outweighs the purely physical substance of earth, mountains, and sky. The point gains biblical reinforcement in the context of Isaiah's Poem of Divine Majesty (Isa. 40.12–26), where the Hebrew prophet declares that in balance with the power of God the earth itself weighs out to a particle of dust. In the New Covenant dispensation, Taylor's grimmer estimates of fallen humanity are outweighed by his antithetical vision of humankind's exaltation through the Incarnation. Influenced by the "deification" theories of Greek fathers of the church, such as Origen and Clement of Alexandria, Taylor went so far as to show human nature advanced above angelic nature and seated, through its conjunction with Christ, in the Trinity.[9] Not only within his own person but also through his covenantal Word and Sacrament, Christ, the ultimate metaphor, had bridged the great gulf fixed between humanity and God.[10] The gracious alchemy effected in Christ's "Humane Frame" promised to transform the poet's fallen words with a touch from "That Golden Mint" issuing from a "Mouth Divine." In sum, the hopeful point of the "Prologue" is to answer the queries of the opening stanza with a potent though qualified "yes."

The qualifications remain crucial, however. Even if generally persuaded of his regeneracy, the poet could not hope to complete his transformation from ignoble dust to glorified gem in this life. Until the Kingdom had fully come, he would continue to feel the law of sin warring against him in his members. Still infected by depravity, his writing too would betray that weakness endemic to the Flesh. To invoke that favorite Puritan metaphor from Isaiah, the poet's proudest verbal craftsmanship looked like a filthy rag

9. On the sources and implications of Taylor's language of human deification, see John Gatta, "Little Lower than God: The Super-Angelic Anthropology of Edward Taylor."

10. In *God's Altar: The World and the Flesh in Puritan Poetry*, 181, Robert Daly proposes that for Taylor, Christ was the essential metaphor.

when contrasted by its natural merits with heaven's perfection. Humbled by this ludicrous disparity, Taylor asks in the "Prologue" that the Lord not laugh his efforts to scorn in the way their inherent demerits would dictate.

The poet comes here to an ambiguous view of his ability to sing the Lord's songs worthily while in earthly exile. On the one hand, he must value the creations of human wit in their embodiment of God's gracious designs. As the Incarnation had sanctified and uplifted human nature, so also Christ's example in Scripture had ratified the legitimacy of figuralism in sacred verse: "For Christ in his parables doth illustrate supernatural things by natural, and if it were not thus, we could arrive at no knowledge of supernatural things, for we are not able to see above naturals" (*TCLS*, 43). Taylor felt duty-bound to offer praise and to practice meditation. On the other hand, he could never ignore the persistence of depravity, the inexpressibility of God, or the failure of language to resolve the mystery of God's silence.[11]

Confronted by this aesthetic dilemma, Taylor confesses in *Meditation* 1.17 that he "can, yet cannot tell this Glory just, / In Silence bury't, must not, yet I must." Likewise in *Meditation* 1.22 he finds that "Whether I speake, or speechless stand, I spy, / I faile thy Glory: therefore pardon Cry." For Taylor, any motion beyond the impasse depended first on acknowledging a double standard of poetic decorum that embraced two distinct scales of judgment, human and divine. He knew that even his most "Sparkling Eloquence" must "appeare as dawbing pearls with mud" (1.13) in comparison with the divine glory. As Charles Mignon observes, Taylor understood that "earthly rhetorical figures simply will not do" and that all his hyperboles must fail within the "decorum of imperfection" falling from Adam.[12]

Having once accepted the futility of touching divinity with human tropes, the sacred poet determined to write had two strategic options. One choice would be to pursue some version of the spiritual approach known classically as the Affirmative Way,

---

11. On the issue of God's silence, see Patricia Caldwell, *The Puritan Conversion Narrative: The Beginnings of American Expression*, 138.

12. Mignon, "A Decorum of Imperfection," 1425.

using natural vehicles to transfer as much sense as possible of the transcendent tenor within the scope of analogical discourse. Figures become the rungs, as it were, on a linguistic ladder reaching toward the ineffable. The elevated grandeur of Milton's hymn to light in Book XV of *Paradise Lost* can be taken as a choice illustration of *via affirmativa* rhetoric. Still, a major discontinuity stands between even the most exalted signs of human language and their divine referent.

More from personal inclination than from theological necessity, neither Herbert nor Taylor characteristically sought to compensate for the natural infirmity of rhetoric by aspiring toward a high-mimetic mode. Herbert's variant aesthetic of the Affirmative Way, as glimpsed in poems such as "Jordan I and II," "Dulnesse," "A true Hymne," "The Forerunners," and "A Wreath," centers on the ideal of simplicity of spirit. Far from technically artless, his pursuit of this principle involves what Louis Martz calls a stylistic "movement from elaboration to restraint" after the model of Sidney. And as Joseph Summers points out, Herbert's "impression of astonishing simplicity" is something "earned," the very "opposite of naivety." This developed poverty of rhetoric is rooted ultimately in an ideal of self-naughting poverty. If the poet could not frame language suitable to heaven, he could at least insure its consonance with his own project of self-purification. "The finenesse which a hymne or psalme affords," wrote Herbert, "Is, when the soul unto the lines accords"; "Beautie and beauteous words should go together." A "plaine" rhetoric would aptly embody this trait of devoted concentration, warding off pride and the blighting effects of the Fall:

Lord, cleare thy gift, that with a constant wit
          I may but look towards thee:
Look onely; for to *love* thee, who can be,
          What angel fit?[13]

But though Herbert abjured the "quaint words and trim inven-

13. *Works of George Herbert*, 168, 177, 116; Louis Martz, *The Poetry of Meditation: A Study in English Religious Literature of the Seventeenth Century*, 260–61, 272, 313; Joseph H. Summers, *George Herbert: His Religion and Art*, 187.

tion" of high rhetoric, so evolving his own specialized use of the second or "mean" option among the traditional three styles,[14] he was not thereby abjuring every form of Affirmative Way theology. His rhetorical doctrine of simplicity may be seen instead as a negative qualification that left him free to pursue positive analogy in the form of deliberately modest tropes like the pulley and the flower. Whatever botched signs of his sinful nature remained in the writing might be subsumed into a larger pattern of sacrifice and self-offering, consecrated to gain a new, though contingent, value as song of praise.[15]

Taylor shared Herbert's hope that his flawed productions might gain divine acceptance when offered sacrificially as his "Penny Prize" (2.106). As God received the widow's mite to be a sanctifying token of self-offering, so he might receive Taylor's "little mite of Love" as a source of "musick sweet . . . that heaven shall greet"—or even, by punning discovery, as a might more awesome than a mountain (2.97). But otherwise the poet in Westfield reached a different solution to the problem of artistic imperfection from the one his predecessor had marked out at Bemerton.

In a few of his poems, Taylor strains to extend his positive metaphors into a high-mimetic mode that Herbert would openly reject. *Meditation* 2.128, for example, part of Taylor's series of reflections on Canticles, magnifies the person and soul of Christ through well-worn tropes of "Precious Stones and Spirituall Jewells." *Meditation* 2.127 labors in vain to convey the heavenly rapture of the Saints with faint exclamations like "Oh. Loveliness. Desirable and high." But such poems, with their vocabulary of surfeiting hyperbole, invariably fall among Taylor's worst.

More characteristically, Taylor admits that his most opulent expression could appear no better than "A pack of guilded Non-Sense" to God (2.35). The effort to weave his verses "with an angelick skill" only leaves his language in "rags, and jags: so

14. On *catachresis* and the Three Styles, see Tuve, *Elizabethan and Metaphysical Imagery*, 130–38, 230–47, and Augustine, *On Christian Doctrine*, trans. D. W. Robertson, Jr., 145–66.

15. Rosemond Tuve has written usefully of Herbert's self-immolation and self-forgetfulness in *A Reading of George Herbert*, 195–97; Stanley E. Fish offers a largely parallel view of Herbert's self-diminishing sensibility in chapter 3 of his *Self-Consuming Artifacts: The Experience of Seventeenth-Century Literature*.

snicksnarld to the thrum." Persuaded he could never manage to sound the Spirit with "A Damask Web of Velvet Verse" (2.56), Taylor shows a general refusal to try. That he should forego the search for "Spangled Flowers of sweet-breathd Eloquence" (2.44) would seem to have been a strategic consequence of his aesthetic. It was not solely determined by Puritan theology—as witnessed by contrast in the frankly epic ambitions of Wigglesworth in *The Day of Doom* or Bradstreet in her *Four Quaternions*. Neither does Taylor, aside from a sport like "Huswifery," try to emulate Herbert's calculated simplicity or a literalized version of the Puritan "plain style." As we have already found, the poet inclines rather toward a reflexive, *via negativa* principle of wit in which he seeks to transcend his verbal failure by exposing it to mockery. Though exploited more fully outside the "Prologue," the negative strategy of reverent parody is briefly suggested there in the energetic alliteration with which Taylor makes his imagined angelic quill "blot and blur yea jag, and jar."

This Negative Way dimension of Taylor's aesthetic is substantially implicated in his peculiar roughness of style. Yet the two Ways are not mutually exclusive, either in spirituality or in creative art. Accordingly, Taylor's aesthetic incorporates as well elements of the Affirmative Way, including the previously mentioned deification doctrine and the affirmation of Christ as mediating Word. Another relevant dimension is the poet's affirmative disposition toward verbal play, as discussed in chapter 1. For though he clearly perceived that words and tropes could not fill the "gaps in the text of the world" when invoked as static signs, he sustained greater confidence—as Michael Clark has effectively shown—in the discursive power of language as relational grammar: "for Taylor, phonemes, syntax, and grammar accomplish what metaphors and images cannot: they establish a connection between the divine and human."[16] Demonstrating the point with reference to Taylor's linguistic manipulations in poems like *Meditations* 2.35, 2.48, and 2.79, Clark is in effect analyzing the poet's play. Language in play accomplishes what words at rest cannot.

Taylor's play of signifiers nonetheless differs, as one might

16. Clark, " 'The Crucified Phrase,' " 280; "The Subject of the Text," 127.

expect, from that reflected in the Derridean model of nonteleological freeplay in a decentered and secular cosmos. [17] For Taylor, the Affirmative Way aesthetic of linguistic play is founded on teleological ritual, in the form of speech-act performance and the ultimate ritual of the Lord's Supper. His play of grace also assumes a creative dependence on the open but nonautonomous text of Scripture. In *Meditation* 2.156, for example, Taylor plays over the word *friend* until it becomes a functional referent for his relation to God, an audacious gesture made possible only because the word and its sacred grammar have already been given him in more than one locus of Revelation:

Callst thou me Friend? What Rhetorick is this?
. . . .
'Twould be too much for Speeches Minted Stamp.
    Sure it would set sweet Grace nigh on the Wrack
To assert I could befriend thee and her Cramp.
    Methinke this tune nigh makes thy Harp Strings crack.
    Yet Graces note claims kindred nigh this knell
    Saying Eate Oh Friend, Yea drinke Beloved Well.

Friend, and Beloved calld to and welcom'd thus
    At thy Rich Garden feast with spiced joy.
If any else had let such Dainties rush
    It would be counted sauced blasphemy.
    But seeing Graces Clouds such rain impart,
    Her Hony fall for joy makes leape my heart.

The Problem of Audience and Expression

Returning to the "Prologue" for a look at its conclusion raises yet another question about Taylor's theoretical intentions, the problem of audience. To speak of the poet's rhetorical wit would seem to imply some context of communicative address. Yet Taylor published neither his verse nor his prose treatises during his lifetime. Though the dramatically framed poetry in *Gods Determinations* is demonstrably related to public issues and reveals a clear sense of

17. See James S. Hans, *The Play of the World,* especially xii, 10, 86, 92, 100.

audience, the meditative poems focus on the individual's spiritual quest and sometimes appear esoteric.[18] Moreover, the fable that Taylor left his heirs a distinct prohibition against publication, though now discredited as fact, has proved oddly resilient.[19] So the prevailing image of Taylor, based mainly on the *Meditations*, remains that of the solitary singer.

Without specifying Taylor's attitude regarding publication, the concluding lines of the "Prologue" do suggest a qualification of this image:

> Thy Crumb of Dust breaths two words from its breast,
>   That thou wilt guide its pen to write aright
> To Prove thou art, and that thou art the best
>   And shew thy Properties to shine most bright.
>   And then thy Works will shine as flowers on Stems
>   Or as in Jewellary Shops, do jems.

Taylor wrote of manifesting the divine nature as openly as a jeweler would display his finest wares. The expired expression of the grace-filled poet is supposed to "prove" and "shew" God's excellency—but to whom? No doubt the poet's own heart is a prime target of the demonstration. The ongoing argument with oneself pursued throughout the *Meditations* is squarely in the tradition of meditative practice urged by Richard Baxter and others. It is also fair to suppose in general that Taylor wrote to a divine audience, as the immediate address of the "Prologue" makes plain.

Yet Taylor's rhetorical voice, even in the *Meditations*, has a further interpersonal resonance echoing from the communicative

18. Beyond certain technicalities of content, the language of the *Meditations* raises problems of intelligibility even for a reader of Taylor's time. The range of Taylor's diction—including archaic terms, dialect, Americanisms, and special language—is evidently broader than that of his fellow versifiers in New England, as discussed by Charles W. Mignon in "Diction in Edward Taylor's *Preparatory Meditations*."

19. For an effective deconstruction of the legend, see Francis Murphy, "Edward Taylor's Attitude toward Publication: A Question Concerning Authority"; another address to the problem appears in Emmy Shepherd, "Edward Taylor's Injunction Against Publication."

vocation of his pastoral and homiletic office. The poems in the *Meditations* are not public, certainly, in the sense of reaching toward a collective audience, but neither are they secretive in the sense of revealing intimate details of the minister's private life. Instead of naming concrete sins, they dwell in a generalized language of depravity and grace symbolically shared by Everysaint in the covenanted community. Thus, though the *Meditations* sound a range of private and public tonalities, their primary speaker is less the romantic solitary than a representative self.[20] The ease with which the poet slips from the *I* to *we* pronoun in *Meditation* 1.31 gives only a hint of his deeper absorption of identity into the representative sinner-saint.

Despite the undeniable circumstance of first-person meditation in the *Meditations*, Taylor's wit projects the sense of a human listener almost everywhere shaping or at least overhearing his discourse. We are dealing, in other words, with an art that is self-consciously rhetorical in its whole orientation, not only in its use of individual rhetorical figures drawn from tradition.[21] And Taylor's intent to communicate must be clearly distinguished from his presumed reluctance to publish. Accordingly, the *Meditations* occupy a mediate position on the social scale of private to public discourse. As a practical, objectified rehearsal of interior rhetoric, their "preparatory" function would lie somewhere between the private work of self-examination and the public challenge of stirring the affections of parishioners. Preaching, then, provides the most obvious rhetorical model for Taylor's communicative voice in the *Meditations*. Two other relevant models are the narrative form of the conversion "relation" and the poetry of the biblical psalms.

Critics have long perceived a close generative correlation between Taylor's meditative poems and his Sacrament day ser-

20. That Taylor's speaker carries a representative or self-mythologizing identity has been recognized before, as by Norman S. Grabo, *Edward Taylor,* 74–75, and Karl Keller, *The Example of Edward Taylor,* especially 75–78. On American and Reformed contexts for Taylor's collective voice, see Sacvan Bercovitch, *The Puritan Origins of the American Self,* especially 2, 8–28, 122.

21. Studies analyzing Taylor's use of formal rhetorical figures include Kenneth R. Ball, "Rhetoric in Edward Taylor's *Preparatory Meditations,*" and William R. Manierre, "Verbal Patterns in the Poetry of Edward Taylor."

mons, however they may differ on the precise chronology of composition.[22] By further implication, the minister's peculiar program of creativity suggests the rhetorical continuity of his homiletic and "personal" exercises despite notable differences in emphasis. And in fact the near-conflation of sermon and meditation, summed up in Baxter's famous account of meditation as preaching to oneself, is a central characteristic of Protestant meditative theory.[23]

As the Lord's Supper "sets out" the image of the Savior "in lively colors" (*TCLS*, 203), so the poet-preacher serves instrumentally to display "Graces bright Shine"[24]—to himself, first of all, lest he become "a castaway" while preaching to others (1 Cor. 9.27), but then by immediate extension to the community. Thus the poet-priest is, in Herbert's relevant image, "a brittle crazie glasse" conveying divine illumination to the world ("The Windows"). If "Gods Altar needs not our pollishings,"[25] God's Word yet needs to be opened and applied. And the early Puritans, endorsing Herbert's dictum that "A verse may finde him, who a sermon flies," readily acknowledged the evangelical uses of poetry.

One way of appreciating the communicative link between Taylor's public preaching and private meditation is to ponder the obvious fact that Taylor troubled to write down his meditations. Though it is useful to understand the transfer of sensibility encapsulated in the phrase "poetry of meditation," it is also worth

22. The sermon-poem relation has been variously defined by Norman Grabo in his introduction to Taylor's *Christographia*; by Robert Benton, "Edward Taylor's Use of His Text"; and by Thomas M. Davis, "Edward Taylor's 'Occasional Meditations.'" Benton finds the poems less derivative from sermon doctrine than does Grabo; Davis finds them less regularly paired to the schedule of Sacrament days.

23. Expounded in Lewalski, *Protestant Poetics*; in Lewalski's earlier *Donne's Anniversaries and the Poetry of Praise: the Creation of a Symbolic Mode*, especially 73ff.; and in U. Milo Kaufmann, *The Pilgrim's Progress and Traditions in Puritan Meditation*, especially 23–24. Even beyond the Puritan context, Tuve remarks that in Renaissance poetic "no one seems to hit on the solution of thinking of poems independently of readers" (*Elizabethan and Metaphysical Imagery*, 180).

24. *A Transcript of Edward Taylor's Metrical History of Christianity*, ed. Donald E. Stanford, 9. The motif of shining or display is persistent in *Metrical History* and in *Meditations*, Second Series.

25. Preface to *The Bay Psalm Book*, in Miller and Johnson, *The Puritans*, 2:672.

recalling the critical distinction between private acts of prayer or meditation, on the one hand, and acts of literary composition on the other. It is, after all, the normative process to engage in serious meditation, including meditation before celebrating the Lord's Supper, *without* recording the process on paper. And though Taylor no doubt drew on his own spiritual exertions in composing his written meditations, he did not produce a poem from every session of private meditation or before every Sacrament day. His art and interior life did not connect so mechanically as that. From the standpoint of the purely private process there is little reason to write in the first place, less reason to do stylistic revision, and no reason at all to seek preservation of the manuscripts beyond one's lifetime. Taylor did all three. When seventeenth-century Christians transferred spiritual exercises from the privacy of the heart to the inevitably more objective medium of written discourse, they did so for reasons that were usually in some sense social.

By way of elucidating this point Joseph Hall, a seminal figure in the Protestant meditative tradition before Taylor, draws a pointed distinction between secret and shared, written meditation in the dedicatory epistle to his *Meditations and Vowes, Divine and Morall*. Extolling the latter, Hall argues that

hereby we make others partners of those rich excellencies, which God hath hid in the minde. And though it be most easie and safe, for a man, with the Psalmist to commune with his owne heart in silence; yet is it more behouefull to the common good, for which (both as men and Christians) we are ordained, that those thoughts which our experience hath found comfortable and fruitfull to our selues, should (with neglect of all censures) be communicated to others. The concealement wherof (mee thinkes) can proceed from no other ground, but either timorousnesse, or enuie. Which consideration hath induced me to clothe these naked thoughts in plaine and simple words, and to aduenture them into the light, after their fellowes.[26]

That Taylor did not publish is no proof of his urge toward "concealement." In fact, to suppose it suspicious that his works never came to press is to presume a norm anachronistic to the seventeenth century. John Fiske, a decent if unremarkable New England poet, never published though he wrote mostly in formal public modes. John Saffin, another respectable writer, published only one or two of his. And major English devotional poets like Herbert and Donne—writers closest in temper to Taylor, though removed in time and cultural ambience—did not usually publish verses during their lifetime either. Typically they thought of addressing their readers through the civilized vehicle of hand-copied manuscript rather than the brasher medium of printed page; and there is reason to believe that Taylor too circulated poetry in manuscript. There is even recent evidence that Taylor knowingly supplied an elegiac poem destined for publication.[27] Herbert's final intentions respecting publication of *The Temple* are still about as obscure as Taylor's respecting the "Poetical Works" manuscript.[28] And yet, for reasons only partly intrinsic to the poetry, Herbert's conscious appeal to an audience in his meditative verse is not nearly so apt to be ignored or denied.

As an intermediate extension of the pastor's homiletic office and as a vividly repeated drama of the representative soul, Taylor's verse therefore answers the imperative to "prove" and "shew" the glory of Christ to His struggling New England saints. This rhetorical claim obtains regardless of actual publication or circula-

27. For description of the "common practice" of circulating unpublished manuscripts in colonial New England, see Harrison T. Meserole, *Seventeenth-Century American Poetry*, xxi-xxii, 491. Taylor may not have granted explicit permission to publish the two stanzas of his "Upon Wedlock and Death of Children" that appeared in Cotton Mather's *Right Thoughts in Sad Hours*, as discussed by Thomas M. Johnson, "A Seventeenth-Century Printing of Some Verses of Edward Taylor," but see the recent printing of a Taylor elegy, in Thomas M. Davis, "Edward Taylor's Elegy on Deacon David Dewey." Material for speculation about Taylor's interest in publishing prose works and nonmeditative verse may be found in Keller, *The Example of Edward Taylor*, 81–82, 115, 141; see also William B. Sprague, *Annals of the American Pulpit*, 1:177–81.

28. For further discussion of the print and privacy question as it involved English writers, see J. W. Saunders, "The Social Situation of Seventeenth-Century Poetry," in *Metaphysical Poetry*, ed. Malcolm Bradbury and David Palmer, 237–59; J. Max Patrick, "Critical Problems in Editing George Herbert's *The Temple*," in *The Editor as Critic and the Critic as Editor*, ed. William Andrews, 3–24; and Lawrence A. Sasek, *The Literary Temper of the English Puritans*, 32–34.

tion of the manuscripts. And though much in his sermons must have eluded the Westfield farmers to whom he preached, this preacher did project the wit of affectivity needed to move a congregation. Moved himself by the force of Taylor's extemporaneous performance in Boston, Samuel Sewall testified that "I have heard him preach a sermon at the Old South upon short warning, which, as the phrase in England is, might have been preached at Paul's Cross."[29]

In addition to the sermon, the standard form of the Puritan conversion narrative also helps to illuminate the representative and rhetorical character of Taylor's verse. Particularly in its American version, a salient feature of the genre is its coalescence of personal experience and public performance. In a culture already permeated by biblical language, the expectation that even ordinary persons must frame and deliver a conversion narrative placed unusual emphasis on the exercise of verbal activity. As a collective, stylized form embracing the individual's saga of salvation, the narrative thus bears an evident parallel to the sequence and rhetoric of Taylor's *Meditations*. Consistent with many comparable passages in the poems, the pastor's own public relation offers testimony both of gracious experience "that I am not able to express" and of sin's oppression in the form of "deadness, dulness," and "universall weriness" of self (*UW*, 1:98, 101).

Patricia Caldwell has argued that for the first generation especially, the conversion testimony reflected high confidence in the cohesive force of language. To express verbally the effects of grace offered not only a visible sign of sanctity but also a possible release from anxiety. Much as Taylor looked to receive "New Words" in his new creation (1.30), so John Cotton affirmed the ability of the newly visible saint to speak "a new Language" in the narrative ritual. At the same time, however, Caldwell finds a pervasive "anguish of inexpressible feelings" reflected in the American narratives, an intense and emotional awareness of "the problem of expression." Taylor's poetic complaints of verbal inca-

---

pacity, less literally justified for him than for most of those whose spiritual circumstance he represents, evidently fit this pattern.[30]

But the most imposing rhetorical model for the poet's conflation of personal and collective voices would have been biblical. For Taylor, the Bible was not to be read literally as a static repository of sacred words and signs. It was instead an exemplar of dynamic speech, "a neate Rhetoricall, and Wise manner of Speaking" and a "truth Speaking form" (C, 273). Following established patterns of Reformed devotional practice, the poet looked to the psalms in particular as his central paradigm of personal yet representative spirituality. As Rosemary Fithian has shown, Taylor's poetry is steeped in musical and technical terminology, imagery, and gestures drawn from the psalter. The way Taylor uses rhetorical features such as antithesis, amplification, and interrogatives—as well as his shifts in address and permutations in mood—is exemplified in the inspired poetry attributed to King David.

Understandably, Taylor took on much of the Davidic *persona* and voice in becoming a meditative poet, finding in the psalms a pattern of language and structure to express the interior drama of salvation. In effect, he was indeed writing "his own Book of Psalms" in the *Meditations*.[31] Yet he also recognized that he must apply his own wit to the ancient words if the song of Israel's sweet singer was truly to become his. He must look toward the creation of "New Psalms" (2.2). Thus, the familiar query of Psalm 8— "What is man, that thou art mindful of him? and the son of man, that thou visitest him?"—is turned and revoiced to fit a variety of moods and contexts throughout the *Meditations*. *Meditation* 1.38 begins with a phrasing of the question that recalls paeans to the Law recorded in still other psalms: "What a thing is Man? Lord, Who am I? / That thou shouldst give him Law . . . . " Yet the poem goes on to play off David's precedent against Paul's New Law

30. Caldwell, *Puritan Conversion Narrative*, especially 50, 93, 105, 114, 135–62.

31. Rosemary Fithian, " 'Words of My Mouth, Meditations of My Heart': Edward Taylor's *Preparatory Meditations* and the Book of Psalms," especially 89–90, 110. Herbert May and Bruce Metzger, eds., *The New Oxford Annotated Bible*, observe that "The *I* of this [Hannah's] psalm, as of many others, is the nation as well as the individual worshipper. The group and the individual are often identified in the Bible in a way strange to modern thinking" (332).

Christology in terms dramatized through the use of contemporary courtroom imagery. Elsewhere Taylor variously turns the query of Psalm 8 to draw out its Christological prophecy—"Oh! what a Lord is mine?" (2.90)—or to underscore his natural unworthiness—"But what am I, poor Mite" (2.48).

Beyond specific patterns of wording, the structure of poems in the *Preparatory Meditations* and the shape of the larger collection are both reflected in the psalms. Psalms of lament, of supplication, and of praise and thanksgiving have identifiable counterparts in the *Meditations*.[32] As commonly enacted in an individual psalm, the psalmist's progress from despair toward confidence typifies Taylor's. And the psalms afford ritual precedent for Taylor's persistent threefold meditative formula of presenting a question or problem, developing it thematically, and offering a final gesture of praise and conditional hope.

The ritual element is significant because in Puritan New England the psalms served not only to assist personal meditation but also to satisfy the communal forms needed for public worship. Commonly, psalms were sung as a means of preparing to receive the Lord's Supper.[33] Invoked as a discipline "preparatory" to the feast, they were also sung as part of its actual celebration. Taylor's meditative poetry therefore fills a rhetorical space between the psalter's ritualized lamentations and its concluding rhapsodies of praise read in anticipation of the eucharistic festival.

The Festal Attraction of the Lord's Supper

It was Taylor himself who asserted a causal connection: "this rich banquet makes me thus a Poet" (2.110). That the *Preparatory Meditations*, at least, were in some way inspired by Taylor's devotion to the Puritan Sacrament of the Lord's Supper is too manifest to doubt. As part of the process of preparing himself inwardly to preach and celebrate the Sacrament about every six weeks, Taylor

---

32. Fithian, " 'Words of My Mouth,' " 97.
33. Rosemary Fithian, "The Influence of the Psalm Tradition on the Meditative Poetry of Edward Taylor," 84–85, 106.

composed a new poem on a more or less regular schedule of discipline. Yet the precise nature of the connection is more problematic than may first appear. Only a few *Meditations* are explicitly "about" the Lord's Supper. And though meditative preparation was a prescribed duty for all ministers of the Sacrament in Puritan New England, nearly all felt they could discharge their duty without becoming poets. So questions remain about why the Supper made Taylor a poet and about how it influenced the sort of poet he became. Fundamentally, the problem involves determining just what the Lord's Supper meant to Taylor.

At the level of outward profession, its import seems perfectly clear. While the intensity of Taylor's eucharistic piety struck some early commentators as suspiciously High Church, such zeal sprang in fact from a thoroughly "orthodox" attachment to the doctrine embodied in the Westminster Confession and matched the general renaissance of sacramental piety overtaking New England during the late seventeenth and early eighteenth centuries.[34] The Lord's Supper was a sign and seal of the covenant in which "worthy receivers" became "partakers of the body and blood of Christ to their spiritual nourishment and growth in grace." Unlike Zwinglian memorialists, Puritans like Taylor regarded the Sacrament as an authentic occasion for believers to enjoy union with Christ. The ritual yielded a divine presence that might be called "real," though it was decidedly "spiritual" and apprehended "by faith" rather than "after a corporal and carnal manner."[35]

In their immediate historical context and in propositional substance, Taylor's views of the Supper were not only orthodox but stubbornly conservative, in ways that Donald Stanford and Norman Grabo have demonstrated.[36] The conclusion derives especially from Taylor's insistence that the requirement of testified

34. The fullest account of the "sacramental renaissance" is that given by E. Brooks Holifield in *The Covenant Sealed: The Development of Puritan Sacramental Theology in Old and New England, 1570–1720*, especially 197–224.

35. Such phrases from the Westminster Confession and *Shorter Catechism* are reproduced by Taylor in *TCLS*, 95, 116.

36. Donald E. Stanford, "Edward Taylor and the Lord's Supper"; Norman S. Grabo, "Edward Taylor on the Lord's Supper."

regeneracy be maintained for those who would approach the sacred banquet. It is also evident that Solomon Stoddard's adversarial championing of "open communion" in nearby Northampton stimulated Taylor toward more passionate and sustained reflection on the nature of the Supper than he would otherwise have shown.

To read Taylor's passionate verses is to suspect, however, that the Supper meant more to him in elusively affective and existential terms than the minimalist category of "orthodoxy" can satisfy. Nor is it possible to propose, as Stanford has done, a simple unanimity of eucharistic belief among John Calvin, the confessional mass of English and American Puritans, and Taylor. Beyond the formally orthodox grounds of Taylor's commitment, we can profitably examine three further aspects of his involvement in the Supper. First, the Sacrament had value for him as a ritual affirmation of New England's sacred errand. Second, it had major pastoral and imaginative worth because of its magnetic power to attract souls to Christ through anticipation. Finally, it consumed the poet's attention as a spiritually festive entertainment and foretaste of final beatitude. Through each of these elements, the Supper exercised substantial influence on the kind of ludic and meditative poet Taylor was to become.

To begin with, the corporate political mythology played a part in stirring Taylor's artistic motivation. More persuaded than many in his generation as to the decisive role of New England's original experiment in Protestant salvation history, Taylor held fast to the founders' provisions for administrating the covenant signs in the face of Stoddard's challenge. In so doing, he "continually reaffirmed the essential rightness of the Puritan errand and claimed his place in it."[37] Stoddard, too, envisioned a special role for the New England churches, and his Presbyterial conception of a

---

37. Thomas Davis, introduction to *UW*, 3:xvii. The successive stages of conflict over sacramental standards between Taylor and the Mathers on the one hand and Stoddard on the other have been extensively analyzed by modern historians. See the convenient summary-chronology in Davis's introduction to *UW*, 1:xviii-xxx, 2:1-57, and the calendar in Karen Rowe's *Saint and Singer: Edward Taylor's Typology and the Poetics of Meditation*, 289-93.

national church covenant looks less parochial than Taylor's defense of the "particular church" polity. Taylor and others of his stamp nonetheless believed that maintaining pure and particular churches was precisely the condition by which the tribal nation witnessed to its redeemed status as a larger body.

Typologically, to be sure, Taylor eschewed the grander sort of historical applications that would make New England an exceptional, antitypal fulfillment of Old Israel.[38] But more than Stoddard, he invested the example of the founders with mythic authority. By 1707, in fact, Stoddard was willing to preach openly of "mistakes" made by the American fathers. Conversely, Taylor warned that God's faithful might in future years "be ready to date the beginning of New Englands Apostacy in Mr. Stoddard's Motions," since it was "to avoid such mixt administrations of the Lord's Supper, and to enjoy an holy administrating of it to the visibly worthy" that the founders undertook their perilous migration in the first place (*UW*, 2:65; *TCLS*, 126). The divinely sketched edifice these builders raised was not to be remodeled after the architecture of human expediency: "God hath measured the width of the doors and gates of His own house. We must keep to God's measures or be measured out for ruin" *TCLS*, 124). To reject the intentions of the founders according to Stoddard's advice was, in Taylor's mind, to accept a logic that would "bring Gods Laws to mans Will, & make them Suite every man" (*UW*, 1:343).

Even though such outbursts of filiopiety indicate a conservative esteem for tradition, Taylor's resistance to Stoddardeanism was motivated by more than a mindless opposition to change. Half a century and more after the fact, Taylor was still engaged by the freshly symbolic meaning of New England's errand in the wilderness, as he probably was by his own renewal of the migration in turning toward Westfield. Indeed it seems that for him the membership specifications of the New England fathers carried historic, revelatory import largely because they *were* innovative.

The irony did not escape Solomon Stoddard. However much Taylor tried to claim continuity with the extended past, Stoddard

38. This point is stressed by Rowe in *Saint and Singer.*

could argue with considerable justice that the opinion requiring conversion testimonies for admission to the Supper was "New, & unheard of in the Churches till of late years" (*UW*, 2:82). In his revised Foundation Sermon, his "Animadversions," and his *Treatise Concerning the Lord's Supper*, Taylor offers no end of proof illustrations that Christians had long enforced a qualification of regeneracy, particularly in less corrupted stages of the church's development. Yet not far beneath his elaborate arguments from scriptural and historical precedent lies his thankful conviction that nowhere else in the Protestant world—including Cromwell's England and Calvin's Geneva—had a whole society institutionalized the conversion relation into a standard for church membership, as had New England. Here, after all, was the nub of God's original relation to America.

So even if New England's verbal rite of initiation had been hinted at in the New Testament record, in the Old Testament types, and in choice episodes from the Christian past, its fulfillment in seventeenth-century America marked a new advance in the divine scheme. Yet to Taylor's deep distress and for God's hidden reasons, this advance had been driven into retreat toward the close of the century. Stoddard's initiatives were only one of many indications that the Lord was withdrawing his favor from the land. By 1675, divine wrath had revealed itself in the bloody chaos of King Philip's War. During the next twenty years, when Taylor was trying to establish his ministry in Westfield, Satanic trouble of all sorts broke in upon God's colonies: fever, smallpox, great fires in Boston, loss of the Massachusetts charter, witchcraft proceedings, and the perceived degradation of morals leading to the 1679 Reforming Synod. Particularly distressing was the scandal of sacramental neglect that occurred when too few "half-way" members of the church—that is, baptized but untestified offspring of believers—came forward to become full communicants.

Taylor responded to the crisis by cultivating his own garden— that is, by keeping green those few acres of the holy plantation left on the good ground of Westfield. He had arrived on the American scene too late to share in the first-generation glories of New England history. Unable to convince Stoddard of his errors and unwilling to accept a highly conspicuous role as polemicist beside the Mathers, he could at least maintain the example of a purified church, perhaps a saving remnant for the future, in his western domain. Even this modest design he did not permanently fulfill. So swiftly was time running against Taylor that Westfield too would quietly approve Stoddardean standards for admission to the Sacrament a year before the poet's death.

He could nonetheless hope to succeed in carrying on his vision of the New England Way within the imaginative sphere of poetry. Out of the troubles of the 1670s and 1680s Taylor derived the stimulus to write serious verse. It was then, quite possibly, that he produced *Gods Determinations*. His earliest *Meditations* date from 1682, after tensions had begun to surface between him and Stoddard; and by 1690, when he set the First Series into final form, the provocation from Stoddard's actions was at its apex. It seems right to suppose, therefore, that not only the Supper but also Stoddard's competing view of the Supper and its relation to the national errand helped to make Taylor a poet. As Thomas Davis explains, the meditative poems "reveal a turning inward" of the poet's "recapitulation of New England's history," an internalization of "his deepest and most personal responses to the encroachment of the secular world" (*UW*, 3:xvii-xviii [introduction]). But in spite of turning his focus inward and adopting a more interior medium than that of prose disputation, Taylor retained a social dimension in his art. The better part of his poetry was still drawing its life from the most social of Christian sacraments.[39]

In socially pastoral and imaginative terms, the fenced table of the Lord's Supper had a second crucial meaning for Taylor because of its role in his understanding of the conversion process. The Supper drew unregenerate souls to Christ by way of anticipatory desire. So long as a church reserved the sacramental banquet for testified saints, the prospect of sharing this privilege induced unconverted souls to pursue the work of spiritual preparation that might initiate their effectual calling. If the Christian religion was in Taylor's view a "Spirituall Magnetick attracting of the heart & affections to God in Christ" (*UW*, 1:10), its lines of

---

39. The inherently communal nature of the Eucharist was reinforced still more by Reformed interdictions of the private celebrations permitted by Rome.

magnetic force commonly passed through the Supper. Once troublemakers like Stoddard opened the meal to externally qualified professors of creedal faith, this magnet of attractive anticipation lost its force—or so Taylor thought. Study of the Taylor-Stoddard controversy from the deeper standpoint of conversion and preparation theology shows that on such grounds Taylor's position was if anything more "liberal" than Stoddard's. Taylor recoiled against the Stoddardean admissions policy not so much because he felt it was breaking continuity with past tradition but because he feared its practical effect would be to deprive the gospel of "one of the greatest inducements it hath to constrain sinners to conversion" (*TCLS*, 143). In counterpoise to his stricter machinery of outward trial, Taylor kept the inducements high in Westfield by holding forth relatively low, optimistic standards of interior judgment for discerning the appearance of saving grace in half-way members.

Against the background of divergent practices sketched by R. G. Pope, Taylor's focus on the meditative incentive of a restricted Sacrament appears as simply one of several evangelical responses to the perceived crisis of declension affecting Connecticut Valley churches following the 1662 synod; Stoddard's revivalism and campaign for "open communion" was another. Less than wholly innovative, Stoddard's "innovations" were startling mainly because he proposed them in the time, place, and manner he did. As Taylor recognized, Stoddard's account of the Lord's Supper as a converting ordinance only revived an earlier strain of sacramental debate that had divided Reformed theologians both in England and on the Continent since the sixteenth century. Stoddard forced his ministerial colleagues to confront vexing questions, such as the qualifications for baptism, that had never been clearly settled from the start of the American experiment. Indeed his understanding of the Lord's Supper was in some ways closer than Taylor's to the conventional Reformed view of the Sacrament as a visible Word.[40] At base, therefore, the Taylor-

---

40. R. G. Pope, *The Half-Way Covenant: Church Membership in Puritan New England*, especially 126–275; Holifield, *Covenant Sealed*, 215.

Stoddard dispute was no simple struggle between old and new. Beneath the surface conflict over formal provisions of church polity, Taylor and Stoddard found themselves deeply at odds over the central Puritan issue of conversion.

As Stoddard later came to describe it, conversion was "the greatest change that men undergo in this world" and was apt to occur in a distinct, emotionally concentrated moment of time. Though he described long and arduous stages of preparation, he insisted that "Preparatory Work" is not, in Increase Mather's phrase, "saving before faith." The great change of conversion is "made at once in the Soul; it is wrought in the twinkleing of an eye." Prior to the climactic instant of infused life the soul contains "not one spark of Grace."[41]

Stoddard based his ministry, then, on a comparatively restrictive and demanding norm of conversion experience. Like John Norton in the first generation, he held that all preparatory work must be seen as quite distinct from the climactic essence of conversion, which he took to be an exceptional thing. One might as well open the Supper to all outwardly conforming Christians because it was impossible to judge reliably who had received the rare inward gift of saving grace. Stoddard also warned his ordained colleagues not to affirm the existence of saving faith in tentatively regenerate souls. "Many that judge that Persons should be Converted before they come to the Sacrament, do run into a great fault," he charged. These faulty shepherds "perswade persons that they are Converted before they are," posing a

---

41. Solomon Stoddard, *The Defects of Preachers Reproved*, 11; idem, *A Treatise Concerning Conversion*, 2–4. Stoddard also wrote of preparation stages in *The Safety of Appearing*, 205, and in *An Appeal to the Learned*, 71–72. For a comparative discussion of Stoddard's views on preparation and conversion theology, see Thomas M. Schafer, "Solomon Stoddard and the Theology of the Revival," in *A Miscellany of American Christianity*, ed. Stuart Henry, 328–62; Norman Pettit, *The Heart Prepared: Grace and Conversion in Puritan Spiritual Life*, 95–101, 133–39, 200–5; and David L. Parker, "Edward Taylor's Preparationism: A New Perspective on the Taylor-Stoddard Controversy." Parker has helped to challenge the conventional reading of Taylor's "conservative" theology as a simple backlash against Stoddard's "liberal" provocations, as has Emory Elliott in *Power and the Pulpit in Puritan New England*, 182–86.

"mighty impediment unto their Conversion," since they no longer "lye open to the threatnings of the Word."[42]

Against such indictments of liberal evangelism Increase Mather leveled the countercharge that Stoddard had defined conversion too inflexibly by the rule of his own impressive faith experience. By the Stoddardean standards Mather labeled a "Judgment of Severity," a whole town would contain too few regenerate persons to make a church, whereas "a Judgment of Charity would find a considerable number." Taylor likewise attacked Stoddard— by name—because his colleague's threshold of grace stood too high to admit St. Paul's conversion of the Gentiles as an instance of saving regeneration, though it might be called "conversion" in a lower sense.[43] To take such a skeptical view of what the apostle's efforts had achieved, suggested Taylor, was to advance an "uncharitable" and "unbelieving" opinion (*TCLS*, 77–78).

Compared with Stoddard, Taylor ordinarily assumed a more protracted and variable model of regeneration. By Westfield's rules of public and private scrutiny, it mattered less whether a person could call to mind the precise time of conversion, whether the episode left enduring emotional impressions, or whether the experience of saving grace conformed to the Pauline model of sudden turning. In poetry as well as in prose, Taylor's metaphors usually suggest the extended, incremental character of the great change, depicting a process in which "The web of grace is wrought in the soul by the shuttles of the Word" (*TCLS*, 40–41). And to judge from the answers given doubting souls in *Gods Determinations* and the 1693–1694 sermons, Taylor's criteria for detecting the first stirrings of the grace needed to claim full membership were lenient indeed. At times these approached the minimal expectations captured in Cotton Mather's reassurance that "Even the Desires of Grace are Grace." Though faith remained an undeserved gift, Taylor's bridegroom giver is "liberal

---

42. Solomon Stoddard, *A Guide to Christ*, 4, and preface, 8; idem, *The Inexcusableness of Neglecting the Worship of God*, 20–21.

43. Precedent for Stoddard's sense of two conversions appears in William Prynne's teaching as described in Holifield, *Covenant Sealed*, 114–15.

handed and open hearted" (*TCLS*, 175) toward those who labor after the wedding garment of salvation.

Extending an impulse already evidenced in first-generation divines such as Thomas Hooker, Taylor reflects a general inclination to blur the distinction between efficacious conversion and preparatory work so as to stimulate the search for early signs of salvation.[44] Like other New England divines of his day, he also interpreted the term *preparation* ambiguously. It might refer in the grander scheme to the soul's preparation for salvation, that process leading toward quickening of the new birth and, ultimately, the eternal sabbath.[45] This more comprehensive sense predominates in Taylor's exhortations in the 1693–1694 sermons to "prepare" for the Supper by seeking the wedding garment of salvation, a preliminary qualification defined as "worthiness of state." The second sense, defined as "worthiness of person" (*TCLS*, 201–2), refers to the more immediate duty of certified saints to re-examine themselves and the redemptive import of the Supper before each celebration. Taylor identifies this repeatable preparation as the chief rationale for his poetic meditations.

But whereas the poems presume a speaker engaged in habitual preparation for communion, their content suggests the longer-term usage as well, since this preparatory activity involves reliving the fundamental experience of conversion again and again, as if expecting the first onset of grace. Half-way members might be encouraged to know that the sort of preparation expected of them for certification as full members did not differ radically from the exercises of piety carried out on a regular monthly basis by veteran saints. As pastor, Taylor would fully exploit the double import of *preparation*, encouraging the doubting and scrupulous

44. See Parker, "Edward Taylor's Preparationism," 263–74, though I think it is going too far to say that Taylor drew *no* "final distinction . . . between preparatory phases and effectual conversion" (270).

45. See Holifield, *Covenant Sealed*, 201. That "preparation for Salvation" had a fuller, more complex meaning in the devotional life of Puritans like Taylor than is implied by its usual identification with eucharistic and conversion theology alone is a major argument of Charles E. Hambrick-Stowe, *The Practice of Piety: Puritan Devotional Disciplines in Seventeenth-Century New England*, especially 203, 208–9.

toward expectant exertion while chiding full members from indolent complacency. Much the same motives that had kindled the first flames of piety might serve also to rekindle and sustain them.

In a sense, therefore, Taylor did conceive the Supper to be a "converting ordinance," albeit not in the directly efficacious manner proposed by Stoddard. Though preaching was the normative method by which God pressed the soul through the early stages of awakening and conviction, a wise minister would know how to pair this driving force of preaching with the more appetitive force of the Sacrament. The Supper offered a meditative magnetism, drawing souls toward that union with Christ realized in the more advanced stages of conversion. If not a means to first conversion in its own right (*ex opere operato*), it was a powerful indirect means when exploited as a psychological lever or motive. Hence Taylor's first answer to the question of why such a feast exists at all is startlingly pragmatic: "To stir up all under the gospel to prepare for it" (*TCLS*, 16). Yet the practical use stands within Providence, for "the method of divine wisdom hath set it as a motive to stir up to the highest gospel qualifications in order thereunto: and these lie in conversion" (*TCLS*, 143–44).

The catalyst needed to release this converting motive was meditation, otherwise named by Taylor as "contemplation" and "consideration." Any half-way member brought to a deep consideration of the joys of sharing the Supper was already close to possessing the coveted wedding garment, "For consideration is a means blessed of God unto conversion" (*TCLS*, 70). One way the unconverted might stir up this meditation in themselves was by watching and listening as others celebrated the Feast. Though the more intimate acts of eating and drinking were reserved for visible saints, half-way members in Westfield were apparently allowed—indeed, enjoined—to remain in attendance while the Supper was administered. Taylor argued that the experience of actually seeing and hearing the Feast take place was "a good means to stir up contemplation" about the mystery of redemption; this, in turn, was "of good use to conversion" (*TCLS*, 138). Contrary to what one might expect of antiritualistic Reformers,

Taylor and other Puritan exponents of sacramental devotion placed great emphasis on seeing, hearing, and understanding the minister's ritual gestures; they were far from discouraging all sense of visual spectacle in the Lord's Supper.[46]

But in addition to setting a physical spectacle before the eye, the minister was called to paint the Feast's lively colors on the mind's eye, or the mystical eye of the heart (Eph. 1.18). He must stir an appetite not only for the seen, the tangible elements of the Supper, but also for the greater mystery of the unseen. Preaching, the aural counterpart and complement of the visible Sacrament, would be his usual means. After all, the prospect of eucharistic fellowship was not an inevitable spur to visible sanctity, as witness the problem of neglect. It was up to the minister to make it so, to dramatize the subjunctive ideal of eating and drinking the Sacrament in a way his parishioners would find irresistibly attractive.

Taylor's own sermons on the Lord's Supper, as well as his *Christographia* discourses on the beauty and worthiness of Christ, illustrate this aim. The minister repeatedly describes his task as one of supplying "motives to move" listeners toward appetency for the Supper and, consequently, toward a claim of regeneracy. Herein the poetic faculties of both preacher and congregation play a conspicuous role. Restricting tangible access to the Supper, Taylor was all the more eager to recreate the Feast in word and image for the "due consideration" of half-way members and was all the more able to appeal to the optative force of imagination.

In all of this one can begin to see an integration of Taylor's vocations as pastor and poet. According to Philip Sidney, imaginative literature has singular power to move us "to doe that which wee know, or to be mooved with desire to knowe." At once teaching and delighting, the poet "dooth not only show the way, but giveth so sweete a prospect into the way, as will intice any man to enter into it."[47] As rhetorical extensions of his homilies,

---

46. See, for example, Cotton Mather's remarks in *Companion for Communicants*, 72, 155, and in *A Monitor for Communicants*, 16.

47. Sir Philip Sidney, *The Defence of Poesie*, E3. For a broader discussion of how this notion figured in Renaissance rhetorical theory, see chapter 8, "The Criterion

Taylor's meditative poems set forth the sweet prospect of redemption. In one way or another they too "move" the implied reader to imagine and meditate on the feast in which "our Savior is set out in lively colors" (*TCLS*, 203). If anything, of course, the poetry— including *Gods Determinations*—stimulates delight as a motive to purchase the metaphorical wedding garment even more than do the prose sermons.

And for imagined readers who have already witnessed to grace but seek further assurance, Taylor's own category, the wit of rhetorical delight generated in poetry like the *Meditations,* might move the heart to "get, and mentain a festival frame of spirit spiritually" *TCLS*, 199). A fruit of meditation, this "festival frame" pertained to the communicant's habitual preparation for the Supper. It embraced a disposition of spiritual "good cheer" antithetical to melancholy. By the same token, a worthy partaking in the feast promised *post facto* to heighten assurance and to relieve lingering symptoms of melancholy.[48] Taylor therefore dismissed Stoddard's charges that the requirement of testified regeneracy must turn Sacrament days into "Days of Torment."

On the contrary, this was a Feast supremely "full of joyous matters" (*TCLS*, 35). It was, Taylor stresses, an occasion of sacred "entertainment." Celebrating here the marriage contract between God's Son and elect humanity, the divine host "entertains" his guests "with the richest provision that heaven itself affords" (*TCLS*, 169). And experiencing the "Spirituall Cheer" of this entertainment in bread and wine, the poet finds "joy up start, / That makes thy praises leape up from my heart" (2.106). Hence this Feast

> yields gracious Laughing ripe
> Wherein its Authour laugheth Hell to Scorn:

of Rhetorical Efficacy," in Tuve, *Elizabethan and Metaphysical Imagery,* 180–91.

48. Beyond its familiar expression in Taylor, this sentiment appears also in Calvin's *Institutes,* 2:1361–62, and in Cotton Mather's *Companion for Communicants,* 72. Though not altogether consistent in usage, Taylor generally argued that the only "assurance" needed to claim regeneracy was a "probable hope," not a certain knowledge.

Lifts up the Soule that drowns in tears, a wipe
    To give th'old Serpent. Now his head piece's torn.
    Thou art, my Lord, the Authour, and beside
    The Good Cheer of this Feast, as Crucifide.

                      (2.109)

It is in the *Meditation* immediately following that Taylor announces "this rich banquet makes me thus a Poet." That the Feast generates in him the Spirit's joy of gracious laughter apparently has much to do with his artistic vocation. From his own blissful experience of grace in the Supper he is incited to "entertain" his Lord "with Delight" (2.131). And he is inspired to cultivate wit as a rhetorical motive of delight, drawing forth and raising the affections of the hypothetically hesitant so they would come forward to eat and drink.

What is more, people did come forward. Perhaps Taylor's creative designs should not be judged by their practical results in gathering souls, but it is worth noting that the poet's evangelical strategy apparently succeeded in bringing a high proportion of Westfield into full membership. Despite the several "harvests" reported in Northampton, it is not clear that Stoddard attracted more members when he lowered the bar to the Supper and stirred up motives of pious dread.[49]

But whatever its practical benefits, the Lord's Supper had supreme value for Taylor as a foretaste of the beatitude he hoped to enjoy in God's eternal festival. If Taylor's first answer to the question of why Christ ordered such an occasion is baldly pragmatic, the second is more sublimely self-subsistent: "To celebrate the soul's espousal unto Himself" (*TCLS*, 17). The Supper existed in part to nourish the soul much as an ordinary meal nourishes the body. Still, the main purpose of a wedding feast or a dinner with friends is not nutritive; no more did Taylor equate the Lord's Supper with its abstracted benefits, spiritual or otherwise. By definition one is to enjoy a "feast," a "celebration," an "entertain-

---

49. Any such conclusion must be tentative, but there is scattered evidence for it, as is suggested, for example, in R. G. Pope, *Half-Way Covenant*, 252–57; see also Caldwell, *Puritan Conversion Narrative*, 84, 99.

ment," as an end in itself. In Taylor's mind, therefore, the spiritually festive "Sabbath Entertainment" (2.108) of the Lord's Supper would rank finally in St. Augustine's higher category of "enjoyment" rather than "use." The Supper marks the Christian Saturnalia of faith.

Because God had ordained the Supper as the most honored link in his chain of earthly ordinances, the "highest glory visible" beneath heaven, it could not be reduced in essence to a merely instrumental function in the sense of Stoddard's "converting ordinance" (*TCLS*, 142–43). Attractive in its own right, the Supper looked toward producing future results even less than did intercessory prayer. And in its American Puritan form, it lacked most of the sacrificial overtones included in the Roman Catholic and even the Anglican ritual. Taylor reminded his parishioners that the Supper was "eucharistical" in the literal sense of rendering thanks in joy and celebration for the work of redemption already achieved (*TCLS*, 89, 90). Though Puritans like Taylor understood the Supper to embrace a serious remembrance of the Passion, they were apt to speak of mystical joy as the proper subjective response of communicants, going so far as to describe the "pleasures" of the sacramental banquet as akin to those exposed in Canticles.[50]

Stoddard complained that sacramentalists like Taylor were setting the Lord's Supper "above all Ordinances both of the Old & New Testament, as if it were as peculiar to Saints as heavenly glory."[51] The charge was substantially accurate. Taylor's effusions of awestruck joy over "the mystical bread" and the table the angels tremble to behold do indeed surpass the conventional bounds of early Puritan thinking on the Sacrament. In denying the Sacrament's unique status, Stoddard could claim to represent the more normative Puritan view. Before the era of sacramental

---

50. Taylor was not alone in his relish for the almost palpable "pleasures" and "entertainment" available in the Sacrament. Comparable language appears in Samuel Willard's *Some Brief Sacramental Meditations*, 5, 11, 14, 15. The "entertainment" theme is also invoked by Thomas Hooker, and by Mather in *Companion for Communicants*, 99, though in a tone decidedly less exuberant than Taylor's.

51. Solomon, *An Appeal to the Learned*, 53.

revival, at least, the prevailing Puritan theology of the Supper stressed its psychological uses as didactic exhibition, as address to the logical understanding, as a kind of audio-visual supplement to homily. The introspective psychology of preparing could over-shadow meditation on the redemptive meaning of the Sacrament, as well as perhaps the Sacrament itself.[52] The Eucharist provoked little sense of ecstatic communion, of the soul's festal espousal to Christ.

But though he agreed that the Supper was in some sense a visible Word and a seal of the covenant, Taylor also insisted it was more. Enlarging a strain of Calvin already improved by English theologians like Richard Vines and John Owen, he stressed the Sacrament's power as a sacred mystery. Christ presented himself here truly and uniquely in a mode of mystical union beyond words, beyond didacticism, beyond the subjective and introspective fancies of the believer. And as E. Brooks Holifield points out, Taylor's focus on the incarnational character of the Supper in conveying both the human and divine natures of Christ placed him in a minority among his contemporaries.[53]

Reformed sacramental theory prevented full realization of the incarnational principle because of its reluctance to affirm a genu-inely *corporeal* presence of Christ's body in the Eucharist. This reluctance caused something of a rupture between the two worlds, even though Cotton Mather called the Sacraments "Engines for a maintaining of a communion between the Visible and Invisible World."[54] Calvin held that Christ's body remained in heaven, physically separated from the communion elements. Sac-ramental union between this body and the believer was effected only through faith, by the interposition of the Spirit moving in accord with God's promise. The Westminster Confession con-firmed that though the body and blood of Christ presented them-selves "really" but "spiritually" to the faith of a believer at the Eucharist, they were not to be sought "carnally in, with, or under

---

52. See Holifield, *Covenant Sealed*, 55, 133, 213–20.
53. Ibid., 223–24, 128–33.
54. Mather, *Companion for Communicants*, 1.

the bread and wine."[55] Even if the eucharistic body of Christ is rightly distinguished from the flesh of the historical Jesus, it is hard to see how one can deny all notion of carnal access in the elements without diminishing their relevance as true vehicles of Incarnation. Depending on how it is managed, the resulting disjunction between corporal and spiritual worlds can inhibit the symbolic imagination.

Whereas much in Taylor's personal theology made up for the general defect of incarnational presence in Reformed theology, this sacramental gap might have had some effect on his framing of metaphors. It has been invoked, for example, to explain the poet's use of a "nontransubstantiating metaphor" distinct from that of Catholic metaphysical verse.[56] It would seem to have had at least some bearing on the peculiar roughness of his metaphorical wit and on the traits of polar hyperbole associated with his reverent parody.

For Taylor, as for Calvin, the reality of the divine presence could not be defined simply in either objective or subjective terms. The Catholic insistence on objective transformation of the communion elements, which made a "monsterous thing" of Christ's body (2.108), threatened to neglect the internal reality of faith. Like the poet's imaginative faculties, the soul's inward senses might half create (through faith) what they perceived and received at the Lord's table. But only half, at the most, lest one succumb to the unsublime egotism of receptionism—that is, make the divine presence too contingent upon the reliability of a person's human faculties. Understanding the Supper to be "a metaphor" in "Some other Sense" than naive literalism, covenant theology empowered worthy receivers to find subject wedded to object and "Signe" to "Signatum" (2.81, 2.106).

Even the central tradition of Reformed sacramentalism therefore offered some slight encouragement toward figurative composition. But Taylor's special investment in an ecstatic and incarnational Sacrament gave major stimulus to his creative

55. Leith, *Creeds of the Churches*, 226.
56. Blake, "Taylor's Protestant Poetic."

imagination. No amount of sacramental devotion could inspire a poetic soul if one regarded the Supper as a purely mental event confined to the logical understanding. By contrast, Taylor's apprehension of the Supper as a profoundly sacred but joyous mystery overflowed naturally into poetic figures. The sacred glory of the "Churches banquet" had been unfolded, after all, under earthly elements "Plain as a pike Staffe" (2.108, 2.109). And the incarnational imagination implies a favorable estimate of the visible world that would seem all but indispensable in a maker of metaphors. Although tropes need not "dash out reasons brains, or blinde its eye" (2.108), they gave full vent to those affective and super-rational facts of sensibility forbidden by didacticism.

Taylor's imaginative writing stands in partial opposition to the deficient incarnationalism of Reformed theology, a privation manifested liturgically in a suspicion of carnal facts and sensuous ritualism. Poetry offered an approved channel for sublimating those carnalizing and ritualizing instincts that found only partial expression in the Puritan sacraments but that seem endemic to the religious nature of humankind. As a ritualistic counterpart to his celebration of the Supper, Taylor's meditative verse fulfills those mythic attributes of repeatability, order, tension, festivity, and limitation of sacred space that Huizinga and others have identified as characteristic of ritual play.[57] Like the Supper, it re-presents the centering event of Anamnesis again and again, interrupting and suspending the profane rhythm of time so as to suggest the more pervasive presence of sacred power in the ongoing process of life.[58]

57. See Johan Huizinga, *Homo Ludens: A Study of the Play Element in Culture,* 28–40, and Robert E. Neale, *In Praise of Play: Toward a Psychology of Religion,* 98–163. In *The Feast of Fools: A Theological Essay on Festivity and Fantasy,* Harvey Cox relates festivity and ritual to meditation and the contemplative life in ways that are sometimes discerning, sometimes trivializing. Insofar as the Supper was for Taylor a kind of repeatable initiation rite, insight can also be gleaned from anthropologist Victor Turner, who considers ludic aspects of ritual, especially in "liminal periods of protracted initiation," in *From Ritual to Theatre: The Human Seriousness of Play,* 32.

58. My formulation here is influenced by the categories of Mircea Eliade as set forth in such classic studies of his as *Cosmos and History: The Myth of the Eternal Return,* trans. W. R. Trask, and *Myth and Reality,* trans. W. R. Trask.

If anything, Taylor's typological license in the verse admits a variety of carnal and sensuous metaphors, including such things as incense and instrumental music, interdicted from his actual celebration of the Sacrament. In its stanzaic pattern and other features, the poetry would seem to approach the highly regularized "festive rhythm" of primordial ritual more closely than did the freer verbal forms of Puritan liturgy. Taylor's poems, in other words, are carnal, festive, and incarnational in ways that his administration of the Supper could not be.

Still, in another important regard the Supper remained for Taylor the only true festival of ritual holiness. Whereas all the poetry stands in one way or another on the order of "meditation," the Supper ritual alone reaches to the wordless and unified apprehension of Reality known technically as "contemplation." Drawn toward the Supper's still dynamism of contemplation, the poems move nevertheless in restless flux, consigned as a lot to the lower case of preparatory work, a mostly comic distortion of the saints' final rejoicing in the eschaton. From this angle too, the Supper stands as the fixed pole that motivates and attracts Taylor's creative artistry.

In sum, there can be no doubt that Taylor's involvement with the Supper and the Stoddardean controversy had a decisive influence on his poetry and his life. But the nature of that influence was subtle and various, considerably more intricate than what is captured in the tale of Taylor's "conservative" reaction to Stoddard's "liberal" innovations. Neither did the poet's response to the Eucharist simply reproduce Puritan orthodoxy of the sort found in the *Shorter Catechism* of Westminster, which speaks of sacramental communion with Christ only in his death, not in his eternal feast of union with God and the human race. The creative nexus between Taylor's devotion to the great Feast of the Lord's Supper and the festive wit of his meditative verse is at once obvious and richly mysterious, like the Sacrament itself.

4 The Comic Design of *Gods Determinations Touching his Elect*

The Character and Precursors
of *Gods Determinations*

Sometime before he had completed the First Series of his *Meditations*, Taylor wrote a curious long poem that appears to be generically unique. *Gods Determinations Touching his Elect* has been usefully compared to a medieval morality play, to a formal Ignatian meditation, and to a standard Puritan homily. It shows some resemblance to hexameral literature, to the epic, to folk and proverbial discourse. And as a drama of salvation and Puritan conversion, this long poem has evident affinities with works like Michael Wigglesworth's *Day of Doom* or John Milton's *Paradise Lost*.[1] But the intricate "needlework of Providence" with which Taylor stitches together these several strands is such that the final artistry bears a pattern all its own. *Gods Determinations* even sets itself apart from Taylor's own *Peparatory Meditations* in its considerably greater range of verse forms, metrics, and literary styles.

Though never published, *Gods Determinations* is also the clearest demonstration of Taylor's rhetorical consciousness, the most

---

1. See Nathalia Wright, "The Morality Tradition in the Poetry of Edward Taylor"; the meditative model is one of several proposed by Norman S. Grabo in *Edward Taylor,* 159–67, while Jean L. Thomas appeals to homiletic precedents in "Drama and Doctrine in *Gods Determinations.*" More restricted comparisons are supplied by Robert D. Arner, "Proverbs in Edward Taylor's *Gods Determinations,*" and by Dennis H. Barbour, "*Gods Determinations* and the Hexameral Tradition." For discussion of the poem in relation to conversion and preparationist theology, see David L. Parker, "Edward Taylor's Preparationism: A New Perspective on the Taylor-Stoddard Controversy," and George Sebouhian, "Conversion Morphology and the Structure of *Gods Determinations.*" According to Thomas M. Davis (*UW,* 3:xvi), *Gods Determinations* had been transcribed in fair copy "by the early 1680s, perhaps even earlier," though some would date the work later.

hortatory and public of his mature poems. As Michael Colacurcio has found, the poem's central occasion was the New England crisis of church membership and sacramental neglect that followed implementation of the 1662 Synod. Taylor was addressing his sweeping discourse most directly to those hesitant half-way members of his Westfield congregation who, though presumably among the Elect, had failed to come forward to share in full membership for fear of their unworthiness and presumption in confessing regeneracy. Like certain of the sermons, *Gods Determinations* seeks to draw timid parishioners through the fearful test of King Philip's War and beyond the still greater torments of self-doubt enlarged by the problematic terms of the half-way covenant.[2] Thus reassured, they might enter the coach of God's covenanted church, their only secure passage toward the heavenly feast enjoyed by foretaste at the Lord's Supper.

Significantly, the poem combines this homiletic motive with artful techniques of psychic therapy. For as pastoral physician, Taylor's implied rhetorical aim was to help the "Poore Doubting Soul" free itself from the state of emotional and spiritual depression traditionally known as scrupulous melancholy. This coalescence of pastoral and therapeutic interests suits an author whose joint offices of minister and bodily physician exemplified in real life what Cotton Mather termed an "angellical Conjunction" of healing roles. If the American jeremiad aimed to chasten yet

2. Michael Colacurcio, "*Gods Determinations* Touching Half-Way Membership: Occasion and Audience in Edward Taylor." The possible relevance of the 1670s Indian warfare as another "occasion" of *Gods Determinations* is indicated by Davis in *UW*, 3:xv, and had earlier been mentioned by Donald Stanford in "Edward Taylor," in *Major Writers of Early American Literature*, ed. Everett Emerson, 84–85, and in *Edward Taylor*, 28–29. That God might use these assaults of "the heathen" as the instrument of his quarrel with New England is a familiar theme in contemporary writings. James Fitch, Taylor's father-in-law, argues thus in *An Explanation of the Solemn Advice* and *The Covenant Solemnly Renewed*. But as Stanford and others point out, Taylor's battle imagery was also well established in literary and devotional convention, appearing in books such as John Downame's *Christian Warfare* and John Bunyan's *Holy War*. Willie T. Weathers thinks Horace may also be lurking behind Taylor's battle scenes; see "Edward Taylor, Hellenistic Puritan," 19. It is therefore hard to say how much of Taylor's images of physical conflict might have been inspired by the plantation's actual experience of warfare.

confirm God's overconfident People of the Promise,[3] Taylor's long poem can be read as a counterjeremiad. Instead of recalling the communal mission through ritual denunciation, it addresses individual souls with intent to repair the bruised reed and revive the smoldering wick. On a meditative plane, *Gods Determinations* therefore represents a kind of interiorized theodicy designed to cast out the evil of spiritual melancholia through the medicine of divine love.

Not the least notable of the restoratives offered the soul (as dramatized character and as outside reader) is the healing therapy of laughter. The disconsolate soul needed to be laughed out of its self-absorbed, melancholic humor, a task the poem itself addresses through its assorted baits of humor and prods of satiric wit. Taylor's version of God's determinations is not only comic in its larger artistic designs and generic flavor but also fairly humorous in its telling.[4]

The poem reveals its comic identity in many shapes. Though relatively few of its lyrics confront us with the compressed style of metaphysical wit, the writing is pervaded by Taylor's characteristically warped mimesis of reverent parody, not to mention his inventive satires on Satan's machinations and on the pitiful reactions of "crippled" humanity. Beyond these strains of holy ridicule, a good deal of jubilant wit is also in evidence: tricks of stage comedy, mock-epic locutions, pleasurably witty repartee, meditative effusions of amazement over the sacred paradoxes, and digressions recreating the extravagant play of grace. Of course, not all of these things will strike the reader as directly amusing. But the poem may otherwise be considered comic because it lines

3. The jeremiad form has received extensive commentary, most prominently from Sacvan Bercovitch in *The American Jeremiad*.

4. As a literary genre, high comedy need not include much humor, though it may and often does; for further comment on this question, see Willard Smith, *The Nature of Comedy*, 167–73. As discussed in chapter 2, there is an ample body of Renaissance literature on the subject of scrupulous melancholy with which Taylor would have been familiar. For instance, the Taylor library included William Ames's *Conscience with the Power and Cases Thereof*, which devotes special attention to analyzing the relation between "melancholy" and "a scrupulous Conscience" (19).

out the divine plot of Christian doctrine while conforming to the narrative plot of serious literary comedy. By divine determination, progress is insured toward a felicitous end, a resolution featuring the redemptive triumph of the protagonist Soul.

The comic spirit most essentially animates Taylor's work as the poem celebrates the ecstatic delight of sharing in the "sumptuous feast" of the Lord's Supper. Having restricted tangible access to visible saints, Taylor unfolded his story of God's electing mercy to draw the contemplative imaginings of his half-way readers at last toward the "joyous matters" of the banquet. Setting their hearts by anticipation on the "Spirituall Cheer" of this sublime "entertainment," they might be moved to purchase the wedding garment of visible conversion that would bring them to the banquet in fact. Taylor regarded the development of such a spiritually festive appetite as crucial for a soul's preparation—both in the saving and in the more immediate, sacramental sense. By spoiling this appetite, Stoddard's innovations threatened to strip the Supper of its imaginative inducements to conversion. It is therefore in defense of the imaginary prospect—not merely of established ways—that Taylor's writing in *Gods Determinations* relies so heavily on the wit of rhetorical delight to inspire hopeful anticipation of the festival and its wondrously "comfortable effects."

Superficially, even the character of Saint seems to endorse the view that presumption is the inevitable opposite of the doubt and despair toward which Soul seems most sorely tempted in this poem. But such a conclusion is one of Satan's delusions. Ultimately the poem shows presumption and despair to be psychic twins, alternative forms of self-absorbing egoism. What the poem finally discloses to be the authentic contrary of despair is eschatological joy, sanguine engagement with glory, the "festival frame of spirit" antithetical to religious melancholy. When Soul takes its place at the feast of holy fellowship to which it had been invited before time began, it finds both despair and presumption dissolved in that "gracious Laughing ripe" which "Lifts up the Soule that drowns in tears" (2.109).

Pointing toward the ripening of the poet's comic imagination in *Gods Determinations* are the samples of his apprenticeship as seen in the extant English poems, Harvard poems, and early Westfield writings. In the earliest case, one can see Taylor sharpening the satiric edge of his humor in his versified complaints on behalf of dissenting religionists in England. The colloquial sarcasms and mock logic of a poem like "The Lay-mans Lamentation" suggest that Taylor, like Nathaniel Ward, may have been influenced either directly or indirectly by the Marprelate tracts.[5] In any event, much of the wit in this early writing is unarresting, forced, or salaciously spiteful, as in "An other answer" to a 1666 pamphlet. In the best of his later work Taylor outgrew the sectarian coarseness of these couplets—but never entirely so, as witness his overfondness for "witty and nippy Epigrams," his late writing on Pope Joan, and his repellent efforts at ecclesiastical mockery in the *Metrical History of Christianity.*

Yet some passages of badinage in Taylor's early "Dialogue between the writer and a Maypole Dresser," to take one instance, show useful training for the dramatic exchanges in *Gods Determinations.* By his wry response to the righteous rebukes of "the writer," the Maypole Dresser provokes comparison with the figure of Satan in Taylor's later poem:

What wee do do, we'll do, whats that to you?
Nor Meddle you with us, but with your shooe.
What wee must have our noses tyde in band,
And pinnd under your girdle by command.
                                        (*UW,* 3:6)

For all its youthful ostentation, the "declamation" that Taylor recited at his college commencement exercises also reveals a resourceful exploitation of verbal humor and an obvious delight with language. Conspicuous as well are the many conceits and ingenuities inserted into Taylor's early verse acrostics. These develop from a slight effort like the preemigration "Letter sent to

5. Edward Taylor, "The Lay-mans Lamentation upon the Civill Death of the late Labourers in the Lords vinyard, by way of Dialogue between a proud Prelate, and a poor Professour Silenced on Bartholomew Day 1662," in *UW,* 3:13–18. See James Egan, "Nathaniel Ward and the Marprelate Tradition," and Raymond A. Anselment, "Rhetoric and the Dramatic Satire of Martin Marprelate."

his Brother Joseph Taylor & his wife after a visit," to the more
elaborate anagram-acrostics and other funeral poems produced at
Harvard. Such specimens of elegiac wit were familiar fare in New
England, and some of Taylor's tribute to the conventions scarcely
rises above false wit. One may fairly wince, for example, at lines
for Francis Willoughby declaring

> Oh! Willoughby IS NOT.
> IS NOT'S the burden of my Song by fate,
> Being of Willoughby the Predicate.
> IS-NOT is not to enter in our eares
> Without heart aching Sighs, & Eyes all tears.
>   (*UW*, 3:22)

In the main, however, Taylor's skill as wit and wordsmith surpasses that of his fellow New England poets even in these early
topical elegies.[6] Also rare is the variety and ubiquity of the comic
spirit in the early verse. "The Lay-mans Lamentation," for instance, has often been described as a mock-elegy for the public
"death" of dissenting clergy because of their silencing after the
1662 Act of Uniformity. In other verses Taylor not only displays the
expected flourishes of New England verbal wit but also fastens
with special zeal on images of gaming and play. After unfolding a
series of mock-epic similes, the elegy for John Allen of Dedham,
minister and overseer at Harvard, adds a sweetly poignant note
to its lament for the fathers by picturing them as fencing masters,
spiritual gamesters.[7] Thus Allen

> Hath now laid down (tho' late he laid at Sin)
> His Gospell Hilts, &'s gone out of the Ring.
>
> How are our Spirituall Gamesters slipt away?
> Crossing their Hilts, & leaving of their play?

6. For more-detailed discussion of ingenuities in the early poetry, see especially
Grabo, *Edward Taylor*, 108–35, together with Austin Warren, *Rage for Order: Essays
in Criticism*, 5–7, and Karl Keller, *The Example of Edward Taylor*, 70–72.

7. Even in a funereal context, such imagery apparently had such a firm hold on
Taylor's mind that it reappears plentifully in the Mather Elegies written toward the
end of Taylor's life (*UW*, 3:241–48).

Leaving the ring to us who'de need before
We take up hilts, the Fencing Schoole implore.
(*UW*, 3:31)

Beyond the sea change of his American migration, Taylor would need several more years of adult responsibility and professional challenge in Westfield before the lighter wit of this student writing deepened into the mature comic stance of *Gods Determinations*.

The Divine Plot and Human Parody of Creation

In broadest outline, the plot of Taylor's *Divine Comedy,* New England style, is both familiar and inevitable. While the poem's smaller progressions may be variously charted, its larger pattern more clearly satisfies the threefold structure augured by its full title. First comes an account of man's creation, fall, and promise of salvation through the Covenants of Grace and Redemption, the pristine essence of "Gods Determinations touching his Elect" (poems 1–6). The long middle section that follows treats the regenerate soul's difficulties in accepting the Covenant of Grace, the "Elects Combat in their Conversion" (poems 7–29). The work concludes with a series of six poems, Nathalia Wright's "choral epilogue," rejoicing over the soul's secure passage on the coach to the heavenly banquet. Declaring the triumph of "Coming up to God in Christ together with the Comfortable Effects thereof," this last section draws the larger poem together into a song of unitive and contemplative rapture, the point of repose identifiable in Norman Grabo's meditative scheme with a colloquy of moved affections. Thus the poem moves inexorably toward a joyously "comic" resolution that many of the *Meditations* suggest only distantly or hypothetically.[8]

8. The tripartite structure assumed here is nearly equivalent to Colacurcio's division and agrees in essence with the more finely divided four- and five-part structures proposed by Wright, Grabo, and Sebouhian. Another pattern useful for explaining the poem's structure appears in William J. Scheick, "The Jawbones Schema of Edward Taylor's *Gods Determinations,*" in *Puritan Influences in American Literature,* ed. Emory Elliott, 38–54.

Though brief, the first "Preface" is crucial, since it enacts in miniature the work's entire course, supplying the theological frame in which the developing human drama must be seen. Its colorful and muscular couplets also represent some of Taylor's finest poetry. One notices immediately the poet's oxymoronic phrasing, his play on the words *all* and *nothing*. On the surface, at least, a line of starkest opposition seems to divide the transcendence of God from the depravity of man:

Oh! what a might is this Whose single frown
Doth shake the world as it would shake it down?
Which All from Nothing fet, from Nothing, All:
Hath All on Nothing set, lets Nothing fall.
Gave All to nothing Man indeed, whereby
Through nothing man all might him Glorify.
                                        (*Poems*, p. 388)

Moreover, the lines beginning "Who laid its [the world's] Corner Stone?" recall a famous passage in the Book of Job (38.4–8) in a way that seems to underscore the awesome distance between God and man—the Creator's majesty, inscrutability, and unimpeachable authority. Yet the mood and context of such queries in Taylor's poem bear even closer comparison to Thomas Shepard's intentions at the outset of *The Sincere Convert*: "Can we, when we behold the stately theater of heaven and earth, conclude other but that the finger, arms and wisdom of God hath been here, although we see not him that is invisible, and although we do not know when he began to build? . . . Who set those candles, those torches of heaven on the table? Who hung out those lanterns in heaven to enlighten a dark world? . . . There is, therefore, a power above all created power, which is God."[9] For Shepard, the

9. Thomas Shepard, *The Sincere Convert*, in *The Works of Thomas Shepard*, 1:10. The connection was first observed by Thomas Johnson in his edition of *The Poetical Works of Edward Taylor*, 191 n. 1. Along with other remarks on the "Preface," Clark Griffith considers the difference in tone between Taylor's questions and those of the Job source in "Edward Taylor and the Momentum of Metaphor," 456 n. 3. Other possible influences on Taylor's rhetorical questions have been proposed: Stanford mentions Joshua Sylvester's translation of Guillaume de Salluste (Du Bartas), *The Divine Weeks*, Abraham Cowley's *Davideis*, and Samuel Lee's *Eleothriambos* (*Edward Taylor*, 30–31); Barbour mentions several hexameral poems in "*Gods Determinations* and the Hexameral Tradition," 215–17.

main point in asking such questions was not to intimidate his audience before the surpassing force and grandeur of God. There is little here of the sarcastic reproof Job receives from the whirl-wind voice. Instead Shepard's chief purpose was to show that humanity could indeed, thanks to a voluntary concession on the part of the Deity, hope to discover evidence of God's existence through an intelligent contemplation of his works.

This comforting provision of the covenant theology likewise manifests itself in the resoundingly affirmative answer Taylor gives to the question "Who? who did this? or who is he?"

> Why, know
> Its Onely Might Almighty this did doe.
> (*Poems*, p. 387)

In fact, the "Preface" reaches well beyond its first superficial image of an Almighty Deity who "Can take this mighty World up in his hande, / And shake it like a Squitchen or a Wand," a God utterly distinct from humanity and his creation. Though all-powerful, the Creator is not wholly removed from the world. The absolute dichotomy between God and sinful humanity is only apparent, a distortion mirroring the faulty eyesight of souls in the current dispensation.[10] And though God might at his pleasure rock the hills and root up rocks with a glance, such destructive gestures are nowhere shown to be his pleasure in the larger poem. Surpassing the original acts of creation, divine *potentia* exerts itself rather in that subtle but miraculous recreation by which elect human beings are converted and sanctified unto communion with God.[11] God's "Onely" might is not only sin-gular in scale, but unifying and centripetal.

Around and beneath its oxymorons, the "Preface" holds out its essential paradox: that the all-powerful Creator of the universe,

10. In appreciating how the theme of unity vs. apparent dualism figures in the poem, I have learned from Scheick's essay "Jawbones Schema." Another pertinent claim for the view that Taylor's "apparent opposites . . . are in fact harmonious" (54) may be found in Sargent Bush, Jr., "Paradox, Puritanism, and Taylor's *Gods Determinations*," *Early American Literature*, 4 (1970), 48–66.

11. In *Christographia*, 452, Taylor proposes that "Conversion of a Sinner is a greater work of power than that of the Creation of the World."

whose most visible sign seems to be brute force, is likewise the all-merciful and human Christ, who is poised to effect the supreme recreative act of spiritual redemption. God therefore wears something of a comic disguise. Behind the mask of fearsome Jehovah lies the preexistent Logos of St. John's Prologue, who "spake all things from nothing," as well as the Holy Spirit, whose wind fills the bellows of the world furnace and whose brooding and sustaining love "lets Nothing fall." Though at first attention is directed toward God's monarchical aloofness, Taylor's wordplay turns the case, by line thirty-seven, to the point where "nothing Man" receives that which should, according to natural logic, escape his grasp, inasmuch as God

Gave All to nothing Man indeed, whereby
Through nothing man all might him Glorify.
In Nothing then imbosst the brightest Gem
More pretious than all pretiousness in them.
(*Poems*, p. 388)

This gem image resurfaces several times in *Gods Determinations*, as when the human soul appears as a "thrice Ennobled Noble Gem" (*Poems*, p. 447), or as a pearl hidden away in a mud puddle. The way Taylor fuses the multiple connotations of the pearl figure typifies his witty handling of scriptural allusions throughout the poem. Thus the gem is, in the first instance, another emblem of the Christ-in-disguise. Set within humanity, it also signifies the human likeness to Christ, the self's mystical potential for union with Divine Wisdom.[12] Then too, the precious stone of the "Preface" is St. Matthew's Pearl of Great Price, which Taylor elsewhere equates with saving faith in Christ: "Nay some men of great worth do take the wedden garment to signify Christ Himself, whom we are exhorted to put on, and then this wedden garment is a pearl, nay the pearl of great price" (*TCLS*, 172–73).

Regarded in its several scriptural settings, the pearl predicts the outcome of *Gods Determinations*. Although man has "darkened that lightsom Gem in him," the pearl is never lost. Darkened and

12. A predictable symbol of Christ and of divine Wisdom, the gem appears often in Taylor's sermons and poetry, as in *Meditation* 2.45 or *C*, 134.

ignobly drenched in mud puddles, the rational soul remains a latent prophecy of Christ's saving act and the ultimate purchase of salvation. Even as the introductory poem recounts a tale of loss and alienation, it foreshadows the story's final comic vision of rebirth and recovery. The "Preface" moves on the surface from "Infinity" (the first word) to "Coalpit Stone" (the last); yet its submerged suggestion is that this "Stone" will become once more a "Diamond"—or, to vary the metaphor, will become communion bread—by Christ's "determination." Having raised the prospect of deceptive division, the "Preface" ends on a note of suspended anticipation. What the carnal faculties perceive to be sheer dichotomy, the inner eye of love, trained in meditative understanding, will replace with figures of enclosure. Enclosure tropes in *Gods Determinations* include "the Pearle within," the Spirit's "Tabernacle," "Graces Spice Box," the walled-in garden from Canticles, and the sumptuous pilgrim "Temple," or coach, that transports the elect to heaven (*Poems,* pp. 431, 416, 451, 454, 400). Even Satan's baneful schemes, one discovers, are ultimately contained within the "All" of God's superintending will.

Another incarnational aspect of the "Preface" that weighs against its reminders of brute force is its anthropomorphic rendering of the creation fable. Despite the poem's affinities with Job, Genesis, and *The Sincere Convert,* much of its imagery swerves strangely aside from these channels. Taylor's God is a skilled artisan who shapes the globe on a lathe, then makes "the Sea's its Selvedge, and it locks / Like a Quilt Ball within a Silver Box."[13] He frames curtains and curtain rods for this creation and into "this Bowling Alley" bowls the sun. He is by turns a blacksmith, carpenter, seamster, weaver, sportsman, and decorator. If all this is a recounting of the Genesis story of Creation reflected through Job and Thomas Shepard, still it surely is—with regard to its imagery, at least—a Genesis writ parodically. In his quaint domesticity and childlike wonder,[14] the poet employs reverent par-

13. For discussion of the syntactical and imagistic questions raised by this section, see J. Daniel Patterson, "A Reconsideration of Edward Taylor's 'The Preface,' Lines 9–12," who proposes that "Sea's" be read as a contraction for "Sea as."

14. On the child motif, see Lynn Haims, "Puritan Iconography: The Art of

ody so as not to imitate too directly the noble cadences and
exalted imagery of his inspired models in Genesis 1 and Job 38.

This anthropomorphic play even implies a subtle mockery of
idolatry. The poet's workman God is, after all, an imitative inversion of the biblical craftsman of idols, the craftsman who "work-
eth in the coals" as a smith, who fashions with planes and hews
down cedars as a carpenter (Isa. 44.9–14). The idol maker's products are "the work of men's hands"; and these empty bodies
"have hands, but they handle not" (Ps. 115.4–7). By contrast,
Taylor's transcendent Might is at the same time an effectually
incarnational Being who does indeed "handle" the creation, as
does the more anthropomorphic Creator of Genesis 2. Though
the world is a "Glorious Handywork not made by hands" of the
idolater's signature, this "noble worke" issues from the "hand" of
an Almighty who "Doth with his hands hold, and uphold the
same" (*Poems*, p. 399). Taylor thereby enforces the crucial paradox
of infinity and finity combined in hypostatic union. God's rushing descent in the "Preface" from abstract "Infinity" to the manual labor of a carpenter epitomizes *kenosis*, the divine self-
emptying. And as yet another play on the manual imagery points
up, this incarnational effusion, a movement in effect from "All" to
"nothing," enables man to possess that salvation that at first "he
cannot have for want of hands" (*Poems*, p. 393).[15]

To dwell so long on the "Preface" is to suppose that what
follows is less enduringly real for Taylor than the opening remi-
niscence of God's "brightest Gem" in its original and complete
setting. Against this divine image sin can infect the course of
things only as a temporary if drastic distortion of reality, more a
privation than a substantive presence. So in the second poem, the
Adamic experience of the Fall resembles nothing so much as a bad
dream. "Vitall Spirits" and the "Vivid hue" of waking health give
way to phantasmagoria, specters of confusion and fear in which

---

Edward Taylor's *Gods Determinations*," in *Puritan Poets and Poetics: Seventeenth-
Century American Poetry in Theory and Practice,* ed. Peter White, 87, 89.

15. The prominence of manual imagery is also discussed, in somewhat different
terms, by Scheick in "Jawbones Schema," 46–47. Yet another probable locus of Taylor's play with biblical imagery is Heb. 9.11–14, where the "more perfect tabernacle"
of Christ's extended body "not made with hands" contains the whole of finite creation and supersedes the handiwork of earthly tabernacles.

"Man at a muze, and in a maze doth stand." We are given to see no dramatized episode of temptation, choice, or sinful deed. Uncertain just what is happening, man faces his obscure calamity of "a thousand Griefs" in "sad amazement." And as with Samuel Coleridge's Mariner, the chief effect of "Apostacy" for Taylor's central man is radical isolation. With Eve nowhere in sight, this Adam is left utterly alone in a "Living Death by Sin." Though he seeks madly about for friends, he sees only enemies in the invading troops of sin and—so he imagines—in the sight of God. He feels isolated even from himself when he "lookes within," as in subsequent poems the plague of alienating division will spread when this central man splits into the several ranks.

Though from one perspective the lapse from felicity is the most "tragic" event in all of *Gods Determinations*, it too develops its comic aspect from Taylor's narration. For one thing, the "Fall" gets teasingly literalized into a report of physical collapse. The sequence, like much else in the poem, is vividly iconographic.[16] After briefly trying to "stand" against the assault of sin, man is absurdly reduced to "Sculking on his face." Later said to be crippled in limb and hand, he "lies" in the dirt—lies, also, in devising "Some Figments of Excuses" for his failure (*Poems*, p. 390). In this graphic spectacle of human weakness Adam is less the dignified first parent of Milton's account than a character out of English realistic comedy. Half seriously, Taylor extends a few epic similes through his story; but instead of the Miltonic "Earth felt the wound," one finds a brief, hardly poignant or epic description of how sin "Beat[s] up for volunteers" and scales the human fort. Taylor's Adam has all the nobility of a naughty child "that fears the Poker Clapp"; and his heart beats so loudly after the event that "it makes / The Very Bulworks of the City Quake." When later called to account, he adopts a posture so pitiful as to seem ridiculous and, like the selfish child he essentially is, blames everything on Eve:

> He on his skirts with Guilt, and Filth out peeps
> With Pallid Pannick Fear upon his Cheeks,

16. See Haims, "Puritan Iconography."

. . . .
This tale at last with sobs, and sighs lets goe,
Saying, my Mate procurde me all this hurt,
Who threw me in my best Cloaths in the Dirt.
                                    (*Poems*, p. 398)

Meanwhile, Taylor has provided a flashback to the eternal
essence of things in "A Dialogue between Justice and Mercy."
From the standpoint of Puritan theology, what goes on here is
conventional enough: God seals the Covenant of Redemption,
and the two sides of His Nature—Justice and Mercy—decide what
each must do to draw man into the Covenant of Grace. Not
surprisingly, a satisfactory plan of atonement is negotiated. These
talking abstractions also have a conventional basis in dramatic
allegories of the Debate among the Heavenly Graces in Medieval
and Renaissance tradition.[17] But the exchange is rendered in a
striking mixture of colloquial and formal allegoric rhetoric, both
sides engaging in a spirited and witty contest of words. Each face
of divinity marshals puns to assert its proper claims. Mercy not
only declares that "Mercy not done no Mercy is" but also more
cleverly assures Justice that the human sinner, once redeemed, is
"just like thee" (*Poems*, pp. 391–94). Then, as if acting through a
comic stage routine, Justice and Mercy momentarily switch roles.
Mercy warns that "Who scants his sin will scarce get grace to
save"; Justice answers consolingly, "Unto the Humble Humble
Soule I say, / Cheer up, poor Heart, for satisfi'de am I" (*Poems*,
p. 397).

The serious point, of course, is that after bestowing the promise
of inherent grace, God must make humbling concessions from
polar sides of the divine nature to fulfill both sides of the Covenant of Grace. Then too, the staged hyperbole and comic jux-
taposition of speaking roles reinforce the inadequacy of any
conceptualization of the sacred identity. The "sign of contradic-
tion" represented in this antiphonal dialogue is further amplified
by the witty content of the speeches themselves. Things become
all too earnest for a moment when Mercy, associated with the

17. Wright, "The Morality Tradition," 3–6.

divine Son, is envisioned departing to "be incarnate like a slave below" (*Poems*, p. 392). But instead of delivering godly pronouncements in the grand epic style, Justice and Mercy more often worry over humankind in tones of earthy and proverbial cynicism:

MERCY
I do foresee Proud man will me abuse,
   He'th broke his Legs, yet Legs his stilts must bee:
And I may stand untill the Chilly Dews
   Do pearle my Locks before he'l stand on mee.
   For set a Beggar upon horseback, see
   He'll ride as if no man so good as hee.
(Poems, p. 394)

At other times their talk suggests the bickering of competitive and complaining parents more than the ring of eternal prophecy:

MERCY
But most he'l me abuse, I feare, for still
   Some will have Farms to farm, some wives to wed:
Some beasts to buy; and I must waite their Will.
   Though while they scape their naile, or scratch their head
   Nay though with Cap in hand I Wooe them long
   They'l whistle out their Whistle e're they'l come.
(Poems, pp. 394–95)

Part of the ingenuity in this farcical dialogue comes from its fusion of scriptural allusion (in this case Luke 14.18–20) with domestic realism. But when the give-and-take fun is over, Mercy has apparently won the upper hand. Its subsuming triumph establishes, in effect, the ultimate ascendancy of the comic over the tragic principle. Elsewhere Taylor can be willing enough to consign to perdition, but in *Gods Determinations*, as in select stages of Puritan homily, the counterjeremiad note of compassion prevails.[18] Even before Mercy appears, its quality of wit tempers

18. Compassion is the poem's "most striking characteristic" according to Herbert Blau, "Heaven's Sugar Cake: Theology and Imagery in the Poetry of Edward Taylor," 341.

the poem's otherwise sharp mockery of depraved humankind. One senses that the Adamic child who runs to lay his head on his mother's lap is tracing a first analogy of the maternally compassionate godhead who later will soothe in Christ's second "Reply" (*Poems*, p. 389). One knows that Christly compassion will eventually make itself one in suffering with the foolish sinner "over Stretcht upon the Wrack of Woe" so that this soul will at last suck the honeycomb and dance to the tune of the "Gospell Minsterill" (*Poems*, pp. 389, 396). Like Satan, the red lion of Justice enters in a blustery rage of fire that seems comically artificial, exaggerated.

But again like Satan, Justice nonetheless plays its part in the holy script beside the white lamb of Mercy. Its impress of the moral law will convict man of the "pickle he is in" during the early stages of conversion; its presence will be needed to capture two of the three ranks of souls. And the aggressive energy of its holy wrath, associated with "Flaming fire," will be mysteriously alchemized, finally, into the holy flames of joy blazing forth from the saints encoached to heaven.

Indeed reprobation has impressively little to do with Taylor's picturing of the divine plan, even granting the titled restriction to "Gods elect." That is not to say that Taylor was a doctrinal universalist in any literal sense.[19] He includes the obligatory scene of mankind splitting "in a Dicotomy," with the strangers sculling to "eternall woe" and the saints called "name by name" into their coach to joy. But in imaginative terms, Taylor comes close to sharing the universalistic vision of his admired church father Origen, for whom God must at last surround even Satan to become "all in all" (1 Cor. 15.28). And so Taylor's hasty tale of reprobation reads like a deviation from the authentic story line.

Perhaps it is simply that the torments of the damned do not matter, cannot be allowed to matter, here. The reprobate are far from heroically fascinating, and even the worst of them have apparently sinned less from malice than from deep-seated ignorance. Since it is they who "do slite the Call and stay behinde"

19. Such was the widely discredited finding of Willie T. Weathers in "Edward Taylor and the Cambridge Platonists."

(*Poems*, p. 400), they suffer no direct curse from double pre-destination. By indelicate analogy, their problem is constitutional indigestion. They have, alas, no stomach for salvation:

Their stomachs rise: these graces will not down.
They think them Slobber Sawces: therefore frown.
They loath the same, wamble keck, heave they do:
Their Spleen thereat out at their mouths they throw. . . .
                                        (*Poems*, p. 401)

Like other discussions in Taylor, "A Dialogue between Justice and Mercy" deals mostly with human nature in the generic, without underscoring intrinsic differences between elect and nonelect. Yet to the extent that *Gods Determinations* grants distinction, it soon establishes its focus on the "Humble Humble Soule" that is redeemable. Taylor's interest lies with the three ranks of souls destined to climb into the royal coach, thereafter to be wheeled to the "mighty sumptuous feast" of heaven and the eucharistic festival of heaven on earth.

Although Taylor's first description of this "Royall Coach" closely matches that given of King Solomon's chariot in Canticles, the handling of it is once again novel, with some touch of the ludicrous. A figure of "the Chariot of the King of Kings," it is presented in anything but regal proportions. It stands instead as a strangely vulgar sign of Christ's agency in the covenanted church. This graphic domesticity is memorably conveyed as the coach sits on display for sinners to gawk at in the marketplace:

Some gaze and stare. Some stranging at the thing.
Some peep therein; some rage thereat, but all,
Like market people seing on a stall,
Some rare Commodity Clap hands thereon
Add Cheapen't hastily, but soon are gone.
For hearing of the price, and wanting pay
Do pish thereat, and Coily pass away.
So hearing of the terms, whist, they'le abide
At home before they'l pay so much to ride.
                                        (*Poems*, p. 400)

Biblical allusions beyond Canticles are evoked here, including an echo of the Parable of the Rich Young Man, but they are again woven into the low-mimetic setting and the tongue-in-cheek style of Taylor's narrative.

Now, by the end of poem 5, every critical event of the plan has been outlined. The action of *Gods Determinations* is, from the standpoint of historical doctrine, complete. But as a combination of meditation and homily, the work still needs to ponder piece-meal the affective, interior implications of the soul's rational knowledge of doctrine. Hence the bulk of the story concerns the varied trials of the saints during and after their experiences of conversion and above all the difficulties faced by saints reluctant to acknowledge their sainthood. With the diagnostic fascination of the mental physician, Taylor looks to see how each species of God's Elect is eventually persuaded to enter the Coach of Salvation.

The Ludicrous Trials of the Doubting Soul and the Unwitting Compliance of Satan

What dominates the long middle section of Taylor's interiorized and strangely mock-epic theodicy, then, is a study of "cases of conscience," a diagnosis of crisis moments in the Puritan psychology of conversion. The American Milton gives short shrift to the philosophic problems of why evil was permitted to enter the world through Adam's original fault or how the fault occurred. The more urgent problem of justification in Taylor's Westfield was why God allowed his saints to suffer Satanic temptation and momentous self-doubt even after their supposed transformation by the Spirit. As the representative Soul protests at one point:

Didst thou thy Grace on Treators arch expend?
. . . .
And hast no Favour for a failing Friend,
     That in thy Quarrell trippeth with his toe?
If thus it be, thy Foes Speed better far,
Than do thy Friends, that go to fight thy War.
                                        (*Poems*, p. 404)

Significantly, what Soul begs of Christ is neither a dogmatic nor a philosophic explanation of evil, but "a Pardon, and a *Remedy*" (*Poems*, p. 405, emphasis added). For Soul is afflicted with a psychic and spiritual illness. Taylor's main task in this middle section is to move his depressed parishioner—through the combined application of practical logic, spiritual direction, and an assortment of comic pills to purge melancholy—to the point where "Desire Converts to joy: joy Conquours Fear" (*Poems*, p. 455). The external shape of this movement is indicated in "The Frowardness of the Elect in the Work of Conversion," where Taylor divides his Elect into four groups. One group, entering the coach immediately, may have some voice later on in the character of Saint. A first rank is won to salvation by Mercy; a second by Justice; and the third by the combined forces of Justice and Mercy. At times, however, all three ranks speak with one voice as "Soul." As Michael Colacurcio points out, the experiences of the various ranks are in many respects similar, since all are confronted with parallel versions of self-doubt and all feel torn between despair and presumption.[20]

The doubts exposed in the central section of *Gods Determinations* also parallel, in substance and in dialogue format, those expressed in the last part of Taylor's *Treatise Concerning the Lord's Supper*. In both cases the disease manifests those physical and emotional symptoms Taylor's audience would have associated with the traditional definitions of scrupulous melancholy. In fact, Taylor was most likely drawing on the written testimony of several eminent spiritual physicians—in particular, on Thomas Hooker's *The Poor Doubting Christian*—in framing his pastoral dialogue with the "Poore Doubting Soul" (*Poems*, p. 448).[21] Like its predecessors, Taylor's analysis confirms that Satan first stirs up the introspective malady in "the Drooping Soul" and then seeks to "thrust / It on Despare." Satan also attacks Soul's "Vitall Spirits," strives against it with "Spite, Spleen, bitter Gall"—all classic signs of melancholia—and raises "a Fog" in it (*Poems*, pp. 406, 447, 442). He plants

20. Colacurcio, "Half-Way Membership," 302–3.
21. For more detailed consideration of this relation, see John Gatta, "Edward Taylor and Thomas Hooker: Two Physicians of the Poore Doubting Soul."

self-doubting phantasms in the victim's brain. As a result, the unfortunate soul begins to "fret," betraying intense "Fear" and "Sad Griefe." It complains of feeling "Lumpish," suspecting its every deed to be hypocritically motivated. Saint's analysis of Soul's sickness matches precisely the descriptions of scrupulous melancholy supplied by ghostly doctors such as William Ames, William Perkins, Timothy Bright, and Thomas Hooker:

If God awakes a Soul, he doth begin
To make him count indifferent things as Sin,
Nay Lawfull things wanting a Circumstance
Or having one too much although by Chance.
And thus he doth involve the doubting soule
In dismall doubts and makes it fear to rowle,
Himselfe on Christ for fear it should presume.
                                        (*Poems*, p. 443)

The process is cumulatively self-destructive, much as bodily illness can grow from annoying minor ailments that sap resistance into major disease. Even—or especially—in the conscientious soul, it is easy to point up failures in performing external deeds. It is still easier to spotlight impurities of motive or inclination in the inner man. While magnifying a soul's moral failings the ill-willed accuser has only to minimize evidence of saving grace. If a soul claims gracious evidence in the form of emotive transport, that can be dismissed as hysterical delusion; if it has never known such sensations of "Assurance Extraordinary" (*Poems*, p. 446), it can be made to fret over the lack thereof. Once infected with fears of unworthiness, bad faith, and possible damnation, a patient with acute melancholy might lapse into despair. And to despair is to seal one's damnation indeed.

It is hard to identify the Satanic author of all this mischief with the ferocious lion, an image from popular tradition, who first rushes bellowing from the wings "in a red-hot firy rage" (*Poems*, p. 403). But Satan, needless to say, is a creature of many faces. While this costume of blustering beast is already a comic reduction from the dignified, epic bearing sometimes allowed the Prince of Darkness, it is also a false front. Whether disguised in

"Angels Coate," lionskin, snakeskin, or canine outfit, Satan "Cannot yet Conceal his Cloven foot" in those awkward scenes of costume change that Taylor includes in the show (*Poems*, pp. 406–7). Satan may pretend to be angry, but he is more nearly worried, afraid that the elect souls he attacks will never be his and that his preliminary setback will lead to final defeat. While he parades as the mighty general, his noisy guns "Shoot onely aire" (*Poems*, p. 406) in the faces of souls shielded by true faith. And in his final shape, the doom of Satan himself is simply to fade into airy nothingness at the close of poem 19, becoming a victim *in absentia* of Saint's one-sided indictments.[22]

Despite the tropes of outward military assault, it is only in their insidiously interior reach that Satan's threats look serious. Accordingly, Satan has no lasting visual presence in the poem. This demon is essentially a mind's voice, a purveyor of words. As such, he tries to mock and invert the creating activity of the Word. William Scheick observes that "Satan parodies Christ's roles as Logos and redeemer."[23] Like his counterpart in Thomas Hooker, Taylor's archenemy appears in the principal guise of a civil and rational gentleman—as an insistent attorney, or what Hooker calls a "wrangling railer."[24] At base he is to be considered less the ferocious "Lion," or a "Rebell Greate," than a "Lyar" (*Poems*, pp. 407, 403, 416). It is therefore as pernicious wit, as one skilled in turning and distorting words, that this devil is most dangerous to the hesitant Soul.

His witty assault takes many forms. Sometimes he is openly satiric, sometimes more subtly destructive. During his attacks on Soul he not only cites Scripture for his own purposes but also

22. In an unpublished seminar paper on "Taylor's Manipulations of Satan in *Gods Determinations*," John Surowiecki discovers a "final irony at Satan's expense" in that "after administering tests to the Souls of all three Ranks, Satan is now on trial, *in absentia*" (24). On this point and on others, Surowiecki's paper has sharpened my later appreciation of how Taylor develops his distinctive characterization of Satan.

23. Scheick, "Jawbones Schema," 42.

24. Thomas Hooker, *The Poor Doubting Christian Drawn Unto Christ* (1629 version), in *Thomas Hooker: Writings in England and Holland, 1626–1633*, ed. George Williams et al., 167. Probably this more civil face of Satan as legal adversary owes something as well to the corresponding personality in the Book of Job.

finds ingenious ways of subverting its real meaning. Toward this end his compendious knowledge of Holy Writ and theology would put many a divinity student to shame. Taunting the three ranks with a distorted version of St. Paul's sentiment in Romans 6.15–23—that conversion frees Christians from the slavery of sin to make them slaves of God—he silently suppresses the slave of sin element to accuse Soul of making a cowardly capitulation to slavery in conversion: "It had been better on the Turff to dy / Then in such Deadly slavery to ly" (*Poems*, p. 403). Or he tries to misconstrue the doctrine of the will's radical renewal by grace by suggesting that conversion is an involuntary rape of Soul's proper faculties, producing only a superficial change in its identity: "Will Wisdom have no better aid than those? / Trust to a forced Faith?" (*Poems*, p. 403).

In his exegesis, as in other appeals to Soul, Satan rarely tempts with bald falsehoods. He is more disposed to deal in half-truths, distortions, inflations. Thus, when he urges the scrupulous soul to take full account of its sinfulness, he observes that "You want Cleare Spectacles: your eyes are dim" (*Poems*, p. 409). In its own right, the line could be taken as sound counsel toward holy introspection and the true sight of sin. The ocular and spectacle imagery has respectable precedent in the Bible, Calvin, and elsewhere. But in the fuller view, true sight consists of seeing God and the Kingdom through eyes of faith; all else, in the gospel parables, is blindness.[25] The tempter himself seeks to blind with "an Ath'istick Hoodwinke" (*Poems*, p. 445). Thomas Hooker's commentary on an equivalent passage helps to expose the real intention behind Satan's words. It is "the policie of the devil," cautions Hooker, to make the sinner "see thorow his own Spectacles" so that he will "see nothing but sin . . . to the end that he may despair for ever," and "Herein the Devil is very subtle."[26]

Subtle is the word. Taylor's Satan closes his ocular discourse with a precise simile: "As to a Purblinde man men oft appeare /

25. See also Scheick's related comments on the spectacles passage in "Jawbones Schema," 45–46.
26. Thomas Hooker, *The Poor Doubting Christian*, 8–9. This particular passage does not appear in the shorter, 1629 version of Hooker's work.

Like Walking Trees within the Hemisphere. / So in the judgment Carnall things Excell" (*Poems*, p. 409). Satan must know, if the Inward Man does not, that the same comparison is a peculiarity of the Marcan evangelist, whose purblind man also reports seeing "men as trees, walking" (Mark 8.24). Though introducing such a detail would not have been crucial to Satan's attack, he must have savored his secret theft with a chortle of pleasure. And one could adduce many more passages where Satan peppers his wit with perverted allusions.

In his attacks against the Second and Third Ranks, Satan points out the inherent "foolishness" of Christian belief. It is "folly," he declares, "to think that Grace was shown, / When in persute thy heart was overthrown" (*Poems*, p. 423). And how, after all, can one believe in a God one has never seen?

What is that fancide God rowld o're the tongue?
Oh! Brainsick Notion, or an Oldwifes Song!
That He should wholy be in e'ry place
At once all here, and there, yet in no space.
. . . .
Nay; what? or where is Hell Can any show?
This Bugbare in the Darke, 's a mere Scar-Crow.
                                        (*Poems*, p. 424)

But whats this Grace, which you, forsooth, so prize,
For which you stand your own Sworn Enemies?
Whoever saw smelt, tasted felt the same?
Its but an airy notion, or a name.

                                        (*Poems*, p. 421)

One can almost forgive the devilish glee with which Satan makes the attempt. Iago, after all, got somewhere preaching this sort of nihilistic materialism, so perhaps it is worth a try with tight-fisted Yankees of the Second and Third Ranks. But the Puritan Iago knows better than to waste his ammunition overdoing the direct appeal to apostasy, especially when campaigning against the First Rank. The few fruits of nominalistic unbelief he will dangle before *them* he offers in a more cautiously hypothetical and sardonically intimate voice: "And if thou saw'st no hell, nor heaven; I see, / My Soule for thine, thy Soule and mine agree" (*Poems*, p. 412). Nor does he lure the devout with promises that they can become like God. He capitalizes instead on Soul's greatest vulnerability by himself playing God. Thus, instead of hellishly impugning the usual standards of Christian holiness, he purports to accept them at face value—only to show how Soul, when weighed in this balance, is found sadly wanting.

If the Evil One cannot convince souls that Christianity is a bad idea, he can hope to convince them that their religion is in vain because they are bad Christians. He can urge them to blur the distinction between temptation and sin, to anguish over failing the Covenant of Works. He can try to interrupt the conversion process, if not to claim them now for his own. And if he cannot immediately draw them to despair, he can at least hope to frighten them enough, by evoking the horrors of despair and damnation on either hand, that they will retreat into a borderland of lukewarm hesitancy and confusion.

For a time this is exactly what occurs as Soul—initially the First Rank, then the Second and Third—is visibly shaken by its infernal antagonist. In his efforts to undermine the assurance of the Elect, Satan relies heavily on the use of barbed witticisms. He charges, for example, that were it not for the terrors of hell and the allurement of heaven "it plainly 'pears / Thy God for servants might go shake his ears" (*Poems*, p. 425). And after reciting a long list of moral failings of each rank, he closes repeatedly with a version of the wry quip, "I am a Saint, if thou no Sinner art" (*Poems*, p. 425).

Particularly damning are the sarcasms he invents to discourage the First Rank. "Is this the fruite of Grace?" he asks, after numbering all the carnal urges of the Inward Man—"If so, how do yee: You and I Embrace" (*Poems*, p. 410). This First-Rank Soul is likewise accused of never having experienced a genuine conversion:

SATAN
Soon ripe, soon rot. Young Saint, Old Divell. Loe
Why to an Empty Whistle did you goe?
What Come Uncalld? And Run unsent for? Stay
Its Childrens Bread: Hands off: out, Dogs, away.
                              (*Poems*, p. 407)

The Soul, of course, is hardly in a position to see anything laughable in these remarks. For Satan's funniness is neither sympathetic nor sanguine but is a calculated assault of ridicule that Christ eventually labels a "Mock" (*Poems*, p. 418). Consequently one is led to ask what, if anything, has Satan's wittiness to do with Taylor's larger design of therapeutic wit in *Gods Determinations*? And why should Taylor allow Satan to speak in the role of, or seemingly to become identified with, Soul's faculty of conscience?

The second question may be answered in part by remembering Bright's theory that some cases of melancholy could be produced by a combination of the Devil's illusion—injected in the form of an excess of "melancholicke humour"—*and* a genuine and warranted remorse for sin.[27] Many, perhaps even most, of Satan's specific moral charges against the Inward and Outward man are based on well-founded evidence. Taylor recognizes that scrupulous melancholy becomes acutely problematic for Soul precisely because the work of Satan and Conscience are, up to a point, identical: both try to discover a "true sight of sin." Only when it comes to assessing the import of sin does the Christian Conscience part ways with Satan by inclining toward the Covenant of Grace. Then too, it is hard to disentangle Satan from Conscience when both are internal antagonists.

To explain the function of Satan's scornful humor in Taylor's larger scheme one must regard Soul not simply as a personage acting within the narrative but also as that implied character who is "outside the poem" looking in at his own sad reflection.[28] The insecure soul who one could imagine reading this poem is presented with a painfully clear impression of his actual plight. But because he sees himself from a fictive distance, he can afford to laugh even at Satan's sardonic jibes and at his own confused response as a character in the story unfolding before him. By laughing at himself, the scrupulous melancholic routs Satan's morbid suggestions and begins to effect a cure of his ill-humored

27. Timothy Bright, *A Treatise of Melancholy*, 190.
28. Norman S. Grabo, "*Gods Determinations*: Touching Taylor's Critics," 23.

condition. From Taylor's standpoint, then, this purgative laughter "justifies" Satan's misanthropic satire, which finds a place in the poet's comic design.

It is in fact a pivotal irony of the poem that Satan imagines himself to be prosecuting his own designs when he is not. More than that, he imagines he might actually "outwit God" and "Spoile God of his design" by destroying man (*C*, 90). For Soul's sake the trickster is nonetheless clever enough to pretend he is only following God's orders by repossessing souls too impure to merit reception in heaven: "I am to make distraint on thee Designd" (*Poems*, p. 408). In an even more distressing turn of speech, he intimates that a secret agreement has been forged between himself and God at Soul's expense:

You'st stand between us two our spears to dunce.
. . . .
    What will you do when you shall squezed bee
    Between such Monstrous Gyants Jaws as Wee?
                        (*Poems*, p. 404)

If such a pact exists, and if Satan has gained equal or superior moral sway in the partnership, Soul knows its predicament to be a cruel joke. Yet the last laugh is on Satan. His hoax of a unified governing order turns out to be right for all the wrong reasons. To rephrase William Blake, he is of the Almighty's party without knowing it. He is unaware of just how his assaults serve God as an agency of conscience and divine justice that tests, purifies, and convicts Soul. As Christ explains, this is a fire to "refine / Thy Soul and make it brighter shine" (*Poems*, p. 418). In his testing role Satan will finally be reduced to something less than the great-jawed lion he at first appears: "loe the Lyon hee / Is not so fierce as he is feign'd to bee" (*Poems*, p. 434). So he becomes only a barking and toothless cur—who is leashed, at that, and is permitted to scare souls from presumption under the watchful eye of the Good Shepherd. In compliance with God's ends, he fills the prescribed role of devil's advocate (and who better for the job?) toward the making of saints. Yet his wit is such an unwitting boon that he has in effect performed much of the preparatory labor in Soul's conversion and sanctification, leaving only the final consolatory work for Saint and Christ to complete.

Thus God's Wisdom exposes all of Satan's "Craftiness" as "mere folly" and "befooles" his "mischievous Design," turning it through redemption to promote "the whole Creation to a greater Glory" than could otherwise be hoped. Not only is "Satans attempt to effect his Design . . . made to Serve to the ruin of his design, and to advance the Contrary to it," but also, through the wit of divine grace, the Serpent's pen is made to write out his own sentence "to be an UTTER FOOLE" (*C*, 90, 95–96, 24–25).

This hidden joke is played out on Satan as his misanthropic satire is loosed to ridicule the sullen side of Soul. Although such satire seems to be exercised throughout at Soul's expense, its real victim is Soul's lesser self and, in particular, the impious products of the splenetic disease. As such, the satire is "optimistic." At the same time the poem fulfills its implied office of therapeutic persuasion through a second treatment, one quite different from satiric wit. This form is amiable humor, which serves more directly to console and amuse the stricken Soul.[29]

In contrast to Satan's derisive wit, Christ's two "Replies" thus offer direct reassurance to Soul—the soul, in this case, both inside and outside the poem. Whereas Satan repeatedly strives to poison Soul's "joy," claiming that true repentance should manifest itself in sorrow and "bitter tears" (*Poems*, p. 412), Christ urges this "Drooping Soul" to "take delight" in Him and in His Holy War against evil. Christ's second "Reply," in particular, tries to cheer up the grieving melancholic. No matter that Soul "was once a Stall/ Rich hung with Satans nicknacks all" (*Poems*, p. 416); with repentance, it will again be a "Tabernacle." "I do in thee delight," Christ insists finally. And throughout this section He seeks to put the overserious Soul in a better humor by adopting a gentle, whimsical affability within the context of a familiar, mother-child relation:

29. The distinction between wit and amiable humor is drawn from Stuart Tave's *The Amiable Humorist*, 43–67; the difference between a "misanthropic" satirist and an optimistic satirist is delineated in Gilbert Highet's *The Anatomy of Satire*, 235–38.

Peace, Peace, my Hony, do not Cry,
My Little Darling, wipe thine eye,
   Oh Cheer, Cheer up, come see.
Is anything too deare, my Dove,
Is anything too good, my Love
To get or give for thee?
                 (*Poems*, p. 414)

As the "lullaby" speech proceeds, it reinforces the impression of
God's sanguine and loving disposition toward souls. Even when
he "Frowns," he does so "with a Smiling Face," just as Mercy had
declared in an earlier speech that "lest the Soule should quite
discourag'de stand / I will step in, and smile him in the face"
(*Poems*, p. 396).

Christ's counsels afford Soul immediate comfort and usher in
the poem's first celebration of triumph in "An Extasy of Joy let in
by this Reply returnd in Admiration." Aptly, the reply indulges in
some good-humored doctrinal punning. But at this point the soul
whose troubles have been relieved consists only of the First Rank.
Presently Satan attacks the Second and Third Ranks, who then
complain to each other in "A Threnodiall Dialogue between The
Second and Third Ranks." Like "A Dialogue between Justice and
Mercy," this is a verbal contest in which the comic effect of the
stichomythic dialogue is heightened through the use of crisp,
tightly rhymed couplets.

To the extent that the scrupulous melancholic here shows itself
to be harboring a delight in its sorrow, it requires more censure
than pity. Demonstrating a humility that is clearly an inverse
species of pride, each rank tries to claim that its spiritual state is
more desperate than the other's. Each laments, "Its worse with
us," and tries to outdo the other in evidences of cursedness. The
Third Rank calls its grace a "Mockgrace" and asserts that "We
dare not wish, as we, our Enemy." To the Second Rank the Third
confides condescendingly, "Would God it was no worse with us
than you," which provokes the retort:

Than us, alas! What, would you fain aspire
Out of the Frying Pan into the Fire?
                 (*Poems*, p. 428)

Taylor's hope, apparently, was that the "Drooping Soul" outside the poem would benefit from seeing how its unholier-than-thou disposition must influence and look to others. A satiric screening of its uncharitable and self-indulgent bearing might be educational, albeit painful.

Still, Soul (consisting now of the Second and Third Ranks combined) is largely in earnest about seeking a "Remedy" for its malady in "Mercies Golden Stacks." Significantly, in looking for a way out of its "wofull Pickle" it turns not directly to Christ, as the First-Rank Soul had done, but to Saint, who represents the "Pious Wise" and the application of redemption available in the earthly church. As classified in the standard literature on religious melancholy, the First-Rank Soul is the patient who is partly able to effect his own cure through prayer. The combined Second- and Third-Rank Soul, on the other hand, may be traditionally diagnosed as the melancholic who, lacking the ability to control his own thoughts, needs to rely on the help of other saintly persons. In having his scrupulous Soul apply to Saint for advice, Taylor is quite literally going by the book—as well as by what one would imagine to have been his own pastoral experience. Saint can speak to Soul with sympathetic authority because it is itself a fully twice-born version of Soul, another Soul advanced in time and experience. In its general manner and couplet-fashioned speech, Saint even seems a thrice-born version of Satan, whom it seems to know all too well and whose role it displaces in the poem.

Saint patiently answers the whole series of Soul's self-doubts: those "touching its Sin," those "from Want of Grace," and those "from Satans Temptations." But though Saint successfully exposes the frail stitches of Satan's logic at every point, his explanations fall short of Soul's needs. "You shew the matter as the matter is," Soul remarks, "But shew me how in such a Case as this, / T'repell the Tempter, and the field t'obtain" (*Poems*, p. 444). What this sick soul wants, in other words, is not simply an explanation but a prescription.

The mere vocal presence of Saint is already therapeutic, recalling Soul to the integrative prospect of a community beyond its solipsistic horizon. But Saint also prescribes certain practical medicines. First, the doubting Soul is to concern itself more with exercising than with discerning its faith:

Perform the Duty, leave th' event unto
His Grace that doth both in, and outside know.
Beg pardon for your Sins: bad thoughts defy,
That are Cast in you by the Enemy.
. . . .
Renew your acts of Faith: believe in him,
Who died on the Cross to Cross out Sin.
. . . .
Do all Good Works, work all good things you know
As if you should be sav'd for doing so.
Then undo all you've done, and it deny
And on a naked Christ alone rely.

(Poems, p. 444)

What seems here a tenuous Augustinian compromise amounts to more than that, and more even than the conditional logic of covenant theology that is likewise implicated. Worthy deeds cannot be considered saving in themselves; but to dismiss them as irrelevant is antinomian. Such is the theological underpinning. More practically and psychologically, Saint's active verbs confirm that the best way to become an honest-to-God saint is to start acting like one. The only way to begin living an identity is to take it up. Though carrying the role may feel like frivolous playacting at first, the soul will in time grow into the part so far as to permit inward detachment from all its external costumes, deeds, and words. Even St. Paul granted spiritual neophytes their need to ripen for a time under the duties of the law before trying to subsist "on a naked Christ."

Active injunctions—"On God in Christ Call hard" (*Poems*, p. 449)—are one antidote to passive introversion. Another requirement is that Soul trust God's promise to accept the smallest sign of visible grace as saving. For Soul to lament that its "measure is so small" is to threaten an ungracious and ungrateful refusal. "You have not what you Would," chides Saint, "and therefore will / Not own you have at all" (*Poems*, p. 440). In most minimal practice, and within a limited sphere of pastoral address, Taylor's Christ can notify Soul that the table of salvation is set for anyone sincerely moved to desire it and to declare that desire. Soul's yearnings to be a saint and its struggles to resist Satan are themselves fair evidence on which to ground an assurance of belonging with God's Elect:

> If in the severall thou art
> This Yelper fierce will at thee bark:
> > That thou art mine this shows.
> > > (*Poems*, p. 414)

Besides performing the duties and trusting the promise, Soul must accept the futility of answering Satan point-by-point and avoid that peril described in the literature of melancholy as "Musings" and "overmuch meditation." Staring into one's heart with single-minded zeal, one can lose sight of God and other Christians. Saint understands well the self-damning effects of morbid introspection and cautions accordingly:

> Deluded Soul, Satan beguiles thee so
> Thou judgst the bend the back side of the bow
> Dost press thyselfe too hard. . . .
> > (*Poems*, pp. 434–35)

One day even the trials and torments of the doubting Soul— "These Crooked Passages"—will be revealed as but "The Curious needlework of Providence." Until then Soul must "Judge not this Web while in the Loom" (*Poems*, p. 449).

The problem of introspection is nonetheless tricky, as the poem gives reason to admit. Despite the dangers of self-scrutiny, Soul cannot give up the sacred duty of examining its state. In his first "Reply," Christ confirms that the unexamined life of the soul is not worth living, as he counsels the First Rank still to "look for Temptations Deep, / Whilst that thy Noble Sparke doth keep / Within a Mudwald Cote" (*Poems*, p. 417). And it is a little too easy to discourage introspection in its excess only. How is Soul to know how much is too much? Never missing a trick, Satan is shrewd enough to attach guilt to Soul's melancholic propensities. If Soul can be brought to see its morose doubts as sinful, as matter for self-reproach, it will have one more reason to descend into melancholy:

To whom . . . [Grace] yields a smile, she doth expect
That with a smile, her smile they soon accept
But you have hitherto like sturdy Clowns
Affronted Grace and paid her Smiles with Frowns.
(*Poems*, p. 422)

Saint turns the indictment around by arguing that Soul would not "sorrow so" in the first place unless it wanted to take true "delight" in God's ordinances (*Poems*, p. 439).

Even with this sort of impeccable reasoning from Saint in the analytic abstract, Soul remains shackled by "Feare," caught emotionally in the "Circular Disputes of Satans Geer" (*Poems*, p. 437). So Saint urges Soul to break the circle of solipsism by sharing its sorrow with others: "Make known thy griefe" (*Poems*, p. 434). To escape its self-centered dilemma, Soul has to turn away from solemn egoism and toward delight in God, joyous participation in the society of the saints:

Fear not Presumption then, when God invites:
    Invite not Fear, when that he doth thee Call:
Call not in Question whether he delights
    In thee, but make him thy Delight, and all.
    Presumption lies in Backward Bashfulness,
    When one is backward though a bidden Guest.
(*Poems*, p. 450)

Thus joy, not despair, is the authentic opposite of self-comforting presumption. Presumption and despair now converge more visibly as Satanic equivalents, in that both are separating and solipsistic. One dare not slight God's invitation to delight by fearing to cross that once awesome threshold dividing preparatory stages from the first signs of salvation. Yet Saint must keep pressing Soul to refuse Satan's heavy spell of sorrow. "Repentance is not argued so from Tears," Saint insists, directly refuting the Evil One's earlier call to sadness, "As from the Change that in the Soul appears" (*Poems*, p. 439).

Taylor also has Saint apply its share of satiric irony to argue Soul out of its morose, self-indulgent conscience. Thus, Saint flings back at the grieving Soul crisp returns like "What Sullen still?"; and "Can't God orefill a little Whimpring Soul?" (*Poems*, pp. 440, 441). Because scrupulosity afflicted the heart, Taylor recognized that theological reasoning applied to the head could never be a sufficient cure. He was equally convinced that "A merry heart doeth good like a medicine" (Prov. 17.22); and besides amiable humor, he could make use also of satiric wit—as wielded both by Saint and Satan—to draw the despondent Soul from self-pity. By indirect cajoling, Soul must be "Coacht along" (*Poems*, p. 401)[30] to release its doubting defenses and repressed emotions. Only then can it respond to intelligible arguments under the Covenant of Grace.

That the theme of social integration has always figured conspicuously in the comic literary genre is also relevant here: "If high comedy can harmonize man's moral nature with the framework of society, if it can make him less selfish, less exclusive of the interests of his fellow men, it has justified its laughter."[31] More narrowly defined, the purpose motivating *Gods Determinations* and much of Taylor's ministry was to harmonize the melancholic soul with the restricted society of the particular church covenant.

Christ's Curious Paradise Regained

Following a bridge passage in "The Effect of this Discourse upon the second, and third Rancks," the felicitous climax to Taylor's poem is supplied by the choral epilogue. This series of six lyrics is at once a single rhapsodic hymn of praise and, as befits the close of a comic drama, a marriage festival. In this case the epi-

---

30. Keller identifies the pun in *The Example of Edward Taylor*, 133.
31. Willard Smith, *The Nature of Comedy*, 173.

thalamium is sung for the apocalyptic marriage between Christ and humanity—or, in mystical terms, the union between the Lamb and his "espoused Wife," Soul (*Poems*, p. 453). "Holy rapture," "Praise," and "Extasies" now accompany the saints as they sing for joy, "Encoacht for Heaven . . . in Christs Coach" (*Poems*, p. 458). Grace has "nullifi'de / Sad Griefe" (*Poems*, p. 451); and formerly melancholic souls breathe their grateful affection "To God, Christ, Christians all, though more, / To such whose Counsills made their Cure" (*Poems*, p. 454). Sharing in the order of purity and holy discipline established expressly by God on earth, in the particular church covenant, they find their former distress converted to spiritual joy.

The first application of this closing celebration is evidently to the present ecclesiastical order, where the sweet singing of the saints in "Acts Divine and Worship" reflects ordinary worship in Westfield's meeting house. Taylor wants to show how "Church Fellowship rightly attended" can turn even the wilds of western New England into the "suburbs here of bliss." The concrete work and worship of the congregational saints embody the nascent Kingdom on earth. After the cosmic sweep with which *Gods Determinations* begins, this end point of the author's vision may seem distressingly parochial, which is literally the case.

But despite the tribal exclusivity of Taylor's Puritan faith, the close of *Gods Determinations* also looks beyond the immediate, as its congregational scenes visibly prefigure life in the New Jerusalem. However remotely, the visible saints singing now echo and anticipate the celestial harmonies of the hereafter, where "Saints, and Angels sing, / Thy Praise in full Cariere, which make / The Heavens to ring" (*Poems*, p. 458). God's preparation of a "mighty sumptuous banquet" likewise has dual reference in time and in eternity. Connected first to the Lord's Supper, Taylor's cherished ritual of church membership, this feast also images the great messianic banquet whose delights may be glimpsed in the joyous merriment of the feast at Cana.[32] For Taylor, the sacramental

32. The abundant New Testament representations of the heavenly kingdom as a great wedding feast, as in Matt. 8.11 and Luke 14.15, correspond to a familiar Jewish image of the messianic era, as seen in Isa. 25.6.

Supper celebrated not only what is and was but also what is still to come. With the early church, he regarded the Eucharist as viaticum, provision along the soul's way. Stocked with this honey-like provision, in the ambiguous landscape between earth and heaven, the itinerant saints ascend out of sight in the poem's concluding tableaux.[33]

Meanwhile, for the reader outside the poem, the choral epilogue continues the poet's therapy for drooping spirits. Just as Bright had urged melancholic patients to embrace "all cheerful sights," Taylor's visual imagery of garden, wedding feast, and a "bespangled" New Jerusalem, together with his auditory impressions of "Sounding Organs," ringing wind and string instruments, and the singing chorus of saints, is calculated to inspire cheering "delight" in the morose parishioner-reader. Fittingly, writers such as Bright and Robert Burton commonly prescribed music as "a sovereign remedy against Despair and Melancholy," a medicine "able to drive away the Devil himself." For Bright, "cheerful" music had special therapeutic merit in diverting the soul's attention from vexing cares, whereas Benjamin Colman would later find there was no better relief for "Grief of mind" than the singing of psalms.[34]

In the tuneful raptures of Taylor's epilogue sequence, psalm-singing is a central metaphor. If the speaking Word provides the original instrument of conversion, the saints' glorified response to grace emerges, like the psalter, as a speech "tassled with praise" in the form of melody (*Poems*, p. 459). Whereas Satan once tried to seduce Soul to the tune of his "Pipes," Soul's new songs are set to the tune of Christ's "Golden Pipes" (in a double sense, as conduits of grace through the church and as musical "Winde Instruments"). Mercy had predicted no less: those "Who mourn when Justice frowns, when Mercie playes / Will to her sounding

33. Taylor discusses manna as viaticum in Sermon #33, "Manna from Heaven," in the Nebraska manuscript "Upon the Types of the Old Testament," transcribed by Charles Mignon, 8.

34. Robert Burton, *The Anatomy of Melancholy*, ed. Floyd Dell and Paul J. Smith, 479; Bright, *A Treatise*, 274; Benjamin Colman, *The Government and Improvement of Mirth*, 3.

Viall Chant out Praise" (*Poems*, pp. 396, 453, 457–58). Even the style of the writing becomes more euphonic in these last poems, as the several ranks are reunited and as Taylor stabilizes his previous variations in rhyme by returning to the favored scheme of *a b a b c c*.

Taylor crystallizes his musical conceit in the reverently facetious lyric, "Our Insufficiency to Praise God suitably, for his Mercy." As Willie T. Weathers has remarked, the poem is notable for its transfer of the traditional music of the spheres to a music of atoms.[35] It is even more intriguing in the euphoric play of its fantasy, its blend of childlike speculation with a Semitic cast of hyperbole ("a thousand times too little," "ten thousand times as much"), represented also in pieces like the "Dialogue between Justice and Mercy":

And had each Tongue, as many Songs of Praise
    To sing to the Almighty ALL
    As all these men have Tongues to raise
      To him their Holy Call?
. . . .
Nay, had each song as many Tunes most sweet
    Or one intwisting in't as many,
    As all these Tongues have songs most meet
      Unparallelld by any?
Each song a world of Musick makes we guess
Whose Tunes in number would be numberless.
               (*Poems*, p. 452)

Much of what Taylor describes here and in "The Souls Admiration hereupon" is what actual church music in Westfield clearly was not: richly polyphonic, diversely instrumental, spontaneously sublime. Yet this negative principle combines with the fancies of exponential division to dramatize an inverting irony characteristic of *Gods Determinations* as a whole. Against the backdrop of Soul's newly rediscovered unity, Taylor reminds us of the comic disparity between sacred melody and "Our Musick," which

35. Weathers, "Cambridge Platonists," 21 n. 55.

"would the World of Worlds out ring / Yet be unfit within thine Eares to ting" (*Poems*, p. 452).

The movement by which the Word becomes song in the epilogue is paralleled by other transformations. The previously masked appearances of Satan, Mercy and Justice, and Saint make way for a more exposed sequence of revelation. Taylor also abandons his cruder theatrics and deliberately obtrusive stage machinery, such as the directions given for Satan's costume change or for moving a desk in the set used by Justice and Mercy.[36] Through earlier scenes of exposition and development, these touches might assure an audience that Taylor's performance was only a comparatively inept staging of the quintessential drama, a lesser play within a play designed to catch the conscience of the doubting Soul. Now obscurity can give way to "open flames" of joy as the poem enters its closing phase of heavenly meditation.

In its transformation symbolism, *Gods Determinations* ultimately points beyond human salvation—in the sense of restored health and wholeness—to "deification." By poem 29 God does more than enable the fallen cripple to stand upright again: in a coach Love "soars the Soul above" its first paradise to greater glories than it had originally lost (*Poems*, p. 451). In this extraordinary, new, and so as yet "curious" garden of Christ, the aspiring Soul can at last know the heavenly enjoyment of true rest in God.

But in its passing growth amid the earthly fellowship, this garden is "curious" as well by virtue of the "Solid Walls of Discipline" that encircle it. Among these fortifications, the church's requirement of testified regeneracy was doubtless for Taylor the cornerstone. By this time Solomon Stoddard would not yet have advanced his theory of the Lord's Supper as a converting ordinance or have begun practicing open communion. But from Northampton and elsewhere voicings of "loose, large Principles"[37] of liberalized admissions already threatened to break down God's fence around the double enclosure of garden and

---

36. Taylor's clowning with stage machinery bears an interesting resemblance to Robert Frost's later treatment of a collapsible plywood throne of God in *A Masque of Reason*.

37. Increase Mather, *A Discourse Concerning the Danger of Apostasy*, 84.

holy city. For Taylor, restricting formal access to the Eucharist
through acceptance rituals—"To open onely to the right"—was
necessary if the genuine corporate meaning of the Sacrament
were to be preserved for experiential access, so that "all within
may have a sight" (*Poems*, p. 454). Without the check of public
relations, the grace Christ offered together "in his Word, and
Sacraments" would be torn asunder, his garden's "Choisest Flowers" trampled underfoot (*Poems*, p. 456).

Yet charity can coexist with vigilance: if the church must maintain its ordinances with "Just Watchmen Watching day, and
night," its gates and "Just Centinalls" nonetheless bear the insig-
nia of "Love Imbellisht plain" (*Poems*, pp. 454–55). Public conversion relations can be maintained without jeopardizing the
membership prospect of worthy souls so long as the attractions of
full fellowship in the feast are vividly dramatized and the relations themselves "charitably" encouraged. Through a riddle of
wit, Taylor brings the whole issue alive:

Hence glorious, and terrible she stands;
    That Converts new
Seing her Centinalls of all demand
    The Word to shew;
Stand gazing much between two Passions Crusht
Desire, and Feare at once which both wayes thrust.

Thus are they wrackt. Desire doth forward screw
    To get them in,
But Feare doth backward thrust, that lies purdue,
    And slicks that Pin.
You cannot give the word, Quoth she, which though
You stumble on't its more than yet you know.
                    (*Poems*, p. 455)

The relations requirement becomes now a kind of convivial joke,
a game of initiation. Specifically, the name of this game is *password*. Soul has to show church sentinels the proper word before it
can pass through the gates, all the while enduring the taunt of
Fear that "You cannot give the word" because "its more than yet
you know." But the outcome is magically fortunate when Desire

supplies the missing word and "joy Conquours Fear." Given the abruptly Herbertian twist and the example of how fear is dispersed in 1 John 4.18, one may suppose at least one version of this password to be Love. From another angle, Taylor's joke is that the convert should be able to find the proper "Word to shew" because it is writ ready-to-hand in the scriptural Word. Even Fear offers a clue in that direction by intimating that Soul's answer is close enough to "stumble on." Effectual calling, that is, should not be judged according to one's own Satanic imaginings but according to a "Faith Ruld by the Word" (*Poems*, p. 439).

Apparently, fearful souls outside the gates can also gather hints of the password by appealing to visible saints they can see inside. New converts demand desperately of others "The Word to shew." Taylor does not visualize for us any human counselors coming forward to meet the demand. But his poem has already demonstrated the usefulness of a saint's testimony and example for a soul trying to resolve its experience into a testifying word of its own. Most optimistically, to conserve the Word within walls of public witnessing means that a soul need not and should not face the crushing dilemmas of conversion in melancholic isolation.

Here then, unfoiled as Taylor's reversed pattern of Satan's game plan, is a more amiable formula of circularity. The would-be Saint must be able to show the proper "Word" to become a full church member. Still, presuming a minimal experience of personal grace in the form of cultivated desire, Soul can gain from association with the corporate body all the word it needs for entry into this curious garden. Taylor thus injects a fresh pattern of semantic play into a controversy that would soon rigidify. His turn of rhetoric shares in that exuberant wedding of divine humor and satiric wit that, retrospectively, one can see enlivening the whole course of "Gods Determinations touching his Elect."

Despite its peculiarities and prolixities, then, Taylor's long poem should not be dismissed as a doctrinal exercise or primitive experiment in early American writing. Nor is it necessary to downgrade the rather different achievement of the *Meditations* in order to admire it. *Gods Determinations* is as searching in its spiritual psychology, as inventively versatile in its rhetoric, as satisfying in its rendering of the comic vision, as anything written on these shores before the age of Emerson. If Taylor had produced nothing else, the artistry of *Gods Determinations* would distinguish him as a leading figure in colonial letters.

5 "A Festival Frame of Spirit": The *Preparatory Meditations*

The Contemplative Spark: Taylor's Poetic Triptych

By the time Taylor began composing the numbered *Meditations*, he had already mastered his medium. From then on his work, like that of many subsequent American authors, would not improve much with time. Some of the earliest poems in the First Series, and sections of *Gods Determinations*, are as successful as anything he would ever write. By 1682, when he began dating his *Meditations*, he had been versifying for more than ten years. In Westfield, he had worked through a number of psalm paraphrases; he had probably completed much or all of *Gods Determinations* and at least some of the eight occasional poems. At one level, then, the *Meditations* should come as no surprise. Plainly inspired by the minister's duty to prepare for administering the Lord's Supper, the numbered devotional poems also reflect the traditional practice of "deliberate" (as opposed to "occasional") meditation.

There is nonetheless something remarkable about the scope and seriousness of a forty-three-year project yielding 217 finished poems. Other ministers, in their preparatory approach to Sacrament days, did not prepare in quite this way. Beyond dutiful perseverance, the *Meditations* project testifies to a fitful passion and urgency of motivation on the part of its author. Having tasted the celestial "cheer" of the Lord's banquet, Taylor found himself enspirited to express the soul's motions toward this festival confirmation of grace. Thus, though duty-bound to meditate, he felt an imperative to write that was more artistic and celebratory than legal. From Taylor's point of view, the wit of his expression was an energy issuing directly from gracious encounter with God. And though he did not publish, he was in principle moved to extend and shape his experience into a verbal construct capable of moving others toward appetency for a feast where they too would find "Inns to entertain them with good Cheere. / That so they may not faint, but upward grow / Unto their ripeness, and to glory Soe" (2.111).

The intensity of personal witness in opening meditations like "The Experience," "The Return," and "The Reflexion" is unmistakable. Despite the uncertainty of biographical conclusions derived from first-person literary expression, such testimony suggests that some particular episode of mystical illumination crystallized Taylor's resolve to begin writing numbered *Meditations*.

Temporal developments had no doubt prepared the atmosphere. As we have seen, the apparent failure of the Puritan plantation to fulfill its national errand led Taylor to narrow his vision of God's imminent earthly Kingdom to Westfield—more especially, to the inner domain of the soul and the imaginative domain of poetry. On these grounds, if nowhere else, the New England Way could be safely preserved from the corruptions of worldliness and newly hatched heterodoxy. By 1682, moreover, Taylor must have felt ready to initiate a long-term writing commitment because his church's covenantal foundation had had three years to settle into place. All the inflammatory ingredients for new composition were there. But a specific occasion of mystical transport may well have lit the flame.

The special incursion of grace is signaled at the outset by Taylor's curious interposition of three unnumbered and undated poems, beginning aptly enough with "The Experience." In a privileged instant, the poet apprehends his human conjunction with God as he never has before:

Oh! that I always breath'd in such an aire,
    As I suckt in, feeding on sweet Content!
Disht up unto my Soul ev'n in that pray're
    Pour'de out to God over last Sacrament.
    What Beam of Light wrapt up my sight to finde
    Me neerer God than ere Came in my minde?

The occasion of this apparently momentous episode is an ordinary celebration of the Lord's Supper. To judge from "The Reflexion," the event is realized most profoundly "Once at thy Feast" as a unique and localized occurrence.

Whether these relations of heightened experience warrant calling the poet a mystic remains a problematic question. Such intimations do not, in themselves, establish a soul's progress beyond the stages of awakening or illuminative spirituality. On the other hand, Taylor was evidently preoccupied with the theme of spiritual espousal. His writing is steeped in the erotic imagery of Canticles and other scriptural founts of traditional Christian mysticism, especially Pauline and Johannine texts. Mystical number symbolism, most obviously centered on the figure seven and its multiple in the forty-nine poems of the First Series, played a role in his thinking.[1] Admittedly, the poet in his private person may never have been gifted to attain that permanently advanced state of unitive love belonging to a mystic in the more exclusive sense. One may nonetheless support Norman Grabo's judgment that the poetry is largely about "the mystical process," together with Donald Stanford's belief that an urge to recapture the crucial moment of illumination could be "the prime motivation for the entire sequence of *Preparatory Meditations*."[2] If mysticism describes "an experimental knowledge of God through unifying love," or the "science of union with the Absolute," then the mystical quest is indeed central to Taylor's *Meditations*.[3] Arguments to the contrary often impose on the poet a model of contemplative experience at odds with testimony by its acknowledged masters in Western spirituality.

When, for example, Taylor betrays a certain suspicion of the charismata—voices, visions, and the like—commonly associated

1. Karen Gordon Grube, "The 'Secret Sweet Mysterie' of Numbers in Edward Taylor's Meditation 80,' Second Series."

2. Norman S. Grabo, *Edward Taylor*, 43; Donald E. Stanford, "Edward Taylor," in *Major Writers of Early American Literature*, ed. Everett Emerson, 70. Grabo's book includes a full chapter, 40–83, on Taylor's "Contemplative Life."

3. The first definition is F. C. Happold's rendering of that produced by medieval theologians, in his *Mysticism: A Study and an Anthology*, 37; the second appears in Evelyn Underhill, *Mysticism: A Study in the Nature and Development of Man's Spiritual Consciousness*, 72.

with William James's "mystical states" or "sporadic mysticism," it is worth remembering that similar skepticisms abound in medieval mystical writings, such as those by Walter Hilton. "We are in the way of ordinary dispensations," Taylor warns his parishioners, "and therefore are not to expect extraordinary communications" to confirm effectual calling (*TCLS*, 157). Not only can feelings of visionary rapture delude, but also too much yearning after them can obscure the less spectacular facts of Christian faith. The almost selfish desire for ecstatic transport leading the poet to lament "Oh! that thou Wast on Earth below with mee / Or that I was in Heaven above with thee" must be restrained by a recognition that he has "thy Pleasant Pleasant Presence had / In Word, Pray're, Ordinances, Duties; nay, / And in thy Graces." So far, in faith, God has indeed "been on Earth below" with him. Worse than living without occasional foretastes of heaven would be "Out of thy Vineyard Work [to] be put away" ("The Return"). And though the poet finds himself longing for unlimited and perpetual enjoyment of heavenly sweetness on earth, he admits the folly of that ambition in *Meditation* 2.96:

But listen, Soule, here seest thou not a Cheate.
   Earth is not heaven: Faith not Vision. No.
To see the Love of Christ on thee Compleate
    Would make heavens Rivers of joy, earth overflow.
    This is the Vale of tears, not mount of joyes.
    Some Crystal drops while here may well suffice.

At the same time, Taylor cherishes his moments of epiphanic insight and rehearses them in ecstatic tones. As he pledges in "The Experience": "Oh! Sweet though Short! Ile not forget the same." Such visitations divulge a glimpse of eternity in time, of the divine image enscribed within the human self. Like the Lord's Supper they accompany, their illumination casts backward in anamnesis and forward in anticipation; they present at once fits of recollection from the soul's first paradise and hints of its final rapture.

Above all, they lend experiential validation to Taylor's doctrinal absorption in the twofold Christian mystery of *theanthropy* and *theosis*. The first aspect, Christ's personal union of human and divine natures, grounds the second, the human soul's "deification," or promise of ideal union with God in love. As Taylor wrote in restatement of Augustine, "God would be the son of man, & would have [all] men the sons of God. Hence he descended for our sake: let us ascend for his sake" (*Harmony,* 2:507). For Taylor this "mystical" incorporation into the divine life, though already achieved ontologically, cannot be fully actualized this side of the grave. Even in the end, the union toward which he aspires would displace the ego-center without obliterating personal identity. Such, after all, is what erotic imagery implies. But it is also doubtful whether the paradoxical unific language of the greatest Christian mystics ever was intended to represent total and simple absorption of the self.[4]

Taylor situates his mystical apprehensions, then, within a carefully conceived doctrinal and intellectual framework. The poetry is no less mystical as a result. Yet this circumstance does identify Taylor more particularly, in the familiar Western mold of Augustine, as an intellectual mystic. Thus, a sensation of pure emotional transport is only the beginning of "The Experience." At an ecstatic instant, while eating the sacramental elements, the speaker finds himself "feeding on sweet Content." A "most strange" radiance momentarily blinds his faculties: "What Beam of Light wrapt up my sight to finde / Me neerer God than ere Came in my minde?" By the second stanza, however, he is able to bring this "vision" into the common light of doctrinal and exegetical teaching:

Most strange it was! But yet more strange that shine
    Which filld my Soul then to the brim to spy
My Nature with thy Nature all Divine
    Together joyn'd in Him thats Thou, and I.
    Flesh of my Flesh, Bone of my Bone. There's run
    Thy Godhead, and my Manhood in thy Son.

4. Dom Cuthbert Butler, *Western Mysticism: The Teaching of Augustine, Gregory and Bernard on Contemplation and the Contemplative Life,* 5.

This consciously intellective reading of Christology serves, if anything, to heighten the affective intensity of the "deification" pronouncement two stanzas later, where Taylor claims superiority over the angels because his nature "doth Unite / Better" than theirs "unto the Deity."

In "The Return" Taylor admits that he cannot return physically and at will to the specific occasion of his "most strange" intimation. But in recollected tranquility he can draw fuller meaning from that sign by turning the mind meditatively upon its corresponding traces in Scripture and in the familiar ordinances of his church. Even glimpsed through the secondary lens of Word and doctrine, the sight of Christ's "Humane Frame" radiates "Glances that enflame" his soul, a joyous "Shine" and "Smile" that "Convayes / Heavens Glory."

The ineffable moment of "The Experience" constitutes, therefore, a sacred center. Around it the poet must be content to let his imaginative wit roam in more mundane, exploratory sallies designed to repossess, internalize, and convey what he can of the divine image. Often, as in *Meditation* 1.17, Taylor's complaint of speechlessness stems more from the constraint of mystical ineffability—"My Phancys in a Maze, my thoughts agast, / Words in an Extasy"—than from that of natural depravity. The final line of "The Experience" finds the poet aware he cannot "ever hold" in secure stasis what he once "had." By recircling motions of mind, he can nonetheless "Return" again and again to the scene of "The Experience" and make oblique, shifting "Reflexion" on what it might reveal in conjunction with the rest of his experience. The triptych presented in "The Experience," "The Return," and "The Reflexion" thus carries some explanation of the repetitive yet digressively varied pattern of the *Meditations* as a whole.

The last poem of the three, "The Reflexion," ingeniously gathers up the optical, food, sexual, and lapidary imagery found in the other two, along with the Rose of Sharon motif explored in the intervening *Meditation* 1.4. As the poem's title suggests, optical figures supply the central focus. This poem may serve as a prime illustration of how Taylor combines theology with affective mysticism, applying verbal wit to shape the fruits of personal meditation into a communicable piece of art.

From the first, "The Reflexion" confronts the reader with an original, graphically absurd concatenation of tropes. Amid the sensuously appealing odors and sights of a banquet hall, Taylor's Lord presents his own substance as "Meat, Med'cine, sweetness, sparkling Beautys to / Enamour Souls with Flaming Flakes of Love." In a reversal of the usual Canticles typology, he also turns out to be "Sharons Rose" presiding as true host at the eucharistic table. Though he "rose" in resurrection, Christ now sits where his guests "do sit" to carve, while the glories of heaven and earth "lie" bundled in this Son like "Sun Beams." As if this much sport with figures and puns were not enough, Taylor adds erotic imagery to describe the soul's desire for "Ravishment" by "Graces Golden Spade."[5] The first-person passion implied in such language seems to lead naturally, by way of retrospective explanation, into the speaker's concrete testimony two stanzas later:

Once at thy Feast, I saw thee Pearle-like stand
   'Tween Heaven, and Earth where Heavens Bright glory all
In streams fell on thee, as a floodgate and,
     Like Sun Beams through thee on the World to Fall.
     Oh! sugar sweet then! my Deare sweet Lord, I see
     Saints Heavens-lost Happiness restor'd by thee.

There is little reason to deny the actuality of the event, perhaps the same one identified in "The Experience." But the "vision" recounted here is something other than a physical apparition projected onto bodily eyes. Instead Taylor records a moment of

5. Karl Keller, *The Example of Edward Taylor*, 214; John Clendenning, "Piety and Imagery in Edward Taylor's 'The Reflexion.'" Clendenning also points out the typological revision in which the Rose of Sharon, usually identified with the female soul or church, is here associated with Christ. Clendenning's further argument—that the speaker's main symbolic role becomes that of bridegroom in relation to God the bride—seems less likely. Some such interchange of gender may surface momentarily in stanza 6; but, in agreement with Keller, I find the speaker of stanza 3 clearly adopting the more traditional female identification of the soul addressing a seducing male God.

decisive insight. This perception comes through the Eye of the Soul, as the *Christographia* sermons term it, but is illuminated by the poet's long-standing "reflexion" on theological doctrine. Theologically, the "Pearle-like" appearance of the Rose-Lord plainly signifies Christ's surpassing beauty and worth. Yet the optical details show more. Standing "'Tween Heaven, and Earth," Christ as pearl reveals himself to be the transparent mediator between God and humankind. Only "through" him does the brilliance of the Logos shine into the world, even when the world—and the poet—know it not. The regenerate looking on him "beheld his glory," outside of which "No man hath seen God" (John 1.14, 1.18). This pearl, as the intervening lens or prism before the illuminative flood, becomes the visible focus of reality. In a lesser dispensation of what the apostolic witnesses received at the mount of Transfiguration, the poet is suddenly graced to "see" history gathered into a pictorial instant as "Saints Heavens-lost Happiness" is "restor'd by thee." This seeing amounts to something more—or less—than extraordinary eyesight. Informed by solid Puritan and Christian doctrine, it also embraces a mystical, supraconceptual knowledge beyond factual understanding.

The startling awareness engendered by the poet's transient experience calls for personal appropriation, an enduring response. Taylor's inability to make suitable response had been, after all, the initiating problem in stanza one and emerges again as the central difficulty in the last two stanzas. The poet's "dull Heart" and temperamental "gloom" obstruct penetration by the visible brightness of God's love. Stricken thus by melancholic depression, he wears the badge of his disease, a "black Velvet Mask," and pleads his release. As the preceding poem informs us, though, a medicinal antidote is available in the blood-red syrup extracted from Christ the Rose, a liquid capable of purging "Ill Humours all that do the Soule inclose." Spreading open this sanguine remedy, we are told, releases the brightness of "Glee" to the heart. A word glossed by the *Oxford English Dictionary* as rich in mirthful and musical connotations, *glee* rarely appears in literature of Taylor's day. Yet it is a pervasive presence in the *Medita-*

tions, where it names the soul's joyous reaction to grace. In effect, the poet takes *glee* to be the emotional incarnation of grace.

Again, however, the key to Taylor's imagistic resolution of "The Reflexion" is optical. As the complaining speaker sees things, his own mask of melancholy blocks his reception of the divine light streaming from his Lord's face. No wonder he perceives too little light emanating from Christ, whose "Sun Beams" appear "bundled" apart at an impenetrable distance. Yet this dimness is something of a self-generated optical illusion, a spiritual far-sightedness that fails to register interior illumination. For Christ is not only humankind's clearest "image of the invisible God" (Col. 1.15) in the objective abstract, but also the New Adam whose radiance reflects the divine image directly into the regenerate soul. As the opening four lines of "The Return" remind us, Christ as pearl not only shows himself as a discrete object of devotion but also casts God's "Image bright" into the praying subject. St. Paul elucidates this dynamic of reflection when he notes that "God, who commanded the light to shine out of darkness, hath shined in our hearts, to give the light of the knowledge of the glory of God in the face of Jesus Christ" (2 Cor. 4.6). So the speaker of "The Reflexion" at last realizes that the fair image he veils—even defaces—under his mask is at once God's and his own:

Shall my black Velvet Mask thy fair Face Vaile?
Pass o're my Faults: shine forth, bright sun: arise
Enthrone thy Rosy-selfe within mine Eyes.

The marvelous, Donne-like twist of the final line is an ocular variation signifying sudden discovery on the part of the speaker. Casting aside his more naive subject-object model of spiritual vision, he abruptly invites Christ's "Rosy-selfe" to shine out from within his "I"—indeed from his "Eyes." In this freshly reciprocal relation, Christ becomes not merely an object of awareness but a way of seeing, a transforming agent of the poet's perception. Already planted as Rose in the poet's garden of the soul, Christ now appears as well in this more dynamic figure of mystical indwelling.

Ultimately, Taylor's brilliant poem is enriched by a reflexive play of imagination between several sets of polarities. The mirror motif helps to order the poem's striking oppositions in imagery, in sensual and theological innuendo, in active and passive moods of response. But Taylor's chief thematic manipulations of the mirror conceit can be identified according to four species of "reflection." First of all, Christ must be regarded as the essential reflection of God in the world. Elsewhere Taylor cites Clement of Alexandria to the effect that "the Eternall Son is the Fathers most Beautifull Looking-Glass"(C, 448). A second mirror is the inward man. This primal self reflects Christ, and God in Christ, as the original image of righteousness is progressively renewed by grace. In a third sense, "the reflection" can be equated with the act of meditation. For to complete the experience of gracious epiphany, one must subsequently reflect on its personal and theological meaning. In this more abstract dimension, of course, the poem is itself the reflection, mirroring as it does a self in the process of meditation.

A fourth and final import of the title refers to the speaker's obligation to reflect before others the glory he has been privileged to receive. The "Eyes" with which the poem ends are also mirrors in which others might glimpse Christ the Rose enthroned. Classic Christian mysticism has never been wholly individualistic and passive in its consequences, as the vigorous careers of well-known Catholic figures like Catherine of Siena and Teresa of Avila demonstrate. Taylor's Puritan version of mystical encounter serves likewise to augment the social and activist strains in historic Puritanism. Even if the soul catches its first flame of reconverting energy in relative isolation, lapsing at intervals into the God-intoxicated woosiness of *Meditation* 2.163 (ll. 25–36), it is bound to spread the fire to "Lighten ery where" ("The Experience"). No doubt Taylor considered his several vocations as clergyman, scholar, physician, farmer, husband, and father to be implicated in that incendiary enterprise.

Evident in much of the prose, especially, is a relentlessly practical, even prosaic side to Taylor's exegetical mind, at first glance antithetical to a contemplative disposition. Yet ordinary means are fully compatible with contemplative discovery, and it is telling that the action of "The Experience" occurs within an ordinary corporate celebration of the Lord's Supper. Later *Meditations*, such as 2.133, affirm that the bride espoused to enjoy communion with Christ is "no Single Person" but "an agrigate." Similarly, the ordinary eucharistic prospect of mystical union includes for Taylor the union of saints in corporate fellowship: the Sacrament "maketh Charity's sweet rosy breath / Streach o're the Whole Society of Saints. / It huggeth them" (2.111).

The missionary tide of Taylor's contemplative experience also overflowed—to invoke the revealing metaphor first appearing in *Meditation* 1.1—into his composition of the *Preparatory Meditations*. Like the psalms, in whose discipline he trained to find his poetic voice, the sequential poems express representative and collective pulsations of the spiritual life through a first-person subject. In stanza five of "The Reflexion," for example, Taylor seems to be narrating an apprehension peculiar to himself. But the earlier query—"Be n't I a bidden Guest?"—has more the accent of a troubled parishioner, whose mood Taylor can so readily reproduce because it overlaps with his own sporadic doubts. Once fired by a personal touch of reconverting grace, the poet is obliged to keep relighting the torch and extending its flame.

Taylor's darting inquisitions of sacred wit aim first to recover and release fiery hints of what Origen called the Eternal Gospel, to reconnect Word and Sacrament, self and the larger Body of Christ. The poet then applies the conjunctive inspiration of "The Experience" to meditative reasoning on the natural world and temporal human events in the case of the "occurrants," or to deliberate meditation on biblical and introspective material in the case of the *Preparatory Meditations*. The end, in either event, is considerably broader than the private and immediate satisfactions of mystical ecstasy.

Patterns of Play in the *Meditations*

Whereas the first several poems of the First Series are charged with freshly awakened conviction of God's overflowing and conjoining Love, it is hard to find a logic of progression persistent throughout the whole of the *Preparatory Meditations*. Often Taylor seems to let his "Wits run a Wooling" (1.29) from one sequence to the next pursuing the natural "Ebb and Flow" of grace. His writing preserves a broad margin of associative spontaneity, in which the soul's "Wondring Contemplations" and "tumbling thoughts" (1.41) can turn with searching abandon. And since Taylor believed the soul's struggle must continue unresolved during this life, he traces the Spirit's action on the heart as an ebb and flow rather than as a simple linear progress.

At the same time, the *Meditations* as a whole contain recognizable clusters of poems related in topic, approach, scriptural texts, or imagery. Certain patterns of order also define the larger course of each series. The First Series begins with strongly emotional responses to the advances of incarnate love as discerned in the sacramental banquet and in the personal attractions of Christ the bridegroom. This section makes abundant use of floral and erotic imagery linked to Canticles and of food and drink imagery linked to the Sacrament. From *Meditation* 1.13 through the account of redemptive triumph in 1.18–22, Taylor shifts into a more objective mode as he considers Christ's prophetic and kingly offices. *Meditation* 1.23 recaptures the mood of exclamatory rhetoric, though subsequent poems are more soberly engaged with the challenge of death and worldly detachment (1.33 and 1.34) or with fears of doubtful election and unworthy response. From *Meditation* 1.41 to the end of the First Series, fear and conflict seem increasingly remote in comparison with the poet's renewed sense of confidence and heavenly joy. Suitably, Taylor's concluding text is from Matthew 25.21, on entering "the joy of thy lord."

More-overt divisions characterize much of the Second Series, beginning with the long and unusually methodical sequence on Old Testament typology in *Meditations* 2.1–30 together with 2.58–60[B] and 2.70–71. *Meditations* 2.31–114 deal in general with Christ's antitypal excellence as Redeemer and the believer's desire to share in a New Covenant relation. Within this transitional section two unified groupings have been identified: the Christology sequence of 2.42–56, connected with Taylor's *Christographia* sermons preached between 1701 and 1703; and the cluster of 2.102–11 expounding the poet's eucharistic doctrine in opposition to Stoddardean and other distortions. Toward the end of the middle section, which Mason Lowance, Jr., considers the most mystical of the three large divisions in the Second Series, Taylor turns increasingly toward texts from St. John and Canticles. A final large group written between 1713 and 1725 (2.115–165) deals almost exclusively with Canticles, including a closely sequential rendering of verses in 2.115–53. In general, the speaker sounds more reposefully assured as he approaches the end of the series in this final Canticles sequence.[6]

Across manifold variations in mood, language, and subject matter in the *Meditations*, Taylor continues his persistent quest for interior evidence of the promise. He never doubts to the point of abandoning faith in his ultimate salvation.[7] Instead, through experimental maneuvers with verbal and imagistic wit, he searches for tokens of congruence between God's scriptural promises and the soul, for personal grounds of response to the great deeds of redemption.

To prosecute his quest, the poet applies a diversity of figures and developmental techniques. As Barbara Lewalski points out, Taylor may develop his figures in analytic or free associative style, in some version of plain-style rhetoric, in meiotic terms, in a more radical mode of metaphoric antithesis, or in a variation of antithesis wherein the figures establish at once the speaker's connection and his contrast with Christ.[8] Most *Meditations* employ some combination of incremental and contrastive-meiotic techniques.

6. Structural sequences in the *Meditations* have been isolated by Louis Martz, Introduction to *The Poems of Edward Taylor*, ed. Donald E. Stanford, xxi–xxiii; Keller, *Example of Edward Taylor*, 75–78; Barbara Lewalski, *Protestant Poetics and the Seventeenth-Century Religious Lyric*, 396–97; and Mason I. Lowance, Jr., *The Language of Canaan: Metaphor and Symbol in New England from the Puritans to the Transcendentalists*, 91. Lewalski finds Taylor reaching a "plateau of assurance" in 2.156; one could locate other high points in poems such as 2.100, 2.139, 2.157[A] and 2.157[B], and 2.163.

7. Taylor's final sense of assurance, though never construed to be absolute, is already suggested in the early manuscript containing his Theological Notes. There he records an affirmative answer to the question "Whether or no a man may be assured in this life he is Elected." Such a belief not only is supported by Scripture and inward tokens but also carries practical sanction because without assurance there could be no "Incouraging others to walke chearfully in the ways of God. Therefore David when he would encourage others said he would declare what God had done for his Soule" (Edward Taylor, "Theological Notes," 27).

8. Lewalski, *Protestant Poetics*, 400–403. Another classification of developmental forms is presented by E. F. Carlisle, "The Puritan Structure of Edward Taylor's Poetry," 151–53.

As for the figures themselves, Taylor records a vast range—from colloquial to elegant—of image patterns. Extended exposure to the poems reveals his fondness for floral, arboreal, alchemical, gaming, writing, and musical tropes; his more domestic weaving, craft, medical, and food references; his frequent mention of jewels, nuts, garments, and perfumes; and his sometimes startling mixture of erotic and scatological images. Much of the imagery, despite its domestic aspect, has a rarefied, ornamental quality; nearly all of it, including the excremental vein, bears some relation to figures sanctioned by prior use of biblical and exegetical authorities.

Amid this varied wealth, two broad categories of metaphor—one signifying containment, the other transmutation—are worth singling out for their relevance to Taylor's major themes. Correspondingly, we have seen how Taylor fed his poetic imagination on the twofold marvel of Christ's "blessed Theanthropie" and humankind's consequent *theosis*. The hypostatic union of natures contained in Christ demanded a "Mysticall Union unto Christ's Person" (C, 102) that would transform the sinful self. Taylor found a joyous convergence of *theanthropy* and *theosis* in his celebration of the Lord's Supper. Though best summed up in the *Christographia*, its accompanying poems, and the *Treatise Concerning the Lord's Supper*, these two enfolding principles animate the entire imagistic body of the *Meditations*.

The containment motif appears in a plentiful assortment of walls, boxes, vessels, cages, tabernacles, temples, nuts, seeds, jars, cabinets, and hearts. Beginning with *Meditation* 1.2, and epitomized in the several poems based on Colossians 2.3, a familiar object of meditation is the pearl lying secretly within the cabinet of Christ. At one level, consistent with John Calvin, the hidden treasure signifies the Redeemer's divine nature concealed within the humbleness of human nature and the cross. Hence the enclosure figure expresses what Taylor called the "inbeing" of *theanthropy,* a meaning overtly represented in *Meditation* 2.45.

The speaker is also apt to identify himself with the container—not merely to enforce a crude body-soul distinction, but more essentially to convey the principle of spiritual indwelling. He is an empty vessel longing to be filled, or a box lodging Christ in the hidden depths of its interior. A poem like *Meditation* 1.2 dramatizes the discovery of deepening layers and shifting manifestations of interiority. Its survey of containers begins with the body's wicker cage, enclosing a cabinet of the soul, enclosing in turn Christ the pearl; and before the poem is through we also hear a self speaking from inside an ointment box, a heart, a pomander, an eggshell, and a purse.

The urge to discover, release, and unite the hidden treasure supplies the affective dynamic behind many *Meditations*. Taylor longs to break open the box (1.3), to solve the riddle (1.36), to decipher the divine love letter (2.8)—or, conversely, to lodge himself inside various containers or under leafy shelters. If he cannot yet enter the secret precincts of glory, as he begs in 2.63, he wants at least to peep over the walls (1.42). So too, a larger poetic aim of the *Meditations* is to find out something of the Word hidden within the indirect verbal expressions of Scripture without tearing away the mystery enveloping its sacred truth.

When discovery occurs, the natural consequence is a transformation of the soul, either gradual or abrupt. In central Puritan terminology, the turning must satisfy some stage of the extended conversion process; in the *Meditations* it likewise represents a quickening of progress toward the conjunctive union of "deification." The subjective and emotive corollary of progress toward the soul's imparadising, a spiritual ideal conveyed in enclosure tropes, is a transmutation of "temper." The *Meditations* express this transmutation through several symbolic modes, notably through the interrelated schemes of alchemy and Galenic humoral medicine.

In Taylor's semiotic scheme, the self's alchemical refashioning from a "leaden" to "golden" substance runs in symbolic tandem with its humoral progress from "gall" to "glee." Some poems allow the two symbol systems to intersect: in 1.33, for example, the "golden Arke" of divine life is equally a "Store-House full of Glee"; in 2.32, the poet prays God to turn his "Leaden Whistle" into an instrument sounding "full of glee." We already have discussed the pervasiveness of humoral symbology in the *Medita-*

tions and *Gods Determinations* and have considered how the polarity between melancholy and sanguinity informs the poet's festive theory. Here we may note especially how Taylor Christianizes the traditional terms. He eschews all reference to black bile, for example, in favor of its equivalent, *gall*. Beyond its usual Galenic import, *gall* has evident biblical overtones through the crucifixion narrative and, typologically, through Psalm 69.21. In *Meditation* 1.18 Taylor pictures Christ facing the world's "Woes in Pickle . . . whose Gall / He dranke up quite." Taylor's poetic term *glee* is still more of an invented composite, connecting as it does with the sanguine temper of Galenic tradition as well as with specifically evangelical qualities of "good cheer," "holy cheer," and grace. In the audaciously playful typological exercise of *Meditation* 2.30, the temperamental and spiritual conflation is evident, as Taylor wrote of how Edenic man "lost God, and lost his Glee."

The devotional meditations embody, then, a play of expression designed to raise affections into that "festival frame" of "glee" suitable for partaking of the eucharistic banquet. The interior discoveries of conjunction most apt to produce "glee" involve apprehensions of *theanthropy* (hypostatic union), *theosis* (deifying communion), and the confirmation of personal election. The play of erotic seduction, as exemplified in the biblically based flirtations of *Meditation* 1.12, is one way Taylor courts spiritual communion. Sexual imagery also allows the poet to combine his metaphorical category of static containment with that of transmutative movement toward union.

Not surprisingly, the eucharistic elements themselves afford the matter for some of Taylor's best *Preparatory Meditations*. As instances, *Meditations* 1.8, 2.60[A], and 2.60[B] reward close scrutiny because they show the poet's comic imagination at play in both its meiotic and festive modes. *Meditation* 1.8 is the outstanding case. It expresses the full range of Taylor's ludic and witty impulses, including his reverent parody of scriptural figures and episodes and his comic inversions of expectation. Here also he celebrates grace's extravagant freeplay in the sacramental antitype and rejoices with astonishment for the humanity on whom it is bestowed. Beneath all of this, the poem illustrates Taylor's meditative technique of manipulating the vast network of imagistic interplay already contained in Scripture. The governing image of food, centered on Christ's presentation of himself as "the living bread . . . of heaven" in John 6.51, is developed against the backdrop of a rich variety of other scriptural allusions—most notably, the Old Testament manna typology—and ends up carrying eucharistic implications as well.[9]

Yet the poem begins with the poet's bemused attempt to comprehend God's truth through exertions of human will and reasoning:

> I kening through Astronomy Divine
>   The Worlds bright Battlement, wherein I spy
> A Golden Path my Pensill cannot line,
>   From that bright Throne unto my Threshold ly.
>   And while my puzzled thoughts about it pore
>   I finde the Bread of Life in't at my doore.

Though the syntax is confused,[10] Taylor seems to be saying that neither the "Astronomy Divine" of theological inquiry nor the high-flying fancies of imaginative writing offer access to God's saving sustenance. Stretching beyond all reach of human merit or calculated ambition, the path from the divine throne to the poet's threshold is one his "Pensill cannot line." Straining his "puzzled

9. As such, the poem and the two others Taylor wrote on the same verse from John (*Meditations* 1.9 and 2.60[A]) are appropriately glossed by exegetical commentary on the Old Testament manna episodes, including the sermon Taylor himself later wrote to accompany *Meditation* 2.60 [A]: Sermon #33, "Manna from Heaven," in the Nebraska manuscript "Upon the Types of the Old Testament," transcribed by Charles Mignon. Subsequent references to this work will be cited in the text as "Manna." Despite some traditional Protestant reservations about interpreting the St. John text and its manna typology as a eucharistic reference, Taylor clearly had this connection in mind. The sacramental antitype becomes, in fact, a central concern in *Meditations* 1.8 and 1.9, whereas in *Meditation* 2.60 [A] the emphasis shifts somewhat toward finding the "living bread" of Christ's nourishment in the scriptural Word.

10. In "Taylor's 'Meditation 8,'" Gerhard T. Alexis proposes resolving the syntactical difficulty by reading "Divine" as a verb. This interpretation has merit, though there are also good reasons for preserving the sense of "Astronomy Divine" as a compound noun.

thoughts" upward in speculative desire, the poet looks down momentarily to discover a revelation surpassing desire landed miraculously on his doorstep: "I finde the Bread of Life in't at my doore." This undeserved and abrupt turn of things exemplifies the free grace most perfectly bestowed in Christ. Rendered by Taylor as a domestically parodic reenactment of the manna events in Exodus, the line and its subsequent elaboration open to display a range of interlocking scriptural and exegetical allusions.

The next two stanzas are mainly explanatory, reviewing the genetic origin of humanity's plight on forfeiting the first fruit of Paradise:

When that this Bird of Paradise put in
    This Wicker Cage (my Corps) to tweedle praise
Had peckt the Fruite forbad: and so did fling
    Away its Food; and lost its golden dayes;
    It fell into Celestiall Famine sore:
    And never could attain a morsell more.

Alas! alas! Poore Bird, what wilt thou doe?
    The Creatures field no food for Souls e're gave.

And if thou knock at Angells dores they show
    An Empty Barrell: they no soul bread have.
    Alas! Poore Bird, the Worlds White Loafe is done.
    And cannot yield thee here the smallest Crumb.

The account thus far is lively but remote: to the poet now filled with ecstatic wonder, all of this is indeed ancient history. A jaunty delight intrudes in usages such as "tweedle" and "peckt"; "Celestiall Famine" offers a pointed summation of the spiritual case; and the weighted spondees of "they no soul bread have" give one pause to admire Taylor's sonority. The writing sounds less than inspired, however, with the bird and cage figure redolent of cloying artifice despite its precedent in emblem literature.

In the astonishing sequence that follows, the soul-struck poet happens upon his best words:

In this sad state, Gods Tender Bowells run
    Out streams of Grace: And he to end all strife
The Purest Wheate in Heaven, his deare-dear Son
    Grinds, and kneads up into this Bread of Life.
    Which Bread of Life from Heaven down came and stands
    Disht on thy Table up by Angells Hands.

Did God mould up this Bread in Heaven, and bake,
    Which from his Table came, and to thine goeth?
Doth he bespeake thee thus, This Soule Bread take.
    Come Eate thy fill of this thy Gods White Loafe?
    Its Food too fine for Angells, yet come, take
    And Eate thy fill. Its Heavens Sugar Cake.

What Grace is this knead in this Loafe? This thing
    Souls are but petty things it to admire.
Yee Angells, help: This fill would to the brim
    Heav'ns whelm'd-down Chrystall meele Bowle, yea and
        higher.

Both the milling-baking and the excremental imagery have traditional precedent but are developed here in startling ways. As Taylor indicates in his later sermon, the ancient Hebrews often prepared their manna by grinding and baking it, typologically demonstrating that Christ must be "broken to pieces in the Mill or Mortar of the Law" and "baked in the fire of Divine Justice" to become "the Spirituall food of the Church" ("Manna," 15). Beyond the conventional literalization of a *corpus Christi* formula, the poetic details of the Father's preparing his "deare-dear" Son convey something of real-life solicitude, baker's pride, and grace of hospitality. Taylor mixes all of this with a reminder of sacrificial violence in his account of the grinding and kneading procedure. And although his first meaning, in reference to the "Tender Bowells" running out "streams of Grace," is an allegorical allusion to the seat of divine mercy, it is hard to ignore the graphic force of the description. As one critic notes, Taylor's curious inversion implies, in a manner "at once grotesque and wonderfully witty . . . that the highest foodstuff obtainable to man must come to him, after all, through divine defecation." Another interpreter relates the grinding of Christ to a digestive process in God's bowels, from which the excremental bread of life proceeds.[11]

By now Taylor's mood is primed to carry one to the climactic revelation: that God has transformed man's "Soule Bread" of previous acquaintance into a "Sugar Cake" finer than angel food. This transmutation, fulfilling the pattern of divine incarnation-to-human deification, had been foreshadowed syntactically when the bread "from Heaven down came and stands / Disht on thy Table up. . . ." But the most essential shadowings of a sugar cake too fine for angels are scriptural, and elaborately so. As Taylor's later "Manna" Sermon #33 recognizes, Psalm 78.25 calls the ancient manna "angels' food." Although the Bible nowhere equates bread or manna with "sugar cake," some of the texts that Taylor's darting wit conflated to create that image are unmistakable. Exodus 16.31 compares the taste of manna to that of "wafers made with honey"; Numbers 11.8 in the Authorized Version describes manna's preparation into "cakes." Taylor's "cake" may also incorporate an allusion to another miraculous episode of feeding, from the career of Elijah. Spiritually despondent after escaping from Ahab and Jezebel into the wilderness, the prophet looks down to behold "a cake baken on the coals" (1 Kings 19.6).

The uplifting and undeserved shock of surprise Elijah receives is paradigmatic in any case of the effect Taylor wants to achieve. The gratuitous act by which God sent himself to our doorstep as food was above human deserving, above its typological foretaste—and indeed, in its effect of human glorification, above the strictest necessity of salvation. For Taylor, the taste of Christ was palpable and delightful, a sugar cake beyond the requirement of mere bread to assuage spiritual hunger. The grace God volunteered to "knead" into this loaf was something better than our need. As the poet read in his copy of Thomas Taylor's *Christ Revealed*, "nothing was more freely prepared and given by God

11. Clark Griffith, "Edward Taylor and the Momentum of Metaphor," 450; Keller, *Example of Edward Taylor*, 206. See also Austin Warren's reading in *Rage for Order: Essays in Criticism*, 15-16. That the reference to God's bowels might be something of a birthing image as well is suggested by Taylor's remarks in *Harmony*, 1:339-40.

than Jesus Christ for the life of the world; hee came without the worlds seeking, without merit and deserving. . . . And was not this miraculous above that, that he which sent the Manna was the Manna which he sent? The taste of Manna was sweet. . . . So nothing is so sweet as Jesus Christ to an afflicted and hungry heart."[12]

Such is the superabundance of grace delivered in Christ that "Souls are but petty things it to admire," and now toward his closing Taylor expands the point with a new image of spatial amplitude. Against the background of this image one should recall Christ's feeding of the five thousand, the narrative occasion of the poem's epigraph and another sign of plenitude. In a stirring expansion of line driven by the equivalent of Gerard Manley Hopkins's hovering accents, the poet chants:

> This fill would to the brim
> Heav'ns whelm'd-down Chrystall meele Bowle, yea and higher.

This inverted sky bowl is a container, of course, and so holds Taylor's usual connotations of interiorized presence. It is also a rounded form, and hence difficult for an uncompassed pencil to line. As with manna, the rounded form can signify divine perfection: Taylor later confirmed that "a Sphere or Orbicular thing is a Suitable Hierogliphick of Eternity. & so imports Christ as being without beginning & without ending, Eternall, an Eternall person Hebr. 13.8" ("Manna," 10).

Though superabounding and free, Christ's delectable grace does require a response. One has at least to "come, take / And Eate"—to complete the circuit of grace with joyous admiration. Even when bread falls at the doorstep, "We must not think this Angells Bread will drop out of the Clouds into our mouths, if we do not open them, & gather it with our own hands, as it falls about our doors" ("Manna," 15). Taylor's rhetorical questions of the last two stanzas evidence part of the soul's admiring response. They culminate in exclamation: "What Grace is this knead in this

12. Thomas Taylor, *Christ Revealed; or, The Old Testament Explained*, 266–67.

Loafe?" Reappearing in *Meditation* 1.9, the exclamatory *what* may well express a bilingual pun on the word *manna*. Like Samuel Mather, Taylor observes that the Hebrew *Man, Hu* can translate as "What?" or "What is this?" and first arose from the Israelites' amazement "at Such a Strange, & Wonderfull thing." Nor does Taylor's linguistic play stop there. As "Food too fine for Angells" the new manna is distinctively a food for man—indeed it *is* man, in the perfected person of Christ. *Manna*, the Hellenized rendering, was more scrupulously orthographized as *Man* in the Geneva Bible. And in the sermon passage just cited, Taylor observes the accidental man-manna correspondence, linking it in turn with "the Wonderfullness of the Lord Christ when he is held out to be both God & Man in one person" ("Manna," p. 4).

Finally, Taylor indulges in wordplay of another sort in the poem's closing couplet:

This Bread of Life dropt in thy mouth, doth Cry.
Eate, Eate me, Soul, and thou shalt never dy.

This gustatory concreteness and address to an unspecified "thou" blending soul and parishioner can surely be read eucharistically. Moreover, Taylor develops a comically literalized double entendre from the familiar exegetical dualism between the "bread of life" and "living bread." Much of the poem is a meditation on signs of Christ's capacity to nourish spiritual life, sacramentally and otherwise. He is thus the "bread of life"—but is also "living bread," with the verbal participle suggesting once more a dynamic element of indwelling. "Living bread" is itself alive, and endlessly regenerative. In localized yet devout parody of St. John, Taylor therefore exhibits the soul's "living bread" as a fully animated presence, a talking particle of Christ's one loaf with a minor life of its own.

The gastronomic communion with Christ so finely celebrated in *Meditation* 1.8 receives varied dramatization in later *Meditations*. In *Meditation* 1.9, the speaker tendering his accolades to the living bread adopts the pose of a clowning braggart. The atmosphere of farce and fantastic buffoonery is comparable to that which Herbert Blau finds yet censures in *Meditation* 1.3.[13] Sixteen years later, Taylor again took up the eucharistic theme, this time in a paired sequence of poems that could be analyzed as well under the heading of typology: *Meditation* 2.60[A], on the living bread, and *Meditation* 2.60[B], on St. Paul's typology of "spiritual drink." Evidently enough, the binary meditation is structured around the two communion elements rather than a common scriptural text. Though the liquid first mentioned in 2.60[B] is water rather than wine, Taylor's point is precisely to show that the two are typologically "the same spirituall drinke"; and a eucharistic setting is overtly established with the "Sacramentall Cup" and "Lords Supper Wine" of stanza five.[14] The sacramental sense is in fact more overt in 2.60[B] than in 2.60[A], where the application is more immediately scriptural. Beyond the bread and wine linkage, then, the ideal complementarity these two poems express is also that of Word and Sacrament.

Though less compelling artistically than *Meditation* 1.8, *Meditation* 2.60[A] brings another perspective to the previously invoked manna typology of John 6.51. Here Taylor teases out a contrastive analogy between the veiled dispensation of heavenly bread to the Hebrews and the paradox of Christ's obscured revelation to his saints in Scripture. As part of its play, the poem unfolds a riddle of successive enclosures evocative of the containment motif. Just as manna hides typologically the theanthropic mystery of the man-God, so Scripture holds embedded within it the eternal sustenance of Christ as Word. And just as the Israelites came to preserve in memory a portion, or homer, of their miraculous food within "Manna's Golden Pot," so Christ the living bread comes to dwell eternally within the hearts of his saints.

After first bemoaning his own journeying condition of sin-sick hunger, the speaker recalls the Hebrews' discovery of a sweet food covered in dew, as described in Exodus 16.13–14:

13. Herbert Blau, "Heaven's Sugar Cake: Theology and Imagery in the Poetry of Edward Taylor," 352.
14. In his typological sermons, Taylor specifies that both the water out of the rock and the wilderness manna were answered in the Lord's Supper, as does Thomas Taylor in *Christ Revealed*, 205.

This Bread came down from heaven in a Dew
    In which it bedded was, untill the Sun
Remoov'd its Cover lid: and did it shew
      Disht dayly food, while fourty years do run.
      For Isra'ls Camp to feast upon their fill
      Thy Emblem, Lord, in print by perfect Skill.

This hidden manna of Revelation 2.17 typifies Christ, as Sermon #33 explains. Christ's coming was obscure in the humble mode of his nativity, as an infant wrapped in a manger, but no less so in his scriptural manifestation, his "Spirituall coming down in the Dew of his word" ("Manna," 8). Though the divine likeness had been imprinted in him and his presence now offered under the emblems for reading "in print," not all would see to read the signs aright. In the instance of the epigraph, the importuning crowd of John 6 asks Jesus for a sign while failing to see the true meaning of the loaves and fishes miracle set before them, just as many of their ancestors failed to grasp the spiritual sign conveyed by God's wilderness dispensation of manna.[15]

Still, Christ is dispensed as living bread to those capably "anointed with eye Salve," those able to penetrate the Word's "Covering Dew" ("Manna," 8, 20; cf. C, 191). For them, this Son truly is a Sun, and his illumination of the covert text divinizes those who internalize its substance:

Thou in thy word as in a bed of Dewes
    Like Manna on thy Camp dost fall and light
Hid Manna, till the Sun Shine bright remooves
      The Rug, and doth display its beauty bright
      Like pearly Bdellium White and Cleare to set
      The Sight, and Appetite the same to get.
. . . .
Refresh my Sight, Lord, with thy Manna's eye.
    Delight my tast with this sweet Honied Cake.
Enrich my Stomach with this Cake bread high.
    And with this Angells bread me recreate.

15. Much the same point is conveyed in the opening paragraph of Taylor's "Manna."

Lord, make my Soule thy Manna's Golden Pot
Within thine Arke: and never more forgot.
(*Meditation* 2.60[A])

Unlike the old manna, however, the "I" of the New Man contains the essence of eternal life. Instead of simply falling down
from heaven, the new spiritual bread makes "lives that on it live
ascend" (l. 29). It is food not simply for "dayly" nurture but for
"ery day" and lives "that have none end" (ll. 16, 37, 30).[16] This
Christic manna offers not only sweet food but also strong "meate"
(l. 6), in the surplus connotations of flesh and wholly fitting
substance for the soul. And unlike the double enclosure of the
manna pot laid up in the ark (or the ancient "shew bread," which
may be alluded to by pun in line 15), Christ is a dynamic and
originative Living Bread as well as a sustaining Bread of Life.[17]

The vitality of Taylor's poetic treatment is more apparent, however, in his corresponding perusal of the liquid element in *Meditation* 2.60 [B]. Though the poet draws on standard typological
material, the wit of the piece lies in the exuberant abundance of
his allusions and his abandonment to their associative interplay.
When Moses strikes the rock in Horeb, a Reformed figure of the
calcified heart, the water released carries for Taylor a flood of
imaginative stimuli. Starting with his own "muddy Inke," the
poet is led to ponder by comic contrast a stream of common
liquids inferior to the miraculous water of Exodus 17. As the
epigraph from 1 Corinthians 10.4 confirms, the drink Moses taps
is a spiritual fountain rising typologically to Christ the rock and to
the two chief Christian sacraments:

Sea water straind through Mineralls, Rocks, and Sands
    Well Clarifi'de by Sunbeams, Dulcifi'de,

16. Karen Rowe, *Saint and Singer: Edward Taylor's Typology and the Poetics of Meditation*, 157–59, points up the poem's contrast between the temporal sense of the
typological manna and the spiritual, eternal sense of Christ as antitype. She also
remarks on the fall versus ascent pattern and elucidates details of the poem not
discussed here.

17. In "Manna," 2, Taylor expressly contrasts the two bread epithets in this
manner.

Insipid, Sordid, Swill, Dishwater stands.
　　But here's a Rock of Aqua-Vitae tride.
　　When once God broacht it, out a River came
　　To bath and bibble in, for Israels train.

Some Rocks have sweat. Some Pillars bled out tears.
　　But here's a River in a Rock up tun'd
Not of Sea Water nor of Swill. Its beere.
　　No Nectar like it. Yet it once Unbund
　　A River down out runs through ages all.
　　A Fountain opte, to wash off Sin and Fall.

So far the primary sacramental reference seems to be baptismal
rather than eucharistic, despite the focus of the accompanying
sermon. Taylor reminds us of spiritual cleansing through hints of
the Genesis flood, of baptism at the Jordan ("a River"), and of the
Israelites' passage over the Red Sea ("Sea Water"). But as the
original water undergoes a transmutation to aqua vitae, blood,
and wine, so one fact of redemption flows into another. So also
the restorative experience of baptism runs forward in an uninter-
rupted current to the sustaining draught of the Eucharist. Perhaps only the startling declaration "Its beere" forces us to pause.
Yet even this arresting appeal to domestic satisfaction leads, by
way of witty semantics, to spirituality. The *Oxford English Dictionary* lists one currently archaic meaning of the word *beer* as *be-er*—
"the self-existent, the great I AM"—which makes perfect sense in
the context of Taylor's foreshadowing of a divine Christ. Then the
nectar is an apposite reference, of course, because it is a god's
drink. When one considers in addition that "angels-food" was a
term for strong ale, a fascinating interplay emerges between the
beer of 2.60[B] and the manna typology of associated poems.

In his closing stanzas, the poet multiplies his allusions through
both testaments of Scripture. Exploiting the antithetical paradox
of Christ as solid rock and as living water, he includes alchemical
nuance as well to enforce his major theme of interior transmutation:

Christ is this Horebs Rock, the streames that slide
　　A River is of Aqua Vitae Deare

Yet costs us nothing, gushing from his side.
  Celestiall Wine our Sinsunk souls to cheare.
  This Rock and Water, Sacramentall Cup
  Are made, Lords Supper Wine for us to sup.

This Rock's the Grape that Zions Vineyard bore
  Which Moses Rod did smiting pound, and press
Untill its blood, the brooke of Life, run ore.
  All Glorious Grace, and Gracious Righteousness.
  We in this brook must bath: and with faiths quill
  Suck Grace, and Life out of this Rock our fill.

Lord, oynt me with this Petro oyle. I'm sick.
  Make mee drinke Water of the Rock. I'm dry.
  . . . .
  If in this stream thou cleanse and Chearish mee
  My Heart thy Hallelujahs Pipe shall bee.

The vivifying influence of Christ's Passion is shadowed em-
blematically by the blood-grape pounded and pressed on the
cross, by the earlier mention of "tears" and "sweat," and by
thoughts of the double stream of blood and water "gushing from
his side." Taylor equates the blood flow with "Aqua Vitae" and a
"brook," both signifying revivification. The twice-mentioned
brook might well allude to Psalm 42, where the speaker compares
his yearning for a refreshing taste of God his "rock" to a hart's
panting for "the water brooks." These notes of restoration coin-
cide with several clever figures of transmutation. Karen Rowe
discovers, for example, that by the end Taylor has turned his
preliminary quill "as smiting rod and pen" into "a pipe, an
angelic musical instrument releasing floods of psalms and hallelujahs from within a once petrified heart."[18] In taking the transformative promise into himself, the speaker prays for anointing
with "Petro oyle." Taylor turns thus upon Christ's titles as rock
and anointed one, upon the commissioning gesture suited to his
own discipleship, and upon the scriptural gesture of healing
resonant with his own illness of need.

  In both 2.60[A] and 2.60[B] the restorative applied through

18. Rowe, *Saint and Singer*, 162.

Christ, as solid or as liquid, has an aspect of medicinal cure. The first poem finds the speaker desperate for a "cure" from his "Queasy Stomach" and "sickness" of mortality, whereas the second shows the speaker ready to expire from faintness. The illnesses, of course, are more spiritual than bodily but involve a psychic dimension as well. In that Galenic context, the sermon accompanying 2.60[A] insists that the bread of life gives healthful nourishment to "the Person, but not the ill Humours in the person." These it destroys ("Manna," 12, 25). Moreover, aqua vitae was an acknowledged seventeenth-century purgative for melancholy.[19]

Meditation 2.60[B] specifies the Lord's Supper to be the essential link between Christ's purgation of temperamental humors and the soul's subsequent celebration. At this enspiriting festival God gives "Celestiall Wine our Sinsunk souls to cheare." Taylor associates this wine, which the Old Testament says was given to make hearts glad, with the "spirited" matter of beer and brandy (aqua vitae). Typologically, of course, the wine in the "Sacramentall Cup" is also a transformed version of Horeb's water.

Yet Taylor's associative fancy rarely restricted itself to the ready-made bridges of linear typology between Old and New Testaments, and so the water reference here bears as well on at least two New Testament occasions. One, the wedding feast at Cana, is another locus of transmutation. Narrated only in St. John's gospel, the episode shows Jesus performing his first public sign by making wine pour from pots filled to the brim with water. The other sign in St. John that Taylor certainly had in mind, to judge from the sermon paired with 2.60[B], is the Samaritan woman's encounter with Christ's "living water" at the well.[20] "Living water," bearing the sense of animated indwelling, makes another typological correspondence with the Horeb water and a ritualistic one with the "Celestiall Wine." It also draws 2.60[A] and 2.60[B]

19. Kathy Siebel and Thomas M. Davis, "Edward Taylor and the Cleansing of Aqua Vitae," especially 109 n. 3.

20. John 4.7–15; cf. Rev. 7.17. Edward Taylor, Sermon #34, "Water from the Rock," in the Nebraska manuscript "Types of the Old Testament," 1, 4.

together as meditations around the Johannine motifs of living bread and living water.

As a natural point of departure for meditation on *theosis*, the exaltation of human nature through Christ, Taylor could look to the New Testament stories of resurrection and ascension. Within a four-poem sequence written under the Philippians motto, "God hath highly exalted him,"[21] *Meditations* 1.19 and 1.20 sport with drastically incongruent ways of naming and visualizing Christ's elevation. They end up dramatizing thereby the fuller Pauline teaching that Jesus has indeed been given "a name which is above every name" (Phil. 2.9). At the same time, these poems stress humanity's involvement in the divine victory, which elevates human nature and calls for a personal identification with Christ's saving deeds.

Meditation 1.19, on the resurrection, begins by mourning the passion event. "Looke till thy Looks look Wan, my Soule; here's ground," the poet exclaims, for "The Worlds bright Eye's dash't out" and the "Candle of the World blown out." As creation lapses into darkness, hell's devils attack God's innocent lamb,

Whom those Curst Imps did worry, flesh, and fell.
Tread under foot, did Clap their Wings and so
Like Dunghill Cocks over their Conquourd, Crow.

If the story is familiar enough, it is told with some strangely facetious accents. That first ocular imperative, "Looke," leads ironically toward the grotesque violence of an eye gouging. It is as though Christ, in voluntarily consenting to bear all human offense, has literalized his own dictum to "pluck . . . out" the eye that offends (Matt. 5.29). Yet already we sense a sardonic twist, an inverted emblem of resurrectional glee, in the portrayal of "Curst Imps" crowing "Like Dunghill Cocks over their Conquourd." These devils lack all semblance of malicious cunning. They

21. Discussed by James T. Callow, "Edward Taylor Obeys St. Paul," and Michael Schuldiner, "Edward Taylor's Problematic Imagery," 96–101.

remain barnyard ruffians, naive gamesters outmaneuvered by
God's grand ploy:

Brave Pious Fraud; as if the Setting Sun:
      Dropt like a Ball of Fire into the Seas,
And so went out. But to the East come, run:
      You'l meet the morn Shrinde with its flouring Rayes.
      This Lamb in laying of these Lyons dead;
      Drank of the brooke: and so lift up his Head.

Oh! sweet, sweet joy! These Rampant Fiends befoold:
. . . .
      He's Cancelling the Bond, and making Pay:
      And Ballancing Accounts: its Reckoning day.

In portraying the death and resurrection as a "Brave" but
"Pious Fraud," Taylor turns the redeemer's death into a clever
pretense, a *trompe l'oeil* designed to baffle "Rampant Fiends." This
deceptive facade amounts to nothing more, in turn, than a figural
semblance of an ineffable truth. Even in the sphere of theology,
legal theories of atonement cannot be solemnly equated with the
sacred reality of redemption. This piety frees Taylor to picture a
playfully literalized "Reckoning day" in which Christ bursts forth
from his successful transactions in "the Counthouse" (l. 25). But
while devils understand only that this trickster Christ has beaten
them at their own game, more discerning eyes see how "much he
gave," the lodging of death's curse quite palpably "within his
Flesh" (ll. 31–32).

The poem reaches the climax of its emblematic wit at its close,
when the redemptive victim undergoes a sudden transformation:

And like a Gyant he awoke, beside,
      The Sun of Righteousness rose out of's Grave.
      And setting Foot upon its neck I sing
      Grave, where's thy Victory? Death, Where's thy Sting?

Sharing in Christ's miraculous elevation into a spiritual giant,
humanity also grows apace to tower over death and sin as confi-
dently as the crowing imps had done earlier. In the closing cou-

plet, Christ's resurrectional triumph is transferred to the "I" of the speaker, seen iconographically as another giant who stands singing the Pauline victory motto while stopping with one foot the narrow neck of a grave. A poem that began with an act of passive observation turns at last into a demonstration of active, personally realized confidence.

Another witty reading of the race's exaltation in Christ appears in *Meditation* 1.20, starting this time with the ascent to heaven in a cloud (Acts 1). The opening puzzle comes with our noticing that Taylor presents two different, and apparently contradictory, modes of ascent. First Christ rides up in a chariot of "Azure Cloud"; one stanza later he is more laboriously making his way to heaven on a "golden Ladders Jasper rounds."

Taylor's exegetical tradition offers some measure of direct resolution. Read against the language of Psalm 104.3 and associated commentary, the cloud-chariot and ladder images need not be seen as wholly inconsistent.[22] The wind and chariot mode, recalling Elijah's whirlwind chariot in 2 Kings 2.11, would highlight the taking up of Christ's human nature, whereas the ladder ascent, typified in the Bethel theophany of Jacob's ladder (Gen. 28.12), stresses more the capacity of Christ's divine nature to raise itself.

Still, Taylor goes out of his way to underscore the radical paradoxes of redemption, the incongruity of the "Mortall Clod immortalizde" and the "Turffe of Clay" who is "yet bright Glories King." He also underscores the defect inherent in his figures of ascent:

He did not in a Fiery Charriot's Shine,
    And Whirlewinde, like Elias upward goe.
But th'golden Ladders Jasper rounds did climbe
    Unto the Heavens high from Earth below.
      Each step trod on a Golden Stepping Stone
      Of Deity unto his very Throne.

The overt denial of "did not" rules out suspicions of careless inconsistency on Taylor's part: his handling of the sequence hints

22. Schuldiner, "Problematic Imagery," 96–99.

at some sort of deliberate ploy. No sooner are we asked to visualize than our icon is shattered. Yet such is precisely the problem raised by the historical ascension once we have embraced the idea of fleshly incarnation. The point behind Taylor's coy riddling lies here: if the historic ascension gives cause for celebrating the raising up of human nature in Christ, it also requires later disciples to raise their sights above the carnal specter of abandonment by Jesus toward true spiritual discernment of the omnipresent Christ. With Christ they are now united by faith.

Thus, having witnessed the very image of God in the earthly Jesus, the apostles in Jerusalem must reconcile themselves to God's apparent departure and abandonment. The poet too faces a crisis of separation. For a time his soul's eye looks with joyous approval on the spectacle of Christ's ascending. He can see its "flakes of Glory," hear its "Heart Cramping notes of Melody." Soon, though, he comes to the inevitable doubt: "Art thou ascended up on high, my Lord, / And must I be without thee here below?" (ll. 31–32).

To recover hope, he must lift his affections above the absent Jesus of history to set them upon the glorified Christ of faith. There alone the duality of human and divine natures resolves without conflict of images. The poet-disciple must also seek God with confidence that his own nature has been mystically raised with Christ, instead of "seking . . . with carnal eyes" after a figure receding into the clouds.[23] Indeed, the ascension event essentially describes the uplifting of *human* nature in Christ, since "the Divine nature properly neither Ascends nor Descends" (*Harmony*, 2:506).

So *theanthropy*, we discover, is humanity's "ladder" to *theosis*. As the Geneva Bible glosses Jacob's vision at Bethel (Gen. 28.12), "Christ is the ladder whereby God and man are joyned together . . . & we by him ascende into heaven." And Taylor elsewhere proposes that this ladder typifies Christ "as to his Humane Nature the foot . . . standing upon the Earth," and "as to his Divine Nature, the Top," reaching "in & above the Heavens"

23. See Geneva Bible gloss on Acts 1.11.

(*Harmony,* 2:384). Meditated on in this light, the ladder back in stanza three becomes a type not of Christ's divine nature alone, but of the whole glorified Christ who theanthropically unites both natures in the endless flux of Jacob's ascending and descending angels.[24]

In the final turn of identity, Taylor asks to partake of Christ's divinizing Spirit after the model of Elisha's plea to share the spirit of the ascending Elijah:

> Lend mee thy Wings, my Lord, I'st fly apace.
> My Soules Arms stud with thy strong Quills, true Faith,
> My Quills then Feather with thy Saving Grace,
> My Wings will take the Winde thy Word displai'th.
> Then I shall fly up to thy glorious Throne
> With my strong Wings whose Feathers are thine own.

Studded in his "Soules Arms" with God's "strong Quills" of faith and grace, he is now prepared to soar on "the Winde thy Word displai'th" until he reunites with his Lord on the celestial mountain. This bird-man conceit, with its aura of exaltative freedom, obviously creates a different mood from its tweedling counterpart in *Meditation* 1.8. No longer a mourning observer of Christ's ascension, the poet has become by meditation a fellow flier determined to "fly apace." But the motive power for his ascent will be supplied by the Spirit's wind rather than by his own exertions. The same elevating Spirit will, one may deduce, feather the quills with which he composes his praise.

In several passages of the foregoing *Meditations,* Taylor shows an evident fondness for puns. Though punning expresses only one aspect of his meditative wit in the devotional poems, one can often approach the core of a poem's meaning by scrutinizing his pervasive wordplay. Taylor applies puns energetically but not frivolously. Not even the divine name and titles are excluded from this reverent sport: in *Meditation* 2.42, for example, Taylor uses skesis (a pun on unidentical words) to enforce the point that

---

24. Such a view is reinforced by the handling of ladder imagery in *Meditation* 2.44 and in lines 25–30 of "The Return."

Christ's body is not properly part of the godhead by declaring it "not Godded" though it "next to th'Godhead lies." As usages where one meaning is contained in another, puns carry forward the theme of spiritual enclosure or *theanthropy*. At the same time, as conversions of sense, they can convey the transformative possibility of *theosis*. Occasionally the central meaning of a poem or a series of poems will turn on a pun or polyptoton (inflectional variation).

Many of Taylor's favorite puns are obvious and common, though the poet never seems to tire of repeating them. Such locutions include the *sun-son* appellation for Christ and the combined noun and resurrectional verb usage of *rose* (as in "Such Beautie rose in Sharon's Rose," 2.116). The multiple connotations of *mite* and *might* figure notably in several poems, and Taylor enjoys fingering the possessive pronoun's homonymic relation to mineral riches: "Am I thy Gold? Or Purse, Lord, for thy Wealth; / Whether in mine, or mint refinde for thee?" (1.6). Words like *passover* (as in 2.22) or *temple* present irresistible opportunities for wordplay. Predictably too the Puritan poet dwells again and again on *grace, gracious,* and *graciousness*. He uses them to evoke not only the gift of undeserved salvation but also the aesthetic perception of beauty or pleasing movement (2.56), the benevolent bearing of his Lord (2.54), or the act of giving thanks (2.86). And at the close of *Meditation* 2.108, Grace suddenly emerges as the proper (but slightly audacious) name of the woman carving the poet's feast of "A whole redeemer" served up in bloody sauce!

Like George Herbert, Taylor turns the Bible's mercantile tropes of rental, purchase, and redemption to display fresh domestic connotations. Thus, he cleverly manipulates golden coins, the "Angell" and the "Sovereign," to fit the religious semantics of *Meditations* 1.6 and 2.11. In esoteric alchemy, he found another symbol system offering semantic overtones with moral and contemplative theology. Beyond his innumerable allusions to sacred gold, for instance, he poses a verbal dialectic between his personal "guilt" and the pure "Quintessence" of love found in Christ's "guilt o're" beauty and "gilded" grave, or between the aspiration to still his soul and homage to the "Golden Still" of Christ's transmutative presence (1.14–15, 2.158, 1.7).[25]

Given Taylor's disposition to regard his poems as biblically modeled psalmody or song, he is also drawn naturally to exploit the ambiguous connotations of musical references. In *Meditation* 2.129 and elsewhere he takes relish in conflating the aural satisfactions of song with other grounds of rapture when he speaks of "inchantings." Other musically related words like *pipe, quill,* and especially *play* satisfy his punning wit in a wide variety of contexts.

Even an apparently commonplace phrasing, like the remark that Isaac's sacrifice "fore shew" Christ's (2.5), can bear pregnant connotations. The plain sense of *fore* is that Isaac, as a type, precedes the era of Christ chronologically though he is otherwise outshone by the antitype. At the same time, the *shew* element of the compound indicates how in Scripture the spectacle of Isaac's sacrifice is set before us in the demonstrative sense. A third nuance of *fore* supports the poem's larger emphasis on God's deliberate sacrifice *for* us in Christ, a sense echoed in *Meditation* 2.24 in the mention of a Christological marvel "that fore us playes."

Another triple connotation—and associated sign of *theanthropy*—is contained in Taylor's statement that the Spirit "Did overshaddow Mary" in *Meditation* 2.20. The direct sense, of divine force descending on the Virgin, opens secondarily into a kind of typological trope in which Mary's enclosure of God in the womb foreshadows the greater tabernacling soon to be made manifest in Christ. Finally too, the Spirit thus manifested in the God-man overshadows that of the human woman, who is paradoxically contained within the mystery of the Son she bore.

By the same token, several of Taylor's puns are pivotally linked to *theosis*. Altar allusions, as in 2.18 and 2.86, transcend their ritual

---

25. More figurally than semantically, the color symbolism of red, white, and gold persistent in Taylor's later poems on Canticles corresponds as well to an alchemical layer of connotation, since white and red represented the penultimate and ultimate stages of the alchemist's Great Work of generating the philosopher's stone.

typology to suggest as well personal transformation (or altera-
tion) through sacrifice: "Lord let thy Deity mine Altar bee."

In addition to manipulating individual words, Taylor toys with
grammatical constructs and relations. In *Meditation* 2.35, he conducts an elaborate game of relational discovery around the
"Spruice / Peart Pronown MY," with polyptotonic extension to
myselfe, mine (in rhyming dialectic with *thine* and in apposition to
minde), and *me*. The final intent is to establish a grammar of assent
binding the speaker to his Lord, who provides the "Golden Link"
in his transformational quest.

Neither is Taylor's wordplay restricted to the English language.
Well-versed in Hebrew, Latin, and Greek, thanks to his studies at
Harvard, he incorporated this linguistic knowledge into his verse
in the form of a multilingual wit that has yet to be fully explored.
His fascination with Hebrew, the sacred tongue, often led him to
meditate on the original sense of his scripture texts, particularly
in his later poems on Canticles. In *Meditation* 2.125, for example,
his discovery of Christ's aspect in the biblical Lebanon (Cant. 5.15)
confronts us with a verbal puzzle:

If I may read thee in its name thou art
    The Hill, it metaphors, of Frankincense,
Hence all atonement for our Sins thy heart
    Hath made with God: thou pardon dost dispense.
    So thou dost whiten us, who were all O're
    All fould with filth and Sin, all rowld in goare.

Despite the "hill of frankincense" verse nearby in Canticles 4.6,
it is far from apparent—without reference to the Hebraic subtext—
what Lebanon has to do either with Frankincense or with cleansing whiteness. What Taylor read first in the etymology of Lebanon
is its Hebrew root, *lavan* or white, deriving most likely from the
snow peaks associated with this northern mountain region. He
would know that whiteness appears also in the word frankincense (*levonah*), a fragrant gum resin consisting of white particles.
The incense could be used either as a perfume (as it is referred to
in Canticles 4.6) or to accompany cereal offerings in the ritual

cultus of sacrifice. In its aromatic capacity, Taylor uses the frankincense to connote other "Sents" (l. 44) evoked in his poem,
especially the fragrance of the famous gum-exuding cedars of
Lebanon as suggestive of the Bridegroom's comely appeal. At the
same time, in its ritual-sacrificial capacity, the frankincense ty-
pologizes Christ's whitening offer of atonement. Taylor may have
even meant the poem's hill and tree configuration to recall Calv-
ary.

On occasion, Taylor's punning around a key word fills a pivotal
yet subtle role in determining the sense of an entire poem or
group in the *Meditations*. One such word is *kinde,* as developed in
Meditation 1.36. Superficially, Taylor's usage appears to serve as
the vehicle of a simple contrast between divine benevolence and
his own human state of depravity:

> To find thee Lord, thus overflowing kinde,
>> And t'finde mee thine, thus overflowing vile,
> A Riddle seems onrivetted, I finde.
>> This reason saith is hard to reconcile.
>> Dost Vileness choose? Or can't thy kindness shown
>> Me meliorate? Or am I not thine own?

Yet even at the first level of meaning, God's "kinde" bearing
toward the human race would involve considerably more for
Taylor than amiability or "Liberallness" (l. 50). Surely the poet's
"kindness" draws here on the fundamental Old Testament concept of God's "loving-kindness," as it is often called in the Authorized Version. This principle of steadfast love (*hesed*) and mercy
grounds the eternal gift of covenant in which Taylor hopes to
claim saving relation. At another level, however, God risks violating his own nature and character—"overflowing kinde"—to become intimate with such a lesser being as the human.

Taylor's affirmative resolution arises out of yet another import of
kindness, in the sense of family relation. Because God has indeed
transcended his own restriction to divinity in the form of Christ's
theanthropy, human beings have become kindred of the Most
High. Their familial status carries both new claims and new

responsibilities. Though they are "children" now through adoption rather than through natural geneology, they are nonetheless organically connected to divinity through "True Loves Veane" (l. 72). So Taylor's inconspicuous word *kinde* holds the family title that unrivets the opening riddle and extends to the poem's climactic resolution of his personal status: "That I am thine."

The integrative results of discovering one's true family bonds are likewise dramatized by the organic-arboreal images presented in *Meditations* 1.36, 1.37, and many other poems. Accordingly, the *Meditations* exploit a richly diverse vocabulary of stock, sap, root and branch, vine and fruit, and engrafting. This theme of organic kinship is central, in fact, to the developmental logic of Taylor's several compelling poems on the Tree of Life motif, especially *Meditation* 1.29. Unusually astute commentary has already sorted out the tangle of biblical and other allusions operative here.[26] Regarded as a separate external phenomenon, the imposing "Tree of Life whose Bulk's Theanthropie" (2.33) emblemizes Christ as the origin and essence of life in its several forms:

And in Gods Garden [I] saw a golden Tree,
    Whose Heart was All Divine, and gold its barke.
    Whose glorious limbs and fruitfull branches strong
    With Saints, and Angells bright are richly hung.
                    (1.29)

Yet the root of the poem's wit lies in the interior, relational import of this verbal emblem stretching between earth and heaven. Longing to be engrafted into the golden stock of Jesse, the speaker discovers this deed already accomplished in Christ. Even if he remains a comically humble twig of the great tree, he finds himself thus connected to the very "heart" of God. As Ursula Brumm helps us to perceive, the central conceit of this poem is humankind's incorporation into God's family tree.[27] And

26. See Ursula Brumm, "The 'Tree of Life' in Edward Taylor's Meditations," and Thomas Werge, "The Tree of Life in Edward Taylor's Poetry: The Sources of a Puritan Image."
27. Brumm, "Tree of Life," 77, 80.

this family tree emerges as something of an elaborate pictorial pun. In forming a new network of bodily vitality, the divine progenitive at once embraces and transcends the many life connections of ordinary human "kind":

I being grafft in thee there up do stand
    In us Relations all that mutuall are.
I am thy Patient, Pupill, Servant, and
      Thy Sister, Mother, Doove, Spouse, Son, and Heire.
      Thou art my Priest, Physician, Prophet, King,
      Lord, Brother, Bridegroom, Father, Ev'ry thing.

6 Songs and Valedictions:
Later *Meditations* and Other Verse

Typological Wit and the Holy Delight of Canticles

To the end of his long life, Taylor held fast to the ways that had so long sustained him in his post at Westfield. Never modifying his resistance to Solomon Stoddard's innovations in church policy, he likewise continued to compose *Meditations* of much the same character for as long as he was able to carry on ministerial functions. These open-ended poems sustain a dimension of perpetual search, of residual doubt in tension with assurance, that renders early and late productions to some degree interchangeable.[1]

Yet the previously noted clusters and topical cycles of development in Taylor's collection do indicate subtler changes, if not progress, during the course of composition. Thus, eleven years after beginning the work, Taylor decided to initiate a Second Series of *Meditations*. Though his reasons for doing so remain unclear, they apparently had something to do with the new concentration on biblical typology demonstrated in poems 2.1–30, 2.58–60[B], and 2.70–71. In their closing phases, Taylor's *Meditations* then proceed toward a nearly total involvement in the spousal imagery of Canticles. Finally, with his inner eye set steadily on eternity, Taylor wrote some surprisingly playful verse on the occasion of his approaching death.

In broadest terms, we might understand the course of Taylor's lifelong poetic journey as fulfilling a tripartite pattern, beginning with the liberating discovery of saving grace in *Gods Determinations*. From this comedy of grace corporately realized in the church, Taylor comes to stress the soul's celebration of sustaining

---

1. Charles W. Mignon, "A Principle of Order in Edward Taylor's *Preparatory Meditations*."

grace amid conflict through the earlier *Meditations,* and at last the comfort received with confirming grace in the later *Meditations* and Valedictory poems. Though such divisions are scarcely hard and fast, there is at least a discernible movement toward resignation in the final phase of Taylor's career, the phase with which this closing chapter is largely concerned. Increasingly, timelessness and the transcendence of struggle dominate the mood of Taylor's later meditations on types, on Canticles, and on death. Yet even in the "occasional" death poems, the poet remains a wit.

These occasional poems also remind us that though the greater body of Taylor's lyric poetry evidently arose out of what Bishop Hall called "deliberate," biblically directed meditation, some of his more graphic and teachable short pieces derived instead from "extemporall" observation of creatures and events in the natural world. Hence the poet's eight numbered "occurrants" of witty reflection on insects, flash floods, and trivial or tragic phenomena in his own domestic world, though probably composed at an early date, are best examined here. The scriptural text remains an allusive presence in these occasional poems, but the poet more obviously exploits naturalistic uses of emblem, exemplum, and allegory.

Considered together as major groups in the Second Series of *Meditations,* Taylor's poems on types and on Canticles show the poet poised between strict historical typology and atemporal allegory. To be sure, the primary structure of the typological poems highlights the temporal contrast between Old Testament shadows and gospel fulfillment. Poems in the sequence also presume that the ancient types existed in fact and not merely in figure. Even these poems, however, are ultimately less concerned with history than with personal applications and the transtemporal centrality of Christ. And they reveal the operation of Taylor's imagination within Scripture to be more playfully interallusive across the text than temporally bipolar from type to antitype. By the time the poet approached the consummation of his own time in the final sequences on Canticles, he found the gap between temporality and timelessness narrowing swiftly.

The sequence of explicitly typological poems opening the Second Series has already provoked a good deal of careful study, most recently and thoroughly by Karen Rowe. Still more commentary is likely to follow publication of the accompanying sermons *Upon the Types of the Old Testament.* The work of able specialists in the field need not be duplicated here. Still, some organized reflection on the wit of Taylor's typic hermeneutics might usefully complement the previous chapter's analytic references to poems from the sequence. For while interpreters have found a conservative, even pedestrian strain in Taylor's purest exercises in prophetic analogy, they have also remarked on his habitual instinct to play with the conventional types and to personalize them, often by wittily inserting himself as a minor prop into the typological scene.[2] Thus typology too holds a place in Taylor's festival frame.

One way of appreciating the significance of this typological wit is to consider its two main courses of application: affirmative and negative. In the poems, Taylor develops a complex devotional dialectic that both affirms and denies the current spiritual relevance of the types.[3] The affirmative approach satisfies Taylor's festival disposition in its discovery of joyous congruence between old and new covenants. The negative approach, often reflected through some version of Taylor's reverent parody, dramatizes the inferiority of the old cultus to the new spiritual order of worship. Above all, it confirms by way of belittling contrast the supreme antitypal glory of Christ.

In the path of affirmative use, the lesser glories penciled "out in fair Colours" by God in the types supply "beams of Excellency to allure" souls to the Lord. A discerning eye will find in exemplars such as Adam, Abraham, and Samson "pictures" of the "Eternall

2. Karl Keller, "'The World Slickt Up in Types': Edward Taylor as a Version of Emerson," in *Typology and Early American Literature,* ed. Sacvan Bercovitch, 175–90; Barbara Lewalski, *Protestant Poetics and the Seventeenth-Century Religious Lyric,* 406–9; Mason I. Lowance, Jr., *The Language of Canaan: Metaphor and Symbol in New England from the Puritans to the Transcendentalists,* 110; Karen Rowe, *Saint and Singer: Edward Taylor's Typology and the Poetics of Meditation,* 248. See the notes to Rowe's book for documentation of the extensive secondary literature on Taylor and typology beyond the items listed here.

3. See also Rowe, *Saint and Singer,* 34, 106, 114.

Love" centered and fully realized in Christ (2.1). These aesthetically appealing influences contribute to the gospel design by stirring desire, enravishing and entertaining "all Such withall that shall be Heirs" of grace.[4] While pondering "The glory of the world slickt up in types," a new heir of the covenantal promises might well experience that crucial insight of correspondence yielding sanguine "glee." Taylor commonly describes the quickening zeal for which he prays as a flood of light, or as a surge of blood carrying both eucharistic and medical-humoral springs of vitality:

Then Pardon, Lord, my fault: and let thy beams
    Of Holiness pierce through this Heart of mine.

Ope to thy Blood a passage through my veans.
    Let thy pure blood my impure blood refine.
    Then with new blood and spirits I will dub
    My tunes upon thy Excellency good.

                                        (2.1)

Yet let my Titimouses Quill suck in
    Thy Graces milk Pails some small drop: or Cart
A Bit, or Splinter of some Ray, the wing
    Of Grace's sun sprindgd out, into my heart:
    To build there Wonders Chappell where thy Praise
    Shall be the Psalms sung forth in gracious layes.

                                        (2.3)

Even if "the glory of all Types doth meet" in Christ, their subtle dispersion throughout an ancient text presents a teasing "Riddle" that must be meditatively resolved before the brilliance of the divine image shines through (2.1, 2.5). The more abundant and obscure the pieces to a typological puzzle, the more delight its completion brings the inquiring poet. Taylor's pursuit of gleeful correspondences in the Word often runs across the established borderline of comparison between Old and New Testament.

A few poems, written mostly toward the beginning of the

4. "Christ the Glory of All Types: The Initial Sermon from Edward Taylor's 'Upon the Types of the Old Testament,' " ed. Charles W. Mignon, 298; *C*, 269.

Second Series, do restrict their attention to a narrow framework of historical typology. But they are the poorer for it. *Meditation* 2.6, as one instance, works through a fairly pedestrian statement of analogies between Jacob and Christ. Despite several lines of personal application, the poem lacks imaginative persuasion. In more effective *Meditations*, Taylor lets his compounding wit roam allusively after correspondences spreading within and across both testaments. This freer form of meditation extends the field of associative inquiry while giving full and mostly conservative account of traditional typal-antitypal structures.

In the overtly typological sequence, *Meditation* 2.24 on the Jewish Feast of Tabernacles illustrates how Taylor uses allusive wit to expand the traditional analogies even into the domestic sphere. Dated 25 December, the antitypal focus of the poem is God's incarnation in Christ as typified by the ancient tents and tabernacles. During the Sukkoth festival, Jews live in tents constructed of boughs to recall their ancestors' sojourning condition in the wilderness. For Reformed exegetes, the feast in its ceremonial aspect was a "real" type of God's tabernacling among his people in the Incarnation, as Taylor's headnote from John 1.14 makes clear. Taylor even thought, as did Samuel Mather, that the antitypal meaning of the feast argued a September date for the savior's nativity. In the Old Testament field of reference, a "tabernacle" was also the early Hebrew tent of worship, a movable repository of the ark and the sanctuary altar wherein "Godhead Cabbin'd." This tabernacle served, in turn, as a prototype of Solomon's temple, which was dedicated at the Feast of Tabernacles. Thus far Taylor's poem merely reproduces standard exegesis.

But to unveil the "bright Wonder, Lord, that fore us playes" in Jesus' fleshly tabernacle, Taylor plays on images and biblical references outside the usual catalogue for this festival. As a result, his interpretation of the feast gives distinctive emphasis to the themes of *theanthropy* and *theosis*. Starting with a vision of the universe itself as divine tabernacle, the poem's pitch of "Wonder grows" as its measure of God's temple precincts shrinks to "a bit of flesh." The celestial canopy contracts to "Tent cloath of a Humane Quilt." Taylor ransacks a plethora of booths, boxes, and tenement figures to articulate amazement over this marvel of *theanthropy* that "May make bright Angells gasterd, at it gaze." In a bizarre conceit evocative of an improvised and slightly sordid manger, Jesus' birth is visualized to resemble the golden Sun's lying ignominiously "buttond up in a Tobacco box."

No less startling for Taylor is the way this union of "Thy Nature all With Mine" transforms human nature, raising it proportionately as God lowers his cosmic tabernacle to the height of a tent frame: "Thou low dost step aloft to lift up mine." To confirm the New Adam's divinizing link with humanity, Taylor introduces his pivotal pun based on allusion to the Old Adam: "Thy Person infinite, without compare / Cloaths made of a Carnation leafe doth ware." Beyond the evident wordplay on a fleshly flower, the poet makes novel imagistic use of standard typology by developing the leaf covering rather than the enclosure connotations of the festival boughs. As Rowe observes, the pun compares Christ's putting on of humanity to the fig leaf clothing of Adam and Eve, with the poem making an innovative substitution of pine, palm, and other branches for the fig covering.[5]

As Christ clothes himself in human flesh, so in turn must the human saint put on Christ and "get into" him.[6] In 2 Corinthians 5.1–4, St. Paul finds "we that are in this tabernacle" naked in our mortality and groaning to be "clothed upon" by Christ. For Taylor, this new clothing of Adam is a divine trick of typology, and in the relevant sermon he relishes the thought that Christ's nativity and Adam's fall may have occurred on the same September day. Such congruences demonstrate "a wonderfull befooling the Divell in his attempt upon our first parents."[7] Thus, the incarnation offers not only a marvel of *theanthropy* for what it can "hold"

5. Rowe, *Saint and Singer*, 123, together with her "Puritan Typology and Allegory as Metaphor and Conceit in Edward Taylor's *Preparatory Meditations*," 109. Also relevant to my understanding of the poem is Rowe's insight that by "mingling typal analogies with worldly images" throughout the piece, Taylor imitates *theanthropy* in poetic terms (*Saint and Singer*, 124).

6. From Sermon #25, "Feast of Tabernacles," in the Nebraska manuscript "Upon the Types of the Old Testament," transcribed by Charles Mignon, 10, written to accompany *Meditation* 2.24 though developed from another scriptural text.

7. Ibid., 5, 13. Samuel Mather discusses the September dating of Christ's nativity and the Feast of Tabernacles in *The Figures or Types of the Old Testament*, 425–34.

of divinity in flesh but also a gift of *theosis* for what it can "hold out" for human benefit (ll. 17–18).

Neither does Taylor portray this incarnation as a purely generalized involvement in humanity. Besides entering generic human nature, God will enter the poet's own particular "heart": Christ will "Not onely Nature, but my person tuch" (ll. 44–47). The poem reinforces this intimacy of indwelling through its variant manipulations of house imagery, particularly in the earlier assertion that "Together in thy Person all Divine / Stand House, and House holder." The wit here lies partly in the homely, domestic irony of the omnipotent "House holder." But the biblical sources of personal intimacy run deeper still when we recall that Jesus owned no earthly house and knew no settled place to lay his head yet came freely beneath the roofs of Jewish houses to heal and sit at table (Matt. 8.20; Mark 5.35–42; Luke 7.36). So Christ has entered the poet's own person to "tent with in't"—that is, through the Latin *tentare*, to share his human struggle and temptations (ll. 10, 49). Then in return, when Taylor has confirmed the "mutuall wee" of an indwelling connection, he prays to "make mee give / A Leafe unto thy Lordship of myselfe." Apparently the poem itself constitutes one such "leafe."

In the contrary negative way of typology, where the poet eschews elaborative analogy, the Old Testament "shadows" become illuminative by way of denial. In *Meditation* 2.1 the poet's outburst of appreciation at "the glory of the world slickt up in types" is quickly modified by his remembrance of the awesome distance between types and their focal antitype:

> Thy glory doth their glory quite excell:
> More than the Sun excells in its bright glee
> A nat, an Earewig, Weevill, Snaile, or Shell.
> Wonders in Crowds start up; your eyes may strut
> Viewing his Excellence, and's bleeding cut.

Such reminders of the great distance between type and antitype enforce a conviction of sacred awe more emphatically Christological than is characteristic of other New England typologizers.

In contrast to the "recapitulative" or "developmental" typology of historians like John Winthrop, Richard Mather, and Cotton Mather, Taylor's devotional fixation on Christ leaves little room—in the poetry, at least—for discovering an antitypal fulfillment in the New English nation.[8]

Taylor recognized that though the types could be manipulated to release positive correspondences of the Word, they could also serve to accentuate, by negative paradox, the superior mystery of divinity revealed in Christ. He knew that in comparative terms not only his poems but even the New Testament portraits of Christ are mere "shadows" of the Truth.[9] Taylor was so impressed, in fact, by Christ's centrality as the alpha and omega, containing all history, that his writing often qualifies the model of a strictly linear typology. Even the historical types do not, after all, come "before" Christ except in a superficial temporal reckoning. Christ precedes *them* both in rank and in his preexistent identity as Logos. Since Christ is ultimately the first and the last, the scriptural motto to *Meditation* 2.2 can aptly call him "the first born of every creature." Appropriately, this poem comes before *Meditation* 2.3 on Adam and Noah, the "first born" of historical types. Seen in relation to these, Christ paradoxically is the "First Born's Antitype: in whom they're shrin'de" (2.2).

The model of linear fulfillment is thus partially displaced by a circular or spheric paradigm centered in the Logos. This centripetal sense relates to Taylor's special fondness for Origen.[10] It is also connected with the more allegorical and personal strain of

8. This is argued especially by Rowe in *Saint and Singer*, drawing on terms discussed by Lowance in *Language of Canaan*. However, the point that Taylor avoids giving antitypal import to the national mission may need qualification with reference to prose works like the *TCLS*. And as Harry S. Stout points out in *The New England Soul: Preaching and Religious Culture in Colonial New England*, 45, the context of the discourse is all-important: the same preacher who stressed eternal and spiritual typology in his "regular" preaching would probably offer a more temporalized, regional interpretation in his occasional sermons.

9. Considering in the aggregate the gospel parables, the Old Testament prophecies, and the traditional types, Taylor declares "the glory of all" these to be "but a darke Shadow" of "the Loveliness of the Lord Jesus" ("Christ the Glory of All Types," 289).

10. On the Origen link, see Thomas M. Davis, "Edward Taylor and the Traditions of Puritan Typology," 31, 36.

hermeneutics that dominates the later poems on Canticles. *Meditation* 2.4 follows St. Paul in seeing "Abrams Shine" as "an Allegory," rather than a wholly linear prophecy, "to typify / Thee, and thy Glorious Selfe in mystery." And in the poem's central stanza, the temporal progress of history gives way to timeless vision:

> Should all the Sparks in heaven, the Stars there dance
>   A Galliard, Round about the Sun, and stay
> His Servants (while on Easter morn his prance
>   Is o're, which old wives prate of) O brave Play.
>   Thy glorious Saints thus boss thee round, which stand
>   Holding thy glorious Types out in their hand.

The colorful iconography of Old Testament saints encloses revelation's temporal narrative within the timeless moment of the text. Its effect is not unlike that achieved by Dante's image of the Book of Creation at the close of the *Paradiso*. And before the resurrected Jesus the earthly sun holds its forward motion—by one reading, a "stay"—as it did for Joshua. As linear time is caught and held in suspension under grace, the personal types dance festively in orbit round the eternal Logos.

In Taylor's poems on Canticles, especially the closing concentration in *Meditations* 2.115–165, this allegorical strain enlarges as the poet fixes his gaze on an eternally glorified Christ. Even here temporality persists, in the form of a timely momentum toward the saints' rendezvous with God in the coming Kingdom. Indeed, the late series on Canticles shows Taylor eager to embrace his godly bridegroom in the next life, the more so as his aging body deteriorates in this one.[11] But as death approaches during Taylor's last twelve years of composing *Meditations*, this slant toward future eschatology begins to converge with realized eschatology, the sense of tasting the final banquet here and now. Typology largely dissolves into the allegorical continuity of a timeless Christ, while graphic allusion to sin and personal un-

11. This is the main argument of Jeffrey A. Hammond, "A Puritan *Ars Moriendi*: Edward Taylor's Late Meditations on the Song of Songs." Fuller discussion appears in Hammond's "Songs from the Garden: Edward Taylor and the Canticles."

worthiness gives way to a more festive confidence in the soul's mystical marriage to Christ. Less exuberantly witty than earlier *Meditations*, the Canticles writing in the Second Series moves first through a quieter mood of resignation and then finally, in the twelve-year cycle written after 1713, to a stage of deeply internalized celebration marked by subtle identification with the Canticles bride.

Following Arthur Jackson's *Annotations* and James Durham's *Clavis Cantici*, Taylor had solid Puritan precedent for pursuing an allegorical exposition of Canticles. Though a Puritan feared to allegorize historical sections in Scripture, this "dark" book of Solomon's was already allegorical by genre.[12] In Taylor's traditional view of its essential allegory, it is to be read as a sacred epithalamium, a spiritual love song. The union it celebrates between bridegroom and spouse represents the love Christ bears toward the faithful soul as well as that advanced toward the aggregate body of saints in the church.

As Karen Rowe and Jeffrey Hammond have shown, Taylor's poetic treatment of the text is carefully exegetical, especially in the unified sequence of 2.115–153. The reading does not, therefore, open in the manner of a thoroughgoing Platonic or Plotinian allegory. Nor is Taylor's approach to Canticles "mystical" in quite the manner represented by a classic Roman Catholic expositor like St. John of the Cross. The Puritan poet makes little attempt to demonstrate a progression through discrete stages of spiritual advance. And only rarely, as in 2.133, does Taylor presume to identify his speaker's voice directly with that of the Canticles bride. More often he claims a comically insignificant role in the spousal relation: it is enough if he can find himself incorporated in the bridegroom as a toe, a finger, a navel, a nose, even a lock of hair. Or else the speaker seems content merely to come within sight of the bridegroom's ravishing countenance by growing into a lofty cedar of Lebanon, satisfied to smell his Lord by becoming "a grape of Leb'nons Vine" (2.125).

---

12. Lowance, *Language of Canaan*, 94–95; Karen E. Rowe, "Sacred or Profane? Edward Taylor's Meditations on Canticles," 126–29.

Yet even through these whimsically modest expressions, the speaker claims to approach effectual union with God, the end of all contemplative search. Sometimes Taylor defines this unitive goal in objective exegetical language, as in 2.154 where the "Golden Belt" of faith buckles "Christ and the Soule together" in a tight clasp. But the personal, experiential aspect of mystical quest asserts itself throughout the Canticles poems. It is especially prominent in the erotic vocabulary of rapture, enravishment, and ecstasy long associated with mystical uses of Canticles. As Origen believed Canticles to be the contemplative summit of Solomon's expression, beyond the natural and moral explorations of Proverbs and Ecclesiastes, so it was fitting for Taylor to end his *Meditations* with a long sequence on "The Song of Songs." With Protestant adjustments, Taylor pursued the same end Origen had announced in the prologue to his *Commentary*: to show how the soul, having perceived "the beauty . . . of the Word of God" and having sustained "some dart and wound of love," is drawn by the fire of this "heavenly desire and love" to ascend toward pure contemplation of the Godhead. [13]

In Taylor's metaphoric rendering, God's courtship of humanity becomes, in fact, an elaborate love game initiated by an amorous dart from Christ's eyes. One of the Canticles poems sees something positively fetching in the glance from a "pert percing fiery Eye" that holds the poet's "heart and Love in a blesst Chase" (2.119). Other poems stress the coquettish subtlety of the divine seducer, whose Love "play[s] bow-peep" (2.96) with the earthly soul. For his part, the poet ventures to respond in tones of teasing intimacy. "Callst thou me Friend? What Rhetorick is this? / It is a Piece of heavenly Blandishments," he demurs at the outset of 2.156. In 2.115 he sets the problem of doubtful relation to the beloved briefly in abeyance with lighthearted diction around a lock-and-key figure. Here Scripture unlocks his soul to enjoy the kinetic freedom of "play" in yet another sense:

Lord, make thy Hold Word, the golden Key
    My Soule to lock and make its bolt to trig

13. Origen, "Prologue to the Commentary on the Song of Songs," in *Origen*, trans. Rowan A. Greer, 223.

Before the same, and Oyle the same to play
     As thou dost move them off and On to jig.

Satisfying the mood of a festive love-ritual, Taylor also makes frequent allusion to "entertainment" in his Canticles poems, a theme usually occasioned by the text's garden and banquet imagery but naturally linked for Taylor with the communion sacrament. Surprisingly, the sensuous attractions of the love feast afford mutual enjoyment to God and the human soul:

Here thus is Entertainment sweet on this.
     Thou feedst thyselfe and also feedest us,
Upon the spiced dainties in this Dish.
          Oh pleasant food! Both feed together thus;
          Well spicde Delights do entertain thee here.
          And thou thine entertain'st with thy good Cheare.
                                        (2.131)

Naturally, the tenor of the poet's erotic metaphors is always spiritual espousal rather than earthly love. His contemporaries would not think to question his poetic applications of sensuous figures from Canticles, a work deemed particularly appropriate as a text for Protestant meditation. Still, one can overstress Taylor's authorized "spiritualization" of eroticism, as if exegetical scholarship removed all trace of force and passion from the sensual vehicle.[14] In practice, the literary vehicle and tenor, *eros* and *agape*, cannot be separated so easily.[15] Though the poet would consciously deny it, some form of actual if sublimated eroticism was needed to charge his language of love enough "to rouse / The dull affections rich flaming Glee" (2.136). Study of the vast exegetical knowledge Taylor brought to his Canticles writings need

14. It is pertinent to recall in this regard that Taylor allowed himself to become familiar with Ovid's *Art of Love*. The notoriously unspiritualized eroticism of this work was, as Mukhtar Ali Isani observes, "unusual reading in Taylor's time" ("Edward Taylor and Ovid's *Art of Love*: The Text of a Newly-Discovered Manuscript," 69).

15. Thus, though Origen insists that the ordinary and higher scriptural ideal of love is the relatively dispassionate affection of *agape* or *diligo*, he admits that occasionally "Scripture calls love [i.e., *eros*] by its own term and summons and impels souls to it" ("Prologue to the Commentary," 224).

not, therefore, obscure appreciation of the sportive and erotic zeal that informs this substantial portion of the *Preparatory Meditations*.

Occurrants of the Divine Traces

Whether centered on Canticles or another text, both series of *Meditations* expose a meditative imagination provoked more by the world of Scripture than by direct exposure to the Creation. Inevitably, natural figures appear—especially in the form of heavenly bodies, vegetable matter, and gems. Yet they remain figures, arguing little interest in nature for its own sake and virtually none in a full-blown vista of the American landscape. Art may be "natures Ape" (2.56) in abstract theory, but the art of the *Meditations* rarely imitates nature in the field. Seen through the refracting medium of scriptural metaphor, the natural world of the *Meditations* appears quaintly remote, if not at times surrealistic. Despite his speculative interest in natural science and attentiveness to remarkable providences, Taylor never formulated a typology of phenomenal nature in the mood of Jonathan Edwards.

Taylor did, however, come to acknowledge the actuality of the natural world as reflected in his later poetic account of "The Great Bones Dug up at Clavarack."[16] He also responded to natural and creaturely phenomena in his composition of the eight "occurrants" finished sometime before 1689. More emblematic or allegorical than genuinely symbolic, the occasional lyrics stop short of interpreting nature as a second source of revelation. Yet these fruits of "extemporall" meditation stand within a well-established Christian tradition of meditation on the creatures. Here the meditative poet dispatches wit to recover sight of what St. Bonaventure described as the scattered "traces" of God in the creation.

What elevates these poems at fortunate moments above the level of didactic illustration, to which they otherwise incline, is their depiction of an imagination at play. Lacking this lighter charm,

16. Lawrence Lan Sluder, "God in the Background: Edward Taylor as Naturalist." Taylor also recorded elsewhere the conventional argument that God exists as shown "From the glorious frame of the whole universe" and by "every creature" (Edward Taylor, "Theological Notes," 22).

most of John Winthrop's journal exhibits of providential intervention come out looking comparatively unbelievable. Though
applied to the service of spiritual teaching, the *exempla* offered in
pieces such as "Huswifery," "Upon a Spider Catching a Fly," and
"Upon a Wasp Child with Cold" are drawn from homely patches
of experience gleaned apparently from direct observation.

Of the eight pieces, "The Ebb and Flow" compares most closely
in theme and manner to poems collected in the *Preparatory Meditations*. Its central image of the fitful flame could well have been
occasioned by an actual view of the Taylor hearth fire, just as
Donald Stanford hypothesizes that the colorful conceits of "Huswifery" began with a scene of Elizabeth Taylor at her spinning
wheel.[17] Fusing domestic imagery with typological allusion to
incense and altars, Taylor's wit addresses the familiar problem of
doubt stemming from a soul's loss of affective feeling sometime
after the grand conflagration of conversion. In time the flames
once sparked so readily from the heart's "tinder box" are supplanted by the smolder of incense enclosed within a "Censar
trim" (*Poems*, p. 470).

Yet the poem consoles that this change signals maturation more
than simple loss. The censer's "glow" betokens a more "intire"
and enduring spirituality than do those first tinder flashes of the
convert's zeal, though both derive from the one sacred fire. Unlike
the personal tinderbox, the "Censar trim" is used in the social,
self-offering service of God's altar worship, so one could imagine
Taylor's mid-life questions about his own ministerial vocation as
one possible "occurrant" of this poem. In light of the perpetual
divine fire of love, "The Ebb and Flow" disarms the speaker's
demon of doubt by naming it satirically as "a mocking Ignis
Fatuus," a spectral appearance to which only the foolish would
pay heed.

"Upon a Spider Catching a Fly" looks at first to be a much
simpler, two-part exercise in blatant moralism. First we watch a
careless fly fall prey to the familiar and devious spider, on the
basis of which we are then taught the predictable lesson of bewar-

---

17. Donald E. Stanford, "Edward Taylor," in *Major Writers of Early American Literature*, ed. Everett Emerson, 87.

ing Satan's snares. We had better shape up and fly right or we die. But while this deceptively transparent poem is indeed structured upon moral allegory, its wit opens up a complexity of didactic interpretation within the allegory that defeats our natural confidence in self-help moralism.

Influenced by emblem books and, perhaps, by medieval exegesis,[18] the poem becomes problematic once Taylor begins to develop his allegorical use of the natural episode given in the opening five stanzas. Taylor is obvious enough about equating the venomous "Elfe" with "Hells Spider," a little-fingered antagonist addressed with pitying and buoyant sarcasm because he is so laughably ignorant of the role his "play"—or "Ploy"—must satisfy in the divine economy.[19] That humanity needs somehow to escape the "nets" ironically set by hell's fisher of men is likewise plain. But if some form of human insect is raised at last to enjoy the higher animal confinement of a "Nightingaile" singing in "Glories Cage," it is not so clear where the poem's other creature, the wasp, is supposed to figure in this equation. If Satan plays the spider role, does Taylor intend to cast us as the fly or as the wasp? Or is the poet dividing humanity into two distinct classes with different scripts?

By one reading, the "silly" and incapable fly does seem a natural type of the natural man, or of the predestined reprobate. The wasp would then serve as a contrasting image of the regenerate man, armed with the sting and vitalism of grace. Still, this "froppish" animal makes an odd icon of sanctity; nor is it plausible to suppose that conversion effaces all hint of the fly's weakness and folly even from visible saints. So in this scheme the wasp looks more like a hypothetical, idealized version of what the saint aspires to be but usually is not. Moreover, the fate of the captured wasp remains inconclusive. Though it seems able to resist immediate destruction, when last seen in stanza 4 it is still struggling in

18. See Thomas E. Johnston, Jr., "Edward Taylor: An American Emblematist," pp, 186–87, and Judson Boyce Allen, "Edward Taylor's Catholic Wasp: Exegetical Convention in 'Upon a Spider Catching a Fly.'"

19. In their competing editions of the poem, Donald Stanford transcribes "play" and Thomas Davis "Ploy," but either of these readings has ludic significance.

the spider's net, whence its efforts may or may not bring saving release. Still another problem arises when we ask whether Taylor addresses his central lesson to fly, spider, wasp, or some combination of the three:

This goes to pot, that not
    Nature doth call.
Strive not above what strength hath got
    Lest in the brawle
        Thou fall.
           (*Poems*, pp. 464–65)

Such a lesson would seem quite beside the point for the fly, whose negligible strength makes striving useless, and for hell's spider, whose allegorical "fall" has already taken place. It applies better to the wasp, whose blend of discretion and vital exertion is sufficient to delay if not to prevent destruction. Yet even for the wasp, Taylor posits no gracious intervention in the natural scene that would insure salvation. Without it, the wasp could not use the poet's moral rule for anything better than a reprieve. Thus, Taylor's summarizing lesson is most aptly owned by the species of regenerate humanity, whose condition approaches allegorically that of the wasp but is not mirrored precisely in the tale of either wasp or fly.

So interpreted, the entomological analogy impresses us finally as a tease, since it frustrates the sort of one-to-one allegoric equation with the human animal we are drawn to expect. Even regenerate humanity betrays something of the spider's deliberate cunning, and must show something of the wasp's active zeal. To stand solely on one's own strength and rectitude is futile, of course, and to think so is already to have fallen. Only divine grace can break Satan's "Cord." Yet to presume on this grace in quiescent indolence is to refuse the divine gift presented in one's natural faculties, which could assist recovery after a fall. This indolent course is equally damning. Hence the purpose of the poem's not so simple didacticism concerning the spiritual life is to teach a paradoxical discipline of active passivity. In addition to applying a potent self-exertion that is itself born of grace, the soul must learn to wait upon grace without visible proof of its effects.

This last lesson takes us beyond the margins of nature's text in the wasp and spider episode. The covenanted soul can, after all, anticipate a spiritual rescue from sin according to grace, whereas the ensnared wasp can expect no corresponding rescue in the order of nature. So the poem's didactic method is fancifully oblique, an approach reinforced by jocular traits of diction, mood, and stanzaic structure. If the soul as reader learns to stir itself toward vigorous exercise in the deadly warfare of "this Frey," it is also brought to meditate on the grace of spiritual receptivity, a more passive confidence that the "Frey" is ultimately God's game against an elfish opponent.

Receptivity to "a vitall grace" is likewise a chief lesson in "Upon a Wasp Child with Cold." What this poem proffers is less an evidence of special Providence discovered within the primary text of Creation than an artifact of meditative wit shaped from personification. Taylor's self-conscious reiteration of *as if* conjunctions clarifies his true concern: an imaginative turning of natural conceits toward the higher use of speculative play. The poet knows full well that the wasp he observes holds no "Volume of Choice precepts cleare" in her "little brain pan," boasts no human "rationality" in her "velvet helmet high" (*Poems*, p. 466). Indeed the artifice of the comparison is highlighted when he calls attention to the insect's "sattin jacket hot" containing an "Apothecaries Shop / Of Natures recepts," then shows her flying away "in thankfull gails / Unto her dun Curld palace Hall / Her warm thanks offering for all." Yet the very energy of this indulgence in pathetic fallacy testifies to the dynamism of grace. The same vital warmth of "Divinity" perceived in the wasp may be attributed to the poet's "nimble Spirit" engaged in "Acting each part though ne'er so small / Here of this Fustian animall."

The poem teaches the lesson of receptive spirituality most clearly in Taylor's sensuous account of the stiffened wasp recovering her faculties, member by member, as she lies "bathing / In Sol's warm breath and shine as saving." Helpless to produce the warmth she needs, she must content herself with receiving it from the divine fire. Still, the wasp can and must take part, by extending her body "in great desire / To warm her digits at that fire." She must show, at the least, sufficient wisdom and initiative to capture the energy poured upon her. The desire for God, then, is an impulse at once universally grounded in the frame of sensuous brute nature and instrumental in the process of redemption.

The poem teaches further through the "school and schoolmaster" of the wasp that clearing one's "misted sight" to see more of God's worldly presence effects a warming of desire. In the closing lines Taylor looks toward the culmination of his desire in an "enravisht" state of bliss, though even while sounding that lofty note he cannot resist adding the earthy pun whereby his heavenly song is "furrd with praise." Sustaining the paradox of an active passivity, the poem ends by combining the passive image of enravishment with that of Taylor making his own athletic "Climb into / The Godhead."

From a wider angle of vision than the insect meditations, "Upon the Sweeping Flood" searches for traces of divine will in the spectacle of natural disaster. Toward this end the poem applies a decidedly satiric wit to the occasion of an actual flash flood of 1683.[20] One import of the event is predictably brought to mind by biblical allusions and precedent: the "liquid drops" that temporarily "drown" Taylor's corner of New England, like those that flooded Noah's biblical world, come to punish human sin. It is tempting to imagine, as several interpreters have, that the sin in question is sexual. With his illicit lover, the speaker would thus be confessing to an erotically "Carnall love." Perhaps we are even catching a provocative glimpse behind the minister's black veil of secret sin!

But such readings are hardly credible, given the broader context of Taylor's writing as well as the wider application of "carnal" in contemporary usage. More plausibly, the poem's "wee" refers

20. For Taylor's account of the Westfield flood in his "Church Records," see *UW*, 3:179. For a reading of the poem as "intriguing failure," see Sanford Pinsker, "Carnal Love / Excremental Skies: A Reading of Edward Taylor's 'Upon the Sweeping Flood.'"

generically to the human race or, in narrowest terms, to the New England congregational race in some phase of its ongoing controversy with God. And at least one name for the sin that so sorely provokes God's excremental wrath to fall upon "our lofty heads" must be pride, the primal fault leading toward the primal deluge. In essence, "Carnall love" translates into that baser, complacent love of self that obstructs communion with the love of God. Pictured here in the graphic imagery of dry and constipated affections, it also infects the whole of nature, as St. Paul observes in Romans 8.22. Taylor's poem confirms, through its wordplay, that even the aerial reaches of creation are indeed "fallen."

Faced with the obstinacy of human self-love, the poem releases a torrent of sacred sarcasm in its second stanza:

> Were th'Heavens sick? must wee their Doctors bee
>   And physick them with pills, our sin?
> To make them purg and Vomit, see,
>   And Excrements out fling?
> We've griev'd them by such Physick that they shed
> Their Excrements upon our lofty heads.
>
> (*Poems*, p. 471)

Though graphically rendered, the didactic import of the illustration appears again, at first sight, to be too obvious to reward analysis. It should scarcely surprise us to read through Taylor's transparent allegory that human pride will be punished.

The lesson does not stop here, however, because the poem also teaches that nature's divinely meditated punishment acts as a genuine purgative. The lightning "flame" of God's charity is a piercing, regenerative force that will eventually supplant the smoldering passions of carnal love.

Though allegorically structured, Taylor's poem thus offers no simple reading of nature's adversities. Other "occurrants," such as the highly elusive "Let by Rain," shore up a comparable barrier of mystery between their analogical premises and didactic conclusions. If "acts of God" like the sweeping flood are viewed as punishment for sin, fit judgments on humanity's dungish ways, they are more deeply and still more ironically regarded as nature's outpouring of regenerative compassion, vicariously on our behalf out of the bowels of God. Like the first flood, the stream of vomit and excrement dispensed in Taylor's poem must ultimately be read as another line in the incarnational message of God's "rich Love Letter to us from above" (2.8).

Taylor's Wit of Valediction

One subgenre of occasional verse still to be considered is the poetry of death, wit's last expressive challenge on earth. In the tradition of John Donne, Taylor finds room for sacred jest, for festive meditation, even in the feverish precincts of sickness and death. Now and then, to be sure, the elegiac pieces convey an almost overwhelming grief of suppressed rage. An early occasional poem, "Upon Wedlock, and Death of Children," shows Taylor laboring to say that God's will remains his "Spell Charm, Joy, and Gem" despite the untimely loss of two infant children. Here an ingenious metaphorizing of the victims as upsnatched flowers, in whom the poet passes "piecemeale" to glory, seems less affecting than the real-life "tortures, Vomit, screechings, groans" with which young Abigail passes from life.[21] More typically, though, wit surpasses mourning, extending the poet's own chant of salvation to the mouth of the grave. The art of holy dying, as represented poetically by Taylor's art, seeks to combine defiance toward the deathly antagonist with resignation to the divine will.

In the 1689 funeral poem for Elizabeth, "ever Endeared, and Tender Wife," Taylor uses only the gentler forms of conceitist expression to reach beyond the opening mood of impotent anguish toward the closing liturgy of hagiographic celebration. At first the poet is devastated to find marriage's "True Love Knot" all the "harder tide" by death: "My heart is in't and will be squeez'd

21. See Robert Daly, *God's Altar: The World and the Flesh in Puritan Poetry*, 163–65; Karl Keller, *The Example of Edward Taylor*, 46; and, for comment on the poem's submerged biblical and doctrinal wit, Gene Russell, "Taylor's 'Upon Wedlock, and Death of Children.'"

therefore / To pieces if thou draw the Ends much more" (*Poems*, p. 472). In part 2, however, the love knot becomes pivotal to his recovery of thankful utterance. "What shall my Preface to our True Love Knot / Frisk in Acrostick Rhimes?" asks Taylor, in poignant recollection of the Dove Poem he had sent his wife some fifteen years earlier. Now, weighed with "Cramping Griefe" at their parting, the poet finds such buoyant gestures impossible. Still, his love knot to Elizabeth affords him some communication with her saintly glory, on account of which he does not hesitate, Protestant scruples aside, to invoke her intercessory power for his elegiac task: "Thy Grace will Grace unto a Poem bee / Although a Poem be no grace to thee." Thus he is enabled in part 3 to advance a litany of praise for Elizabeth as child, neighbor, housemistress, mother, "Yoake Mate," and "Reall, Israelite indeed." Rather than sounding an elaborately figured melody, Taylor models the more sober tropes of this last section on what he takes to be the "gracious Speech" of Elizabeth herself.

A more sportive, audacious style of wit characterizes poems in which Taylor looks toward his own imminent departure from the world. Nearly eighty, he survived a serious illness in 1720 to take one last and remarkably extended encore as a poet. "Upon my recovery out of a threatening Sickness in December Ano Dmi 1720" expresses resignation to God's will in the awkward interval "untill I / My Quarters moove into Eternity" (*UW*, 3:219). But by now the poet has grown impatient to fulfill his pious death wish, a yearning he subdues in part through joking remonstrance with God. "What, is the golden Gate of Paradise / Lockt up 'gain that yet I may not enter?" he queries, with mock annoyance. In jest, he can at once tease God for holding off his desire to die yet plead his strict acceptance of Providence: "Thy Will be done, I say, do ask me to do the same; / I'de rather dy than cast upon it blame."

In "A Fig for thee Oh! Death," Taylor addresses his plea for speedy release directly to the "King of Terrours" (*UW*, 3:263), whom he also denounces. Personified in a formidable visage of "Gastly Eyes" and "Grim looks," Death first seems to paint itself as a composite icon from emblem books and from the death's-head of a Puritan tombstone.[22] Yet this opening portrait is shaded with suggestions of mock horror, as we notice Death's "Butter teeth" and "bare bones," his overdrawn Satanic costuming in "Grizzly Hide, & clawing Tallons." Thereafter, in the course of the poem's comic reversal, Death's horrid "grimace" is unmasked to reveal "Christ's bright face"; Death's "Gastly Eyes" dissolve within "th'Eye Omniscient" of the Almighty. But because Death does pose a mortal challenge to the self, its defeat is achieved here not mainly through the soul's natural force of immortality—as is often the case, even in ostensibly Christian literature—but through the divine wonder of bodily resurrection. In striking fashion Taylor's poem portrays resurrectional life as a blissfully erotic reunion of soul and body.

Treating the soul-body problem within a complex and slightly confused figural scheme, the poem is in essence dramatizing St. Paul's teaching that Christians must resign possession of the corruptible body before being gifted with a transformed, incorruptible body at the last trump (1 Cor. 15.35–57). "A Fig for thee" describes this process, involving also the reconjoining of body and soul, largely through sexual tropes and figures of nut and seed. St. Paul insists that the natural body is sown as generative seed, the essence of which is raised in power as a spiritual body. Jesus in St. John's gospel concurs that the corn of wheat must "fall into the ground and die" to bring fruit (John 12.24).

In Taylor's rendering, the corruptible body becomes a nutshell, cracked and ground to powdery dust in Death's "Mill the grave." Enclosed within, the seed or "kirnell fair" of the soul is safely preserved. So also grace preserves the poet morally from being "tumbled in Such grave" as mortal sin, a stroke of wit appearing only in the poem's final, revised version. Though the poet yields his unpreservable flesh wholly to devouring Death, this "Mess" is only a "vile harlot," a "Strumpet," a "Fig." Hence the "Fig" Taylor

22. Lewalski, *Protestant Poetics*, 394; Thomas M. Davis and Arthur Forstater, "Edward Taylor's 'A Fig for thee Oh! Death,'" in *Discoveries and Considerations: Essays on Early American Literature and Aesthetics Presented to Harold Jantz*, ed. Calvin Israel.

bequeaths to Death is a worthless trifle—as well as a somewhat obscene gesture of defiance, a *Fica*—and a token on the larger scale of God's Last Judgment.[23] A fig is also a fruit with many seeds, so that the wordplay of the poet's closing taunt recalls his earlier nut and seed figure combined with a possible hint of Christ's resurrectional triumph as the "first fruit" of redemption.

Meanwhile Death, like Satan in *Gods Determinations*, will unwittingly play his part in the divine scheme by grinding in his "Smoky furnace" and then refining, as in the production of glass, the poet's bodily essence. The body will eventually become quite "Christalized" by God, thereby prepared for reconstitution and marriage with the soul at the General Resurrection. Then the sundered members are reknit,

And each to 'ts fellow hath exactly joyn'd,
[I]s raised up anew & made all bright
And Christalized; & top full of delight.
And entertains its Soule again in bliss
And Holy Angells waiting all on this.
The Soule & Body now, as two true Lovers
[E]ry night how do they hug & kiss each other.
[A]nd going hand in hand thus thro' the Skies
[U]p to Eternall glory glorious rise.
                                        (*UW*, 3:264)

This conceit of soul and body as lovers, which does not appear in sources to which Taylor was otherwise indebted,[24] involves a transmutation of the previous brothel imagery. Its Whitmanesque flavor suggests that for Taylor, as for Whitman and in another sense for Freud, the very process of dying could be imagined in erotic terms. Toward the close of "A Fig for thee Oh! Death," spiritualized passion extends its embrace beyond the nocturnal romance of soul and body toward the "bright face" of the heavenly bridegroom.

The three versions of Taylor's poetic "Valediction" show him already dancing by anticipation a "Holy Galliard" in the "Angell

23. Davis and Forstater, "Edward Taylor's 'A Fig,' " 76–77.
24. Ibid., 72–73.

play house" of heaven (*UW*, 3:229, 232). With seeming disdain, the moribund writer takes his leave of the stars, sun, moon, air, and "Terraqueous Globe." All these things, apparently, are readily dismissible vanity and "non-Sense." Instead of uplifting the heart toward eternity, the stars play frivolously "at bow peep"; the sun and moon chase each other "at Barly breaks"; the air carries "nasty speech" jogging at its back; and the whole "mocking Crew" of earth's creatures insinuate the promise of enduring sensual bliss. No wonder the poet looks with eager longing to the next world, bidding farewell to former doubts of regeneracy with "proof well nigh / That mine Election's to Eternall joy" (*UW*, p. 238). In heaven alone the poet's "praise shall Parallel Eternity" (*UW*, p. 239), in contrast to the sorry rhymes he must labor to produce while on earth.

Yet the *contemptus mundi* message is not all we find in this awkwardly whimsical rhetoric. Taylor's words of "Valediction to the Whole World" convey more of a frolicsome and affectionate farewell to nature than a repudiation of all its gifts. It is hard to respond otherwise to the quaint catalogues or to this valediction to air:

But now I bid thee here adjue, adjue
And going off trumpet tantarrow too.
                    (*UW*, p. 221)

To wean the heart from everything earthly is now, after all, a virtue born largely of necessity. Taylor can entertain high spirits only because he imagines himself exchanging the food, drink, and apparel of an earthly paradise for their counterparts in the heavenly Eden:

    . . . hence I say to ye adjue
I am within Gods Paradise's View,
Where my best life is; & no Physick there
Is ever needed. And my Souls good cheere
Is of the Tree of Life, that tree most Choice,
That is within Gods blissfull Paradise.

And of the most Sweet Waters of that River,
Of Gods rich Aqua Vitae I'st drink Ever.
                    (*UW*, p. 236)

If such a prospect makes it easy to forego the "bobbing pleasures" of eating more fruit from earth's "Terren play house," it
cannot be so painless for the poet-scholar to leave behind "study,
Books, Pen" or the world's wealth "Of Sounds & Words," to say
nothing of friends, children, and "Deare, Deare Wife" (*UW*, pp.
235, 224, 233, 236). Taylor has already admitted that an earthly
element like air is not only a channel of iniquity but also a
thoroughfare of angels and a vehicle of sacred speech. That the
poet does affirm the circumstances of his earthly life becomes
apparent by canto 5, where he thanks God for having seated him
in New England's gospel light rather than "in Pagan times" or "in
Pagan Papistick places like / Hells foggy Darkness."

Only in comparison with promises of the next life, then, might
the consolations of this one deserve rhetorical scorn. In fact, the
imagery of Taylor's own expectant singing and jumping in "heart
ravishing joy" (*UW*, p. 239) matches quite plainly the frolicking of
celestial bodies with which the poem begins. Even in the sensuous realm, this Puritan remains enough of a dancer to answer
distant rhythms of the cosmic dance. But the heavenly banquet
festival of the Lord holds a higher appeal for which he can wait no
longer. For Taylor, every delight of life on earth must pale as he
approaches at last the glory streaming from "Christs dining
Chamber that's most high / Wherein he feasts his Guests Eternally."

Epilogue

The object of the preceding analysis has been to clarify Edward Taylor's identity as a religious poet, especially as a Christian poet of meditative wit and comic vision. Though the poet's fascination with wit as the play of grace does not explain the whole of his creativity, it is integral to his artistic grasp of the sacred. In Taylor, a highly theological mind, playfully yet earnestly engaged with ideas, applies itself to the service of a soul questing for assurance of divine love. The study has also aimed to take full account of Taylor's party affiliations as a Puritan poet, though without supposing that this secondary context produces any fixed conclusions about the character of spirituality reflected in his verse. Finally, too, one is obliged to render some response to the textbook naming of Taylor as an American poet.

Except in hindsight, it is hard to make much of a case for the recognizably American quality of Taylor's verse or for the impact of his work on the growth of American letters. Local color is all but invisible in the prose as in the poetry. And until they were published in the last half-century, the poems could not influence literary tradition. It remains a question to what extent the rusticity of Taylor's life on the American frontier may have affected the noted "roughness" of his poetic style. Taylor was surely no sophisticate in the sense of a Jack Donne. The cultural isolation of Westfield must have stamped itself somehow on the artistic consciousness of a preacher-poet whose circle of familiar converse and whose congregation of rude farmers were in another country from Samuel Sewall's Boston, to say nothing of Donne's London.

Still, Taylor's writing is hardly that of the naive primitive. As his well-stocked library testifies, he maintained his long-distance membership in the extraordinarily verbal culture of New England's clerisy and insulated himself from the wilder energies of the frontier. His verse sounds no smoother numbers in its earliest

English phase than when later issued in America. If the apparently crude force of Taylor's wit declares its difference from the style of any English Metaphysical, neither does it invite confusion with the style of any other colonial poet in America. The wilderness hypothesis may therefore come to shed more light on the motivating circumstances of Taylor's large Westfield opus than it has so far on the peculiarities of his style. Despite his Puritan accent and the uncouth mores of his setting, Taylor stands more within than without the impressive tradition of seventeenth-century English devotional verse. To reaffirm as much, with Barbara Lewalski, produces the curious result of drawing Taylor criticism back full circle toward some of its earliest concerns.

Taylor clearly did wear the colors of his adopted land in his struggle to sustain the religious idealism of its New English founders. Even the meditative poems can be regarded as stemming from his commitment to uphold the collective faith of his tribe. To rhyme the fellowship's tale of personal conversion, year after year, was to sign fidelity to that original idea of America, or to whatever local and internalized version of it could be endorsed for the new remnant of second- and third-generation saints.

But in another, more paradoxical way, the national import of Taylor's verse is most noteworthy by way of negation. Having pressed his defense of the fathers' errand in his anti-Stoddardean prose, Taylor was not disposed to set forth grand expectations of national promise in his verse. If the once imagined glory of the New Israel was never to reach fruition in New England as a whole, poetry remained as a vehicle for expressing and discovering other hopes. In the *Meditations* and *Gods Determinations*, Taylor implicitly rejects the sort of nationalized typology or expansive deification of a new American self pursued by other establishment figures like Cotton Mather. Without expressly refuting the myth of American exceptionalism, he pledged primary allegiance to his heavenly country and declined to invest belief in the rising secular nation. In all this he shares something with the great and more vocal naysayers of nineteenth-century American literature.

As in the national context so also more generally, Taylor's disposition to accept limits may have been his greatest asset in transcending them. He was not eager to leave the comparatively cultured Bay Area for Westfield, for example, yet he used his books and writing to make the most of his mentally confining estate on the frontier. Despite his evident faults as an artist, it is unlikely he would have left us better work had he spent all his days in Boston or London. He likewise accepted, to the betterment of his art, the limiting condition of writing the *Meditations* within the calendar of his community's worship. A romantic aesthetic of inspiration would view this sense of obligation to produce poems on schedule as inimical to genuine creativity. Yet the example of someone like J. S. Bach, a greater artist than Taylor who turned out roughly a cantata a month on demand during the early Leipzig years, suggests otherwise. Poetically, Taylor even confined himself to writing the same form of six-line stanza during the more than forty-year span of composing the *Meditations*. And most notably, from the standpoint of present-day interests, he focussed with peculiar intensity upon the limitations of language.

Compared with the partly anachronistic "American" frame of identity, the "Puritan" one may go further toward establishing the substantial unity of Taylor's vocation as pastor and poet, activist and contemplative. As study on Taylor continues, the once broad chasm between the sensuously witty author of meditative verse and the seemingly autocratic defender of an outmoded polity begins to narrow. Taylor was undoubtedly a real Puritan as well as a real poet. Artistically, his involvement in sectarian creedalism probably helped him in some ways, hurt him in others. Thus, if his poetic imagination shows no apparent damage from the iconophobia Puritans often betrayed toward the visual and plastic arts, it manages with only limited success to rise above the recurrent mood of self-absorption to which the Puritan conscience was notoriously prone. Or if mainstream Reformation piety lacked something of the incarnational and ritualistic blood life of Catholic Christianity, Taylor developed a noteworthy compensation for that defect in the ritualized forms of his meditative verse, his own liturgy of the Word.

By the same token, the comic and playful dynamics of Taylor's wit at once issue from and diverge from the core of Puritan divinity. Insofar as the poet's ludic impulse is congenital rather than theoretical, it can even on occasion subvert his own designs, as in some of the unwittingly laughable reprovals of sin in the *Christographia* sermons. But in its best moments Taylor's wit summons up facts of human nature more deeply innate than depravity, reconfirming Aristotle's fitting definition of our kind as the laughing and playing animal.

Appendix
An Edward Taylor Chronology

Life and Prose Productions

1642 Estimated birthdate in Sketchley, Leicestershire, near weaving center in England. Parents are prosperous yeoman farmers.

Educated under nonconformist schoolmaster and academy during Civil War turmoil.

1662 Act of Uniformity: Taylor's refusal to subscribe ends brief career as teacher and spurs American migration.

1668 Sails to America, composing diary en route.

Admitted to Harvard, where serves as college butler; later instituted as scholar of the house.

1669 Westfield, Massachusetts, is incorporated.

1671 Graduates from Harvard and arrives in Westfield after arduous winter journey.

Apparently with reluctance left Harvard to accept call, following gossip from counseling of Elizabeth Steadman, a married woman.

Takes up long-term duties as community minister, physician, and farmer.

Poetic Productions*

English Poems

"A Dialogue between the writer and a Maypole Dresser," "The Lay-Mans Lamentation," and three other pieces in couplet form written perhaps in late 1660s or early 1670s.

Harvard Poems, 1668–1671

Six public elegies on Richard Mather, Zecharia Symmes, Francis Willoughby, and John Allen.

Poetic "Declamation" in praise of English language delivered at Harvard Commencement, 1671.

*The naming of stages in Taylor's poetic writing follows that proposed by Thomas M. Davis and Virginia L. Davis in *The Unpublished Writings of Edward Taylor,* vol. 3.

1674 Marries Elizabeth Fitch of Norwich, Connecticut, daughter of the Reverend James Fitch. Marriage lasts fifteen years and produces eight children, of whom three survive infancy.

1675–1676 King Philip's War disrupts ministry in Westfield.

1679 Conducts Foundation Day ceremonies for covenanting of Westfield Church.

Presents spiritual "Relation" and preaches sermon "A Particular Church is God's House" (later revised), defending current New England Way.

1683 Occasion of "great Flood" and related poem.

1685 Approximate time when began writing exegetical *Harmony of the Gospels,* a work never finished though extended to almost five hundred manuscript pages.

1689 Elizabeth Taylor dies.

1690 Solomon Stoddard commences practice of "open communion" in nearby Northampton.

1692 Marries Ruth Wyllys, who eventually bears six children.

1693–1694 Writes eight Sermons comprising *Treatise Concerning the Lord's Supper,* linked to *Meditations* 2.101–11. Anti-Stoddard argument confirms need to prepare before wedding feast and complements the case made earlier in "Animadversion" and later piece "The *Appeale* Tried" (ca. 1710–1711).

1693–1706 Composes thirty-six sermons "Upon the Types of the Old Testament," linked to poems in *Meditations,* Second Series.

Westfield Poems, 1674–1689

"This Dove & Olive Branch" and love letter to Elizabeth.

Gods Determinations Touching his Elect, possibly completed during this period.

Eight occasional poems, or "occurants," including "Huswifery," "Upon the Sweeping Flood," "Upon a Spider Catching a Fly," and "The Ebb and Flow."

Paraphrases of the psalms.

Begins First Series of *Preparatory Meditations,* 1682.

Elegy on death of Elizabeth Taylor.

Westfield Poems, 1690–1705

Paraphrases on the Book of Job.

Begins Second Series of *Preparatory Meditations,* 1693.

Begins *Metrical History of Christianity,* a lengthy (over 20,000 lines) but inferior work offering a Protestant perspective on the history of horrors, persecution, and martyrdom.

Elegies on Samuel Hooker and on sister-in-law Mehetabel Woodbridge.

"The Great Bones Dug Up at Clavarack."

1701–1703 Produces fourteen *Christographia* sermons, describing the exemplary beauty and character of Christ's person in its union of human and divine.

Associated with *Meditations* 2.42–56.

1712–1713 Preaches two disciplinary sermons related to conflicts with church members.

1720 Suffers major illness.

Returns to Harvard to receive M.A. New meetinghouse in Westfield indicates success of ministry but occasions bickering among townspeople and their aged pastor.

1725 Taylor retires from ministry, in failing health.

1729 Taylor dies, leaving library of over two hundred volumes, many transcribed by hand.

1730 Ruth Taylor dies.

1937 First major publication of Taylor's verse by Thomas Johnson.

Westfield Poems, 1720–1725

"Upon my recovery out of a threatening Sickness," 1720.

"Valedictory Poems" preparatory for death.

Last poem in *Meditations*, 1725.

Elegies for Increase Mather.

Verses on legendary "Pope Joan."

"A Fig for thee, Oh! Death."

Bibliography

Alexis, Gerhard T. "Taylor's 'Meditation 8.'" *Explicator* 34 (1966): Item 77.

Allen, Judson Boyce. "Edward Taylor's Catholic Wasp: Exegetical Convention in 'Upon a Spider Catching a Fly.'" *English Language Notes* 7 (1970): 257–60.

Ames, William. *Conscience with the Power and Cases Thereof.* London, 1639.

———. *The Marrow of Theology.* Translated by John Eusden. Boston: United Church Press, 1968.

Anselment, Raymond A. *'Betwixt Jest and Earnest': Marprelate, Milton, Marvell, Swift, and The Decorum of Religious Ridicule.* Toronto: University of Toronto Press, 1979.

———. "Rhetoric and the Dramatic Satire of Martin Marprelate." *Studies in English Literature 1500–1900* 10 (1970): 103–19.

Arner, Robert D. "Edward Taylor's Gaming Imagery: 'Meditation 1.40.'" *Early American Literature* 4 (1969): 38–40.

———. "Proverbs in Edward Taylor's *Gods Determinations.*" *Southern Folklore Quarterly* 37 (1973): 1–13.

———. "Wit, Humor, and Satire in Seventeenth-Century American Poetry." In *Puritan Poets and Poetics: Seventeenth-Century American Poetry in Theory and Practice,* edited by Peter White, with advisory editor Harrison T. Meserole. University Park: Penn State University Press, 1985.

Augustine. *De Trinitate.* In *Augustine: Later Works,* edited and translated by John Burnaby. Philadelphia: Westminster Press, 1955.

———. *On Christian Doctrine.* Translated by D. W. Robertson, Jr. Indianapolis: Bobbs-Merrill, 1958.

Babb, Lawrence. *The Elizabethan Malady: A Study of Melancholia in English Literature from 1580–1642.* East Lansing: Michigan State University Press, 1951.

Ball, Kenneth R. "Rhetoric in Edward Taylor's *Preparatory Meditations.*" *Early American Literature* 4 (1969/1970): 79–88.

Barbour, Dennis H. "*Gods Determinations* and the Hexameral Tradition." *Early American Literature* 16 (1981/1982): 213–25.

Baxter, Richard. *Preservatives against Melancholy and Over-much Sorrow.* London, 1716.

———. *The Saints' Everlasting Rest.* In *The Doubleday Devotional Classics,* vol. 1, edited by E. Glenn Hinson. Garden City, N.Y.: Doubleday, 1978.

Benton, Robert. "Edward Taylor's Use of His Text." *American Literature* 39 (1967): 31–41.

Bercovitch, Sacvan. *The American Jeremiad*. Madison: University of Wisconsin Press, 1978.

———. *The Puritan Origins of the American Self*. New Haven: Yale University Press, 1975.

Bethell, S. L. "The Nature of Metaphysical Wit." In *Discussions of John Donne*, edited by Frank Kermode. Boston: Heath, 1962.

Blake, Kathleen. "Edward Taylor's Protestant Poetic: Non-Transubstantiating Metaphor." *American Literature* 43 (1971): 1–24.

Blau, Herbert. "Heaven's Sugar Cake: Theology and Imagery in the Poetry of Edward Taylor." *New England Quarterly* 26 (1953): 337–60.

Bright, Timothy. *A Treatise of Melancholy*. Introduction by Hardin Craig. 1586. Reprint. New York: Facsimile Text Society and Columbia University Press, 1940.

Brown, Wallace. "Edward Taylor: An American Metaphysical." *American Literature* 16 (1944): 186–97.

Brumm, Ursula. "Meditative Poetry in New England." In *Puritan Poets and Poetics: Seventeenth-Century American Poetry in Theory and Practice*, edited by Peter White, with advisory editor Harrison T. Meserole. University Park: Penn State University Press, 1985.

———. "The 'Tree of Life' in Edward Taylor's Meditations." *Early American Literature* 3 (1968): 72–87.

Burton, Robert. *The Anatomy of Melancholy*. Edited by Floyd Dell and Paul J. Smith. New York: Farrar and Rinehart, 1929.

Bush, Sargent, Jr. "Paradox, Puritanism, and Taylor's *Gods Determinations*." *Early American Literature* 4 (1969/1970): 48–66.

Butler, Dom Cuthbert. *Western Mysticism: The Teaching of Augustine, Gregory and Bernard on Contemplation and the Contemplative Life*. 2d ed. London, 1922. Reprint. New York: Harper and Row, 1966.

Caldwell, Patricia. *The Puritan Conversion Narrative: The Beginnings of American Expression*. New York: Cambridge University Press, 1983.

Callow, James T. "Edward Taylor Obeys St. Paul." *Early American Literature* 4 (1969/1970): 89–96.

Calvin, John. *Institutes of the Christian Religion*. Edited by John T. McNeill. 2 vols. Philadelphia: Westminster, 1960.

Carlisle, E. F. "The Puritan Structure of Edward Taylor's Poetry." *American Quarterly* 20 (1968): 147–63.

Clark, Michael. "'The Crucified Phrase': Sign and Desire in Puritan Semiology." *Early American Literature* 8 (1978/1979): 276–93.

———. "The Honeyed Knot of Puritan Aesthetics." In *Puritan Poets and Poetics: Seventeenth-Century American Poetry in Theory and Practice*, edited by Peter White, with advisory editor Harrison T. Meserole. University Park: Penn State University Press, 1985.

———. "The Subject of the Text in Early American Literature." *Early American Literature* 20 (1985): 120–30.

Clendenning, John. "Piety and Imagery in Edward Taylor's 'The Reflex-ion.' " *American Quarterly* 16 (1964): 203–10.

Colacurcio, Michael. "*Gods Determinations* Touching Half-Way Member-ship: Occasion and Audience in Edward Taylor." *American Literature* 39 (1967): 298–314.

Coleridge, Samuel T. *Confessions of an Inquiring Spirit.* Edited by H. Hart. Stanford: Stanford University Press, 1957.

Colman, Benjamin. *The Government and Improvement of Mirth.* Boston, 1707.

The Confession of Faith; The Larger and the Shorter Catechisms. London: T. Nelson and Sons, 1860.

Corthell, Ronald J. "Joseph Hall and Protestant Meditation." *Texas Studies in Language and Literature* 20 (1978): 367–85.

Cox, Harvey. *The Feast of Fools: A Theological Essay on Festivity and Fantasy.* Cambridge: Harvard University Press, 1969.

Crane, William G. *Wit and Rhetoric in the Renaissance: The Formal Basis of Elizabethan Prose Style.* New York: Columbia University Press, 1937.

Daly, Robert. *God's Altar: The World and the Flesh in Puritan Poetry.* Berke-ley: University of California Press, 1978.

Davies, Horton. *The Worship of the English Puritans.* Westminster, En-gland: Dacre Press, 1948.

Davis, Thomas M. "Edward Taylor and the Traditions of Puritan Typol-ogy." *Early American Literature* 4 (1969/1970): 27–47.

———. "Edward Taylor's Elegy on Deacon David Dewey." *Proceedings of the American Antiquarian Society* 96 (1986): 75–84.

———. "Edward Taylor's 'Occasional Meditations.' " *Early American Liter-ature* 5 (1970/1971): 17–29.

Davis, Thomas M., and Forstater, Arthur. "Edward Taylor's 'A Fig for thee Oh! Death.' " In *Discoveries and Considerations: Essays on Early American Literature and Aesthetics Presented to Harold Jantz,* edited by Calvin Israel. Albany: State University of New York Press, 1976.

Dryden, John. *The Works of John Dryden: Poems 1649–1680,* edited by Edward Niles Hooker and H. T. Swedenberg, Jr. 19 vols. Berkeley: University of California Press, 1956–1987.

Egan, James. "Nathaniel Ward and the Marprelate Tradition." *Early Amer-ican Literature* 15 (1980): 59–71.

Eliade, Mircea. *Cosmos and History: The Myth of the Eternal Return.* Trans-lated by W. R. Trask. Paris, 1949. Reprint. New York: Harper and Row, 1959.

———. *Myth and Reality.* Translated by W. R. Trask. New York: Harper and Row, 1963.

Elliott, Emory. *Power and the Pulpit in Puritan New England.* Princeton: Princeton University Press, 1975.

Emerson, Everett. *Puritanism in America: 1620–1750*. Boston: G. K. Hall, 1977.

Fender, Stephen. "Edward Taylor and the Sources of American Puritan Wit." Ph.D. diss., Manchester University, 1962.

Fish, Stanley E. *Self-Consuming Artifacts: The Experience of Seventeenth-Century Literature*. Berkeley: University of California Press, 1972.

Fitch, James. *An Explanation of the Solemn Advice* and *The Covenant Solemnly Renewed*. Boston: J. Green, 1683.

———. *The First Principles of the Doctrine of Christ*. Boston, 1679.

Fithian, Rosemary. "The Influence of the Psalm Tradition on the Meditative Poetry of Edward Taylor." Ph.D. diss., Kent State University, 1979.

———. " 'Words of My Mouth, Meditations of My Heart': Edward Taylor's *Preparatory Meditations* and the Book of Psalms." *Early American Literature* 20 (1985): 89–119.

Gatta, John. "Edward Taylor and Thomas Hooker: Two Physicians of the Poore Doubting Soul." *Notre Dame English Journal: A Journal of Religion in Literature* 12 (1979): 1–13.

———. "Little Lower than God: The Super-Angelic Anthropology of Edward Taylor." *Harvard Theological Review* 75 (1982): 361–68.

Gelpi, Albert. *The Tenth Muse: The Psyche of the American Poet*. Cambridge: Harvard University Press, 1975.

The Geneva Bible. Introduction by Lloyd E. Berry. Facsimile of 1560 edition. Madison: University of Wisconsin Press, 1969.

Gilman, Ernest B. *The Curious Perspective: Literary and Pictorial Wit in the Seventeenth Century*. New Haven: Yale University Press, 1978.

Goodman, William B. "Edward Taylor Writes His Love." *New England Quarterly* 27 (1954): 510–15.

Grabo, Norman S. "Catholic Tradition, Puritan Literature, and Edward Taylor." *Papers of the Michigan Academy* 45 (1960): 395–402.

———. *Edward Taylor*. New York: Twayne, 1961.

———. "Edward Taylor on the Lord's Supper." *Boston Public Library Quarterly* 12 (1960): 22–36.

———. "*Gods Determinations*: Touching Taylor's Critics." *Seventeenth-Century News* 28 (1970): 22–24.

———. "Puritan Devotion and American Literary History." In *Themes and Directions in American Literature*, edited by Ray B. Browne and Donald Pizer. Lafayette, Ind.: Purdue University Studies, 1969.

Griffith, Clark. "Edward Taylor and the Momentum of Metaphor." *ELH* 33 (1966): 448–60.

Grube, Karen Gordon. "The 'Secret Sweet Mysterie' of Numbers in Edward Taylor's 'Meditation 80,' Second Series." *Early American Literature* 13 (1978/1979): 231–37.

Haims, Lynn. "The Face of God: Puritan Iconography in Early American Poetry, Sermons, and Tombstone Carving." *Early American Literature* 14 (1979): 15–47.

———. "Puritan Iconography: The Art of Edward Taylor's *Gods Determinations*." In *Puritan Poets and Poetics: Seventeenth-Century American Poetry in Theory and Practice,* edited by Peter White, with advisory editor Harrison T. Meserole. University Park: Penn State University Press, 1985.

Hall, David D. *The Faithful Shepherd: A History of the New England Ministry in the Seventeenth Century.* New York: Norton, 1972.

Hall, Joseph. *The Works of Joseph Hall.* 3 vols. London: M. Fletcher for R. Moore, 1628.

Haller, William. *The Rise of Puritanism.* New York: Columbia University Press, 1938.

Hambrick-Stowe, Charles E. *The Practice of Piety: Puritan Devotional Disciplines in Seventeenth-Century New England.* Chapel Hill: University of North Carolina Press, 1982.

Hammond, Jeffrey A. "A Puritan *Ars Moriendi*: Edward Taylor's Late Meditations on the Song of Songs." *Early American Literature* 17 (1982/1983): 191–214.

———. "Songs from the Garden: Edward Taylor and the Canticles." Ph.D. diss., Kent State University, 1979.

Hans, James S. *The Play of the World.* Amherst: University of Massachusetts Press, 1981.

Happold, F. C. *Mysticism: A Study and an Anthology.* Middlesex, England: Penguin, 1970.

Herbert, George. *The Works of George Herbert.* Edited by F. E. Hutchinson. Oxford: Oxford University Press, 1941.

Herrick, Marvin T. *Comic Theory in the Sixteenth Century.* Urbana: University of Illinois Press, 1964.

Highet, Gilbert. *The Anatomy of Satire.* Princeton: Princeton University Press, 1962.

Holifield, E. Brooks. *The Covenant Sealed: The Development of Puritan Sacramental Theology in Old and New England, 1570–1720.* New Haven: Yale University Press, 1974.

Hooker, Thomas. *The Poor Doubting Christian.* London: 1646.

———. *The Poor Doubting Christian Drawn Unto Christ.* (1629 version). In *Thomas Hooker: Writings in England and Holland, 1626–1633,* edited by George Williams et al. Cambridge: Harvard University Press, 1975.

———. *The Soul's Vocation.* In *Salvation in New England: Selections from the Sermons of the First Preachers,* edited by Phyllis Jones and Nicholas Jones. Austin: University of Texas Press, 1977.

Howard, Alan B. "The World as Emblem: Language and Vision in the Poetry of Edward Taylor." *American Literature* 44 (1972): 359–84.

Huizinga, Johan. *Homo Ludens: A Study of the Play Element in Culture.* 1949. Reprint. London: Temple Smith, 1970.

Hyers, M. Conrad. "The Dialectic of the Sacred and the Comic." In *Holy Laughter: Essays on Religion in Comic Perspective,* edited by M. Conrad Hyers. New York: Seabury Press, 1969.

Isani, Mukhtar Ali. "Edward Taylor and Ovid's *Art of Love*: The Text of a Newly-Discovered Manuscript." *Early American Literature* 10 (1975): 67–74.

Israel, Calvin. "Edward Taylor's *Barleybreaks*." *American Notes and Queries* 4 (1966): 147–48.

Johnson, Parker H. "Poetry and Praise in Edward Taylor's Preparatory Meditations." *American Literature* 52 (1980): 84–96.

Johnson, Samuel. *Lives of the English Poets,* edited by George Birbeck Hill. 2 vols. New York: Octagon, 1967.

Johnson, Thomas. "A Seventeenth-Century Printing of Some Verses of Edward Taylor." *New England Quarterly* 14 (1941): 139–41.

———, ed. *The Poetical Works of Edward Taylor.* Princeton: Princeton University Press, 1943.

Johnston, Thomas E., Jr. "Edward Taylor: An American Emblematist." *Early American Literature* 3 (1968/1969): 186–98.

Kaufmann, U. Milo. *The Pilgrim's Progress and Traditions in Puritan Meditation.* New Haven and London: Yale University Press, 1966.

Keller, Karl. *The Example of Edward Taylor.* Amherst: University of Massachusetts Press, 1975.

———. "'The World Slickt Up in Types': Edward Taylor as a Version of Emerson." In *Typology and Early American Literature,* edited by Sacvan Bercovitch. Amherst: University of Massachusetts Press, 1972.

Kierkegaard, Soren. *Concluding Unscientific Postscript.* Translated by David Swenson and edited by Walter Lowrie. Princeton: Princeton University Press, 1941.

———. *The Journals of Soren Kierkegaard,* edited and translated by Alexander Dru. London: Oxford University Press, 1938.

Leith, John H., ed. *Creeds of the Churches.* Garden City, N.Y.: Doubleday, 1963.

Lewalski, Barbara. *Donne's Anniversaries and the Poetry of Praise: The Creation of a Symbolic Mode.* Princeton: Princeton University Press, 1973.

———. *Protestant Poetics and the Seventeenth-Century Religious Lyric.* Princeton: Princeton University Press, 1979.

Lowance, Mason I., Jr. *The Language of Canaan: Metaphor and Symbol in New England from the Puritans to the Transcendentalists.* Cambridge: Harvard University Press, 1980.

Lyons, Bridget G. *Voices of Melancholy: Studies in Literary Treatments of Melancholy in Renaissance England.* London: Routledge and Kegan Paul, 1971.

McNeill, John T. *The History and Character of Calvinism*. New York: Oxford University Press, 1967.

———. *A History of the Cure of Souls*. New York: Harper, 1951.

Mahood, M. M. "Something Understood: The Nature of Herbert's Wit." In *Metaphysical Poetry*, edited by Malcolm Bradbury and David Palmer. Bloomington: Indiana University Press, 1971.

Manierre, William. "Verbal Patterns in the Poetry of Edward Taylor." *College English* 23 (1962): 296–99.

Martz, Louis L. *The Paradise Within: Studies in Vaughan, Traherne, and Milton*. New Haven: Yale University Press, 1964.

———. *The Poetry of Meditation: A Study in English Religious Literature of the Seventeenth Century*. 2d ed. New Haven: Yale University Press, 1962.

Mather, Cotton. *Bonifacius: An Essay upon the Good*. Edited by David Levin. Cambridge: Belknap Press of Harvard University Press, 1966.

———. *A Companion for Communicants*. Boston: B. Green, 1690.

———. *A Monitor for Communicants*. Boston: B. Green, 1714.

Mather, Increase. *A Discourse Concerning the Danger of Apostasy*. Boston, 1679.

———. *The Mystery of Christ*. Boston, 1686.

Mather, Samuel. *The Figures or Types of the Old Testament*. 1705. Facsimile reprint. New York: Johnson Reprint Corp., 1969.

May, Herbert, and Metzger, Bruce, ed. *The New Oxford Annotated Bible*. New York: Oxford University Press, 1977.

Mazzeo, Joseph Anthony. "A Critique of Some Modern Theories of Metaphysical Poetry." *Modern Philology* 50 (1952): 88–96.

Meserole, Harrison T. "'A Kind of Burr': Colonial New England's Heritage of Wit." In *American Literature: The New England Heritage*, edited by James Nagel and Richard Astro. New York: Garland, 1981.

———. *Seventeenth-Century American Poetry*. 1968. Reprint. New York: W. W. Norton, 1972.

Mignon, Charles W. "Diction in Edward Taylor's *Preparatory Meditations*." *American Speech* 41 (1966): 243–53.

———. "Edward Taylor's *Preparatory Meditations*: A Decorum of Imperfection." *PMLA* 83 (1968): 1423–28.

———. "A Principle of Order in Edward Taylor's *Preparatory Meditations*." *Early American Literature* 4 (1969/1970): 110–16.

Miller, Perry. *The New England Mind: From Colony to Province*. 2 vols. Cambridge: Harvard University Press, 1939–1954.

Miller, Perry, and Johnson, Thomas, eds. *The Puritans: A Sourcebook of Their Writings*. 2d ed. 2 vols. New York: Harper and Row, 1963.

Miner, Earl. *The Metaphysical Mode from Donne to Cowley*. Princeton: Princeton University Press, 1969.

Morgan, Edmund S. *Visible Saints: The History of a Puritan Idea*. Ithaca, N.Y.: Cornell University Press, 1963.

Morison, Samuel Eliot. *Harvard College in the Seventeenth Century.* 2 vols. Cambridge: Harvard University Press, 1936.

———. *The Intellectual Life of Colonial New England.* Ithaca, N.Y.: Cornell University Press, 1956.

Murdock, Kenneth B. *Literature and Theology in Colonial New England.* 1949. Reprint. New York: Harper and Row, 1963.

Murphy, Francis. "Edward Taylor's Attitude toward Publication: A Question Concerning Authority." *American Literature* 34 (1962): 393–94.

Neale, Robert E. *In Praise of Play: Toward a Psychology of Religion.* New York: Harper and Row, 1969.

North, Michael. "Edward Taylor's Metaphors of Promise." *American Literature* 51 (1979): 1–16

Origen. "Prologue to the Commentary on the Song of Songs." In *Origen,* translated by Rowan A. Greer. New York: Paulist Press, 1979.

Parker, David L. "Edward Taylor's Preparationism: A New Perspective on the Taylor-Stoddard Controversy." *Early American Literature* 11 (1976/1977): 259–78.

Parker, Gail T. "Jonathan Edwards and Melancholy." *New England Quarterly* 41 (1968): 193–212.

Patrick, J. Max. "Critical Problems in Editing George Herbert's *The Temple.*" In *The Editor as Critic and the Critic as Editor,* edited by William Andrews. Los Angeles: Clark Memorial Library, 1973.

Patterson, J. Daniel. "A Reconsideration of Edward Taylor's 'The Preface,' Lines 9–12." *Early American Literature* 20 (1985): 64–65.

Perkins, William. "Concerning Recreation." In *English Puritanism from John Hooper to John Milton,* edited by Everett H. Emerson. Durham, N.C.: Duke University Press, 1968.

———. *The Whole Treatise of the Cases of Conscience.* London, 1611.

Pettit, Norman. *The Heart Prepared: Grace and Conversion in Puritan Spiritual Life.* New Haven: Yale University Press, 1966.

Pieper, Josef. *Leisure the Basis of Culture.* London: Faber and Faber, 1952.

Pinsker, Sanford. "Carnal Love / Excremental Skies: A Reading of Edward Taylor's 'Upon the Sweeping Flood.'" *Concerning Poetry* 8 (1975): 53–54.

Pope, R. G. *The Half-Way Covenant: Church Membership in Puritan New England.* Princeton: Princeton University Press, 1969.

Quarles, Francis. *The Complete Works in Prose and Verse.* Edited by Alexander Grosart. 3 vols. Edinburgh: Edinburgh University Press, 1880.

Riverius, Lazerius. *The Practice of Physick.* London, 1672.

Rowe, Karen E. "Puritan Typology and Allegory as Metaphor and Conceit in Edward Taylor's *Preparatory Meditations.*" Ph.D. diss., Indiana University, 1971.

———. "Sacred or Profane? Edward Taylor's Meditations on Canticles." *Modern Philology* 72 (1974): 123–38.

————. *Saint and Singer: Edward Taylor's Typology and the Poetics of Medita-tion.* Cambridge: Cambridge University Press, 1986.

Russell, Gene. "Taylor's 'Upon Wedlock and Death of Children.'" *Expli-cator* 27 (1969): Item 71.

Rutman, Darrett. *American Puritanism: Faith and Practice.* New York: J. B. Lippincott, 1970.

Sasek, Lawrence A. *The Literary Temper of the English Puritans.* 1961. Reprint. New York: Greenwood, 1969.

Saunders, J. W. "The Social Situation of Seventeenth-Century Poetry." In *Metaphysical Poetry,* edited by Malcolm Bradbury and David Palmer. Bloomington: Indiana University Press, 1971.

Schafer, Thomas M. "Solomon Stoddard and the Theology of the Reviv-al." In *A Miscellany of American Christianity,* edited by Stuart Henry. Durham, N.C.: Duke University Press, 1963.

Scheick, William J. "The Jawbones Schema of Edward Taylor's *Gods Determinations.*" In *Puritan Influences in American Literature,* edited by Emory Elliott. Urbana: University of Illinois Press, 1979.

————. *The Will and the Word: The Poetry of Edward Taylor.* Athens: Univer-sity of Georgia Press, 1974.

Schuldiner, Michael. "The Christian Hero and the Classical Journey in Edward Taylor's 'Preparatory Meditations. First Series.'" *Huntington Library Quarterly* 49 (1986): 113–32.

————. "Edward Taylor's Problematic Imagery." *Early American Literature* 13 (1978): 92–101.

Sebouhian, George. "Conversion Morphology and the Structure of *Gods Determinations.*" *Early American Literature* 16 (1981/1982): 226–40.

Sewall, Samuel. "The Letter Book of Samuel Sewall." 2 vols. *Collections of the Massachusetts Historical Society* 50–52 (1886–1888).

Shepard, Thomas. *The Works of Thomas Shepard.* 3 vols. Boston: 1853.

Shepherd, Emmy. "Edward Taylor's Injunction Against Publication." *American Literature* 33 (1962): 512–13.

The Shorter Catechism with Scripture Proofs. Edinburgh: Banner of Truth Trust, n.d.

Sidney, Sir Philip. *The Defence of Poesie.* London: For William Ponsonby, 1595.

Siebel, Kathy, and Davis, Thomas M. "Edward Taylor and the Cleansing of Aqua Vitae." *Early American Literature* 4 (1969/1970): 102–9.

Slethaug, Gordon E. "Edward Taylor's Copy of Thomas Taylor's *Types*: A New Taylor Document." *Early American Literature*: 8 (1973): 132–39.

Sluder, Lawrence Lan. "God in the Background: Edward Taylor as Natu-ralist." *Early American Literature* 8 (1973): 265–71.

Smith, Willard. *The Nature of Comedy.* Boston: R. G. Badger, 1930.

Sprague, William B. *Annals of the American Pulpit.* 9 vols. 1886. Reprint. New York: Arno Press and New York Times, 1969.

Stanford, Donald E. *Edward Taylor.* Minneapolis: University of Minnesota Press, 1965.

———. "Edward Taylor." In *Major Writers of Early American Literature,* edited by Everett Emerson. Madison: University of Wisconsin Press, 1972.

———. "Edward Taylor and the Lord's Supper." *American Literature* 27 (1955): 172–78.

Stoddard, Solomon. *An Appeal to the Learned.* Boston: B. Green, 1709.

———. *The Defects of Preachers Reproved.* New London: T. Green, 1724.

———. *The Efficacy of the Fear of Hell.* Boston, 1713.

———. *A Guide to Christ.* Boston: Draper for Henchman, 1735.

———. *The Inexcusableness of Neglecting the Worship of God.* Boston: B. Green, 1708.

———. *The Safety of Appearing.* Boston: Samuel Green, 1687.

———. *A Treatise Concerning Conversion.* Boston: Franklin for Henchman, 1719.

Stout, Harry S. *The New England Soul: Preaching and Religious Culture in Colonial New England.* New York: Oxford University Press, 1986.

Sudol, Ronald A. "Meditation in Colonial New England: The Directives of Thomas Hooker and Ebeneezer Pemberton." *Christianity and Literature* 28 (1979): 36–43.

Summers, Joseph H. *George Herbert: His Religion and Art.* Cambridge: Harvard University Press, 1954.

Surowiecki, John. "Taylor's Manipulations of Satan in *Gods Determinations.*" MS, n.d. Photocopy in possession of author.

Tave, Stuart. *The Amiable Humorist.* Chicago: University of Chicago Press, 1960.

Taylor, Edward. "Christ the Glory of All Types: The Initial Sermon from Edward Taylor's 'Upon the Types of the Old Testament.'" Edited by Charles W. Mignon. *William and Mary Quarterly* 37 (1980): 286–301.

———. *Edward Taylor's Christographia.* Edited by Norman S. Grabo. New Haven: Yale University Press, 1962.

———. *Edward Taylor's Treatise Concerning the Lord's Supper.* East Lansing: Michigan State University Press, 1965.

———. *The Harmony of the Gospels.* Edited by Thomas M. Davis and Virginia L. Davis, with Betty L. Parks. 4 vols. Delmar, N.Y.: Scholars' Facsimiles and Reprints, 1983.

———. *The Poems of Edward Taylor.* Edited by Donald E. Stanford. New Haven: Yale University Press, 1960.

———. "The Pouring of the Sixth Vial: A Letter in a Taylor-Sewall Debate." Edited by Mukhtar Ali Isani. *Massachusetts Historical Society Proceedings* 83 (1971): 123–29.

———. "Theological Notes." MS, Redwood Athenaeum, Newport, R.I., n.d.

————. *A Transcript of Edward Taylor's Metrical History of Christianity.* Edited by Donald E. Stanford. 1962. Facsimile Reprint. Ann Arbor, Michigan: University Microfilms, 1978.

————. *The Unpublished Writings of Edward Taylor.* Edited by Thomas M. Davis and Virginia L. Davis. 3 vols. Boston: G. K. Hall, 1981.

————. "Upon the Types of the Old Testament." MS edited into typescript by Charles W. Mignon. University of Nebraska, Lincoln, Nebraska, n.d.

Taylor, Thomas. *Christ Revealed; or, The Old Testament Explained.* Introduction by Raymond A. Anselment. 1635. Facsimile reprint. Delmar, N.Y.: Scholars' Facsimiles and Reprints, 1979.

Terrien, Samuel. *The Elusive Presence: The Heart of Biblical Theology.* San Francisco: Harper and Row, 1978.

Thomas, Jean L. "Drama and Doctrine in *Gods Determinations.*" *American Literature* 36 (1965): 452–62.

Thrall, William F.; Hibbard, Addison; and Holman, C. Hugh. *A Handbook to Literature.* 2d ed. New York: Odyssey Press, 1960.

Turner, Victor. *From Ritual to Theatre: The Human Seriousness of Play.* New York: Performing Arts Journal Publications, 1982.

Tuve, Rosemond. *Elizabethan and Metaphysical Imagery: Renaissance Poetic and Twentieth-Century Critics.* Chicago: University of Chicago Press, 1947.

————. *A Reading of George Herbert.* Chicago: University of Chicago Press, 1952.

Underhill, Evelyn. *Mysticism: A Study in the Nature and Development of Man's Spiritual Consciousness.* 1911. Reprint. New York: E. P. Dutton, 1961.

Vincent, Thomas. *An Explicatory Catechism.* Boston, 1711.

Walker, Jeffrey. "Anagrams and Acrostics: Puritan Poetic Wit." In *Puritan Poets and Poetics: Seventeenth-Century American Poetry in Theory and Practice,* edited by Peter White, with advisory editor Harrison T. Meserole. University Park: Penn State University Press, 1985.

Warren, Austin. *The New England Conscience.* Ann Arbor: University of Michigan Press, 1966.

————. *Rage for Order: Essays in Criticism.* Ann Arbor: University of Michigan Press, 1948.

Weathers, Willie T. "Edward Taylor and the Cambridge Platonists." *American Literature* 26 (1954): 1–31.

————. "Edward Taylor, Hellenistic Puritan." *American Literature* 18 (1946): 18–26.

Werge, Thomas. "The Tree of Life in Edward Taylor's Poetry: The Sources of a Puritan Image." *Early American Literature* 3 (1968/1969): 199–204.

Westgate, Sam. "George Herbert: 'Wit's an Unruly Engine.'" *Journal of the History of Ideas* 38 (1977): 281–96.

White, Helen C. *English Devotional Prose: 1600–1640*. Madison: University of Wisconsin Studies in Language and Literature, 1931.

Wigglesworth, Michael. *The Diary of Michael Wigglesworth, 1653–1657*. Edited by Edmund S. Morgan. New York: Harper and Row, 1946.

Wiley, Elizabeth. "Sources of Imagery in the Poetry of Edward Taylor." Ph.D. diss., University of Pittsburgh, 1962.

Willard, Samuel. *Some Brief Sacramental Meditations*. 2d ed. Boston, 1743.

Williamson, George. *Six Metaphysical Poets: A Reader's Guide*. New York: Farrar, Straus and Giroux, 1967.

Wilson, Thomas. "The Art of Rhetorique." In *The Renaissance in England: Non-dramatic Prose and Verse of the Sixteenth Century*, edited by Hyder E. Rollins and Herschel Baker. Boston: D. C. Heath, 1954.

Wright, Louis B. *Middle-Class Culture in Elizabethan England*. Ithaca, N.Y.: Cornell University Press, 1958.

Wright, Nathalia. "The Morality Tradition in the Poetry of Edward Taylor." *American Literature* 18 (1946): 1–17.

Ziff, Larzer. "The Literary Consequences of Puritanism." In *The American Puritan Imagination: Essays in Revaluation*, edited by Sacvan Bercovitch. Cambridge: Cambridge University Press, 1974.

———. *Puritanism in America: New Culture in a New World*. New York: Viking, 1973.

Index